Fragile Success

Fragile Success

Ten Autistic Children,
Childhood to Adulthood

Second Edition

by Virginia Walker Sperry, M.A.

·P A U L·H·
BROOKES
PUBLISHING C°

Baltimore • London • Toronto • Sydney

Paul H. Brookes Publishing Co.
Post Office Box 10624
Baltimore, Maryland 21285-0624

www.brookespublishing.com

Copyright © 2001 by Paul H. Brookes Publishing Co., Inc.
All rights reserved.

Typeset by Argosy, West Newton, Massachusetts.
Manufactured in the United States of America by
The Maple Press Company, York, Pennsylvania.

All photographs and text in this book have been used by written
permission of the parents and/or guardians of the children
discussed or of the children themselves. The names of both
the parents and the children have been changed to protect
their privacy.

Library of Congress Cataloging-in-Publication Data

Sperry, Virginia Walker, 1915–
    Fragile Success : ten autistic children, childhood to adulthood /c
  by Virginia Walker Sperry.—[2nd ed.].
     p. cm.
    Includes bibliographical references and index.
    ISBN 1-55766-458-7
     1. Autism in children—Case studies. 2. Autism in children. I. Title.

RJ506.A9 .S682 2001
618.92'8982—dc21
                                                00-56466

British Library Cataloguing in Publication data are available from the
British Library.

Contents

To Sally A. Provence, M.D.
September 4, 1916–February 6, 1993
This book would not have been written
without her wisdom and guidance,
and constant encouragement

About the Author

Virginia Walker Sperry, M.A., was director of the Elizabeth Ives School for Special Children in New Haven, Connecticut, from 1966 to 1972. A graduate of Bryn Mawr College, she also received her master's degree in early childhood education from Peabody Teacher's College in Nashville, Tennessee. She currently is Research Affiliate at the Child Study Center, Yale University School of Medicine.

Mrs. Sperry has three children, six grandchildren, and one great-grandchild. She lives in Hamden, Connecticut, with her husband.

Foreword to the First Edition

Fragile Success tells about the lives of people: about children who, when very young, were found to be very different from their peers in ways that perplexed and pained their parents and confounded their doctors and teachers; about how they changed, while remaining very much the same, over a time span of 25 years[1]; about the philosophy, skill, warmth, and motivation of a dedicated teacher, Virginia Walker Sperry, who has remained in touch with them and who knows them as adults. Through this book, Mrs. Sperry makes us very aware of the value of a teacher's knowing a child well and daring to be creative in using and modifying educational methods.

In the late 1950s, just before the children portrayed in this book were born, there were very few clinical or educational resources to serve autistic children[2] and their parents and, indeed, few clinicians who recognized the characteristics that distinguished these children from those suffering from other severe childhood developmental and behavioral disorders. During the nearly 40 intervening years, there have been hundreds of studies aimed at improving diagnosis and treatment of the group of clearly related disorders called by various names: infantile autism, childhood autism, infantile psychosis, childhood schizophrenia, atypical personality development, and, more recently, pervasive developmental disorder.

In their *Handbook of Autism and Pervasive Developmental Disorders*, editors D.J. Cohen and A.M. Donnellan explain:

Those disorders were first described in the medical literature only 40 years ago. Thirty years ago [the 1960s], treatment was focused almost exclusively on young children and consisted of attempting to use psychotherapeutic techniques developed for the therapy of

xi

neurotic children. Twenty years ago, behavioral and educational interventions were initially attempted, bringing along with them scientific interest in behavioral mechanisms. Concurrently, neurochemical and other biomedical efforts were initiated, and autism became conceptualized as a disorder reflecting abnormalities in brain maturation and function. (1987, John Wiley & Sons, p. xv)

The contrast between the 1950s and 1990s is worthy of note. Now, there is much greater understanding of the natural history of the syndrome than there was in the 1950s. Parents today, especially in the United States, England, and Canada, can expect to find specialized diagnostic, treatment, and educational programs. A child now can receive a detailed and comprehensive assessment of his or her intellectual and adaptive competence, and any associated medical conditions can be accurately identified.

Currently, too, there is agreement on the heterogeneity of autism, that autism is not a single disease entity with a single cause. Children diagnosed as autistic vary widely in intellectual ability, adaptive and defensive capabilities, general level of personality organization, and severity of symptoms.

The various chapters of this book show clearly the wisdom of the teaching approach used by Mrs. Sperry in her years at the Elizabeth Ives School for Special Children in New Haven, Connecticut: that, really, to help a child learn how to cope with the world, one must look for and nurture a child's strengths at the same time as one attempts to alleviate his or her problems. The statement of Mrs. Sperry's philosophy, the story of the work at Ives School, and the individual case studies that follow here make the reader vividly aware of how puzzling and hard to reach and influence these children were and of the patience and resourcefulness that were required of their teachers and therapists.

In addition to these case studies, several parents have written about their children: of the emotional stress of caring for an autistic child; of the strain to which the families are subjected; of the long, hard road to understanding and acceptance. While there are unique features in the experiences of all families with autistic children, there are many shared ones: the search for answers and understanding; the feelings of despair and hope; the pain, anger, sadness, and frustration. To a greater or lesser extent, these all are a part of the experience of these families.

Particularly poignant are the accounts written by two mothers about their autistic daughters. Karen's mother's eloquent account covers 25 years and tells of the perplexity and pain as well as the efforts, successful and unsuccessful, she and the rest of the family have made to help Karen and to live with her day by day over the years. Polly's mother's story has a special vividness in the description of the effect Polly's problems have had and continue to have on the lives of her parents and brothers. By her own admission, Polly's mother is angry and embittered. She despairs of things ever being better for her and Polly. When asked if she had anything to add to her account, she said she did not, because "it hurts me too much to write any more about it."[3] The other parental accounts show the possible variety of emotional reactions of having an autistic child, from gratitude and hopefulness to frustration and embitterment.

The nine[4] case studies—Tom, Jimmy, Polly, Bill, David, Karen, John, Larry, and Eric—illustrate the similarities and differences of the syndrome in children who in early childhood would be considered moderately to severely dysfunctional. Through the stories set down in these pages, it is not difficult for the reader to identify how the parents and teachers experienced being with these children as they grew up. It is less easy to imagine the thoughts and feelings of the children/young adults themselves except at moments when their panic, fear, anger, or pleasure is apparent in their behavior. So, though this book is about the children and their afflictions, it is also about the caring adults who, as parents and teachers, sought to understand, nurture, and help them.

Sally A. Provence, M.D.
Former Director
Sally Provence–Irving B. Harris
Child Development Center
Yale Child Study Center
New Haven, Connecticut

ENDNOTES

1. At the time this Foreword was written, this time span was correct. The author's relationship with these individuals has, of course, lengthened from that described here by the late Sally Provence.

2. The terminology used in this Foreword was acceptable at the time it was written; it may not always conform to the more "person-first" language preferred today.

3. Since the time this Foreword was written much of the bitterness and frustration experienced by all of the parents in the study, including Polly's mother, has been replaced by a growing sense of pride and acceptance of their children's accomplishments.

4. This Foreword does not reflect the addition of another case study, which tells the story of Jane, a young woman who has pervasive developmental disorder-not otherwise specified (PDD-NOS).

Foreword to the Second Edition

In her foreword to the first edition of *Fragile Success,* my colleague and teacher, Sally A. Provence, reviewed the development of autism as a diagnostic concept and traced its history into the late 1980s. As she noted, autism has been the focus of much clinical and research interest since its first scientific description by Leo Kanner.[1] Dr. Provence rightly emphasized the unusual social development that is the hallmark of the disorder. The social difficulties observed in autism are, as the case histories here so vividly demonstrate, the most perplexing and challenging aspects of the disorder. Although these problems have generated increasing interest, both in the areas of psychology and of neurobiology, they remain, in some ways, poorly understood.[2]

Other aspects of development in autism also are perplexing. Although some skills are delayed, others may be advanced (e.g., some children with autism have an early interest in letters and numbers and may be early readers; others may have unusual abilities in calculating dates or drawing).[3,4] Various theories have arisen attempting to explain the source of these uneven patterns of development and the associated social difficulties, including impairments in "theory of mind,"[5] "central coherence,"[6] or "executive functioning."[7] Probably even more important, these theories have, in turn, led to increasingly focused and precise research studies.

Advances in research have been made on numerous fronts. One major area has been the development of better and more precise methods of defining and characterizing autism. Autism was not even recognized as an "official" diagnostic category until 1980. Since that time, steady improvement has been made in the definition of autism.[8] This has been important in furthering the efficacy of research in many ways, for example, in helping to ensure the comparability of research studies.

The internationally accepted definition of autism in use at the beginning of the 21st century, as outlined in the *Diagnostic and Statistical Manual of Mental Disorders, Fourth Edition* (DSM-IV),[9] was developed based on a large study in which nearly 1,000 individuals from around the world were evaluated.[10] According to this definition, in order for an individual to be diagnosed as having autism, by age 3 he or she must exhibit or have exhibited a specified number of problems in social interaction, in communication, and in imaginative play, as well as unusual behaviors and restricted interests and activities. Another major advance is the inclusion of other varieties of pervasive developmental disorder in addition to autism (e.g., Rett's disorder, Asperger's disorder, childhood disintegrative disorder, and pervasive developmental disorder-not otherwise specified [PDD-NOS]). The inclusion of these "new" conditions speaks to what likely will be a trend in the future, that is, the delineation of more subtypes within the broader autism spectrum. Advances in biology, especially in genetics, may help us better understand the relationships of these conditions to autism and may also, of course, lead us into totally new areas of research.

Beginning in the 1990s, remarkable advances have been made in our understanding of the neurobiology of autism. Even before the 1980s, various factors suggested the neurobiological basis of autism (e.g., high rates of association with mental retardation and seizure disorder and other medical conditions).[11,12] The high rate of seizure disorder in autism was particularly noteworthy, but clinicians and researchers also realized that there were various, if not always very specific, signs of neurological difficulties. For example, in young children with autism researchers have found a persistence of many reflexes that would typically have disappeared in early infancy, as well as delayed development of hand dominance.[13]

Some controversy surrounds the frequency with which autism is associated with other medical conditions in a *causal* way. For example, although it is likely that seizures and autism originate from the same fundamental cause, some claim that medical conditions might cause autism. For example, studies from the 1970s indicated that children who suffered from congenital rubella were more likely to have autism; however, as time went on, these data were questioned as the children included in the studies were followed and seemed to lose some of their "autistic features."[14] Although it has been argued that as much as one third of all cases of autism can be associated with an identifiable medical condition, it now seems that a more likely figure might be 1 in 10 cases.[14] The conditions that seem most strongly related to autism include fragile X syndrome and tuberous sclerosis; although these conditions account for only a small number of individuals with autism, they are of special interest because both fragile X syndrome and tuberous sclerosis have strong genetic components.

Fortunately, great advances in our understanding of the genetic basis of autism have occurred over the past decade. In some ways this seems paradoxical because at first there seemed to be very little genetic contribution to autism. The condition was (relatively) rare, however, because individuals with autism often did not marry and reproduce. The first evidence for a genetic basis for autism, or at least some cases of autism, was found in twin studies in which it was clear that identical twins (who have exactly the same genes) are much more likely to be "concordant" for autism; that is, if one twin shows autism, so does the other. It has now become apparent that there is an increased risk for recurrence in brothers and sisters of the child with autism—probably a 2%–3% risk. On the one hand, while this risk may not, absolutely, seem great, it is much higher than the rate expected in the general population—approximately 50–100 times greater. The observation that siblings also may be at risk for other developmental difficulties (e.g., in reading or language) suggests that what is inherited might well be a more general risk for developmental problems.

It now appears that several genes are likely involved in causing autism; the search for these genes is advancing every day, and it is possible that within the first few years of the 21st century the genetic basis for at least some cases of autism will be found. This will open up new possibilities for both research and clinical care.

Another active area of work has been the study of the brain in autism. The focus here has been to clarify those areas of the brain that are responsible for features of the disorder. Interest has understandably focused on the areas of cerebral cortex that we know relate to language and social interaction (frontal and temporal lobes), as well as other brain areas.[15] Another line of work has focused on the cerebellum, the portion of the brain that is very involved with coordination of movement; however, early reports of abnormalities here using magnetic resonance imaging (MRI) scans have proven difficult to replicate.[15]

Relatively recently, researchers have found unusual head sizes in individuals who have autism. In the past, studies that grouped children with autism together reported average head size, but it now appears that this is misleading because some individuals with autism have larger heads and brain size, while others, particularly the more intellectually challenged, may have smaller head sizes.[16] Studies of actual brain tissue based on postmortem studies have noted some changes in certain areas of the brain, such as the hippocampus and amygdala; these are areas involved in the storage of memory and emotional information. The advent of newer techniques, such as functional magnetic resonance imaging (fMRI), offers the potential of considerable progress in the relatively near future as individuals with autism actively engage in various tasks.

Various studies of brain chemistry have been conducted. One of the most extensively studied systems has been that which involves the brain transmitter *serotonin*; it is now well established that about one third of children with autism have increased blood levels of serotonin. Unfortunately, this finding is not specific to autism, and the real importance of this observation is not clear.[17] Studies of other neurotransmitter systems have produced conflicting findings.

The interest in the neurobiological aspects of autism has paralleled the increasing sophistication of drug treatments for autism. Although much work remains to be done, significant progress has been made in the treatment of the various symptoms associated with autism and the other conditions, such as depression, that are sometimes associated with it.[18]

In the field of autism, some of the greatest advances of the 1990s to the present, other than in genetic implications, have come in the areas of behavioral and educational interventions. For children with autism and related conditions, structured and individualized intervention programs are now available that teach social, communication, and other skills.[19] It now appears that early identification and intensive intervention significantly improve outcomes.[20] Although goals for intervention understandably vary depending on many factors, several generalizations can be made. Children with autism do best with structured programs and explicit teaching. Such programs must recognize a child's strengths as well as weaknesses. Various skills can be taught; for example, for the youngest and those with the most severe impairments, "learning to learn" skills are important; whereas, for older and more able individuals, social skills training may be more central. Various behavioral procedures can be used to help the child learn by decreasing problem behaviors and helping the child to develop alternative behaviors.

Once learning has taken place, generalizing skills to different settings is the next key aspect of education programming. For all individuals with autism, fostering speech and communication skills is important. There is general acceptance that levels of speech and communication skills are two of the greatest determinations of adult outcome. Accordingly, there is considerable emphasis on helping the child acquire language or, when this seems unlikely, fostering more general communication skills in other ways.[21] Various nonverbal methods, such as sign language, picture exchange, and so forth, can be very beneficial in helping nonspeaking individuals learn to communicate.

Similarly, behavioral teaching methods used for individuals with autism can help them to develop both cognitive and communicative skills (e.g., discrete trial training). These methods are useful for individuals diagnosed with various types of autism spectrum disorders (i.e., throughout the range of syndrome expression in autism) but are particularly needed for younger individuals and those with more challenging behaviors who need special help to enable them to learn from both the social and nonsocial world. Although there is some disagreement about the extent to which progress can be made, there is little doubt that such methods are extremely useful.[22, 23]

For the higher functioning individuals with autism, various curricula for teaching social skills are available. The use of structured rehearsal, role playing, small-group teaching, and social scripts can be very helpful. While teaching must be explicit, the use of natural environments can help foster generalization of skills.[24]

Over the past decade, another major area of work has been with the families of children with autism. The birth of a child with a serious disability is always a major event in the lives of family members. As Sally A. Provence notes in Chapter 1, in the first years after autism was described, there was the notion that perhaps poor parental interaction with children caused autism; a very considerable body of work has shown that this is not the case, but this early mistake really haunted the field and significantly delayed the study of effects of autism on other family members. The study of families of individuals with autism has been further stimulated by recent genetic research on autism. The growing appreciation of the importance of supporting family members as well as the child with autism is a welcome phenomenon.[25]

This impact has probably been most dramatic with the implementation of the Education for All Handicapped Children Act of 1975 (PL 94-142), which mandated that schools provide services for all children with disabilities, including those with autism. Although support services can, unfortunately, be spotty and inconsistent, they are, in general, much more available in the United States than they were even 20 years ago. This has eased the burden on families as have the various efforts to provide health care providers and others basic information on autism to facilitate early detection and early implementation of services. Families also have been helped by the development of numerous models of supportive living and employment arrangements and better and more effective drug treatments, among other supports.[26] At the same time, of course, the impact of having a family member with autism remains major.

The case histories in this book demonstrate that autism and related disorders are serious, lifelong conditions. Although important gains can be made with intervention, particularly with early intervention, and although there are definite changes with development, autism is an enduring condition that challenges many aspects of our existing system of care. The needs of the individual and family change over time and as a function of the specific areas of strength and weakness exhibited by the person with autism. Because autism affects multiple aspects of development, it also is the case that various professions and professionals are involved in the care of the person with autism (e.g., educators, psychologists, physicians, speech-language therapists, occupational and physical therapists, social workers, lawyers, vocational counselors). Probably more than any other disorder, autism has helped foster the multidisciplinary approach to developmental disabilities.

Parents and professionals have been working more and more effectively with individuals with autism to help them develop their autonomy and capacities for self-sufficiency. As a result, many individuals with autism now are living productive adult lives and are participating more actively—and effectively—in both family and community life. At the same time, as this book demonstrates, some support often is needed. The differences among individuals with autism are quite marked and must be respected; from the point of view of social policy, an awareness of such differences is crucial.

In summary, the decade leading into the 21st century has witnessed tremendous progress on both the scientific and clinical fronts. Genetic research has provided new information about the origins of autism and may, even within the next few years, yield fundamental knowledge about the cause(s) of autism. It is hoped that such knowledge can be translated into more effective interventions as well as into prevention. More and more studies of various drugs have appeared; this growing body of work suggests that while these agents do not produce a magic cure, they can significantly alleviate symptoms that are a source of distress to the individual or that interfere with the benefits of a good program. Studies of psychological development have become increasingly precise as investigators have developed specific theories or "models" of autism; such theories are helpful to refine the questions researchers ask and to develop more effective interventions. Advances have been made on the education front, and more children with autism are receiving services in their local schools, often in inclusive environments. As adults, more individuals with autism are able to achieve some degree of personal independence and self-sufficiency.

Although much progress has been made, much remains to be done. The recent increase in support for research at the federal level is very important in helping sustain this momentum. Programs of care remain costly both in the monetary and psychological sense. Thus, it is critical that funding for research in autism continues at a reasonable level. Much remains to be learned. In the meantime, these 10 case histories provide a vivid testament to the efforts of individuals and their families who are coping with autism.

Fred R. Volkmar, M.D.
Yale Child Study Center
New Haven, Connecticut

ENDNOTES

1. Kanner, L. (1943). Autistic disturbances of affective contact. *Nervous Child*, 2, 217–250. This paper remains the "classic" description of autism.
2. Volkmar, F.R., et al. (1997). Social development in autism. In D.J. Cohen & F.R. Volkmar (Eds.), *Handbook of autism and pervasive developmental disorders* (pp. 173–194). New York: John Wiley & Sons.
3. Whitehouse, D., & Harris, J.C. (1984). Hyperlexia in infantile autism. *Journal of Autism and Developmental Disorders, 14*(3), 281–289.
4. Treffert, D. (1989). *Extraordinary people.* New York: Ballantine Books.
5. Baron-Cohen, S. (1989). The autistic child's theory of mind: A case of specific developmental delay. *Journal of Child Psychology and Psychiatry, 30*(2), 285–297.
6. Jarrold, C., & Russell, J. (1997). Counting abilities in autism: Possible implications for central coherence theory. *Journal of Autism and Developmental Disorders, 27*(1), 25–37.
7. Ozonoff, S., Pennington, B.F., & Rogers, S.J. (1991). Executive function deficits in high-functioning autistic individuals: Relationship to theory of mind. *Journal of Child Psychology & Psychiatry and Allied Disciplines, 32*(7), 1081–1105.
8. Volkmar, F.R., Klin, A., & Cohen, D.J. (1997). Diagnosis and classification of autism and related conditions: Consensus and issues. In D.J. Cohen & F.R. Volkmar (Eds.), *Handbook of autism and pervasive developmental disorders* (pp. 5–40). New York: John Wiley & Sons.
9. American Psychiatric Association. (1994). *Diagnostic and statistical manual of mental disorders* (4th ed.). Washington, DC: Author.
10. Volkmar, F.R., et al. (1994). Field trial for autistic disorder in DSM-IV. *American Journal of Psychiatry, 151*(9), 1361–1367.
11. Minshew, N.J., Sweeney, J.A., & Bauman, M.L. (1997). Neurological aspects of autism. In D.J. Cohen & F.R. Volkmar (Eds.), *Neurological aspects of autism* (pp. 344–369). New York: John Wiley & Sons.
12. Dykens, E.M., & Volkmar, F.R. (1997). Medical conditions associated with autism. In D.J. Cohen & F.R. Volkmar (Eds.), *Handbook of autism and pervasive developmental disorders* (pp. 388–410). New York: John Wiley & Sons.
13. Minderaa, R.B., Volkmar, F.R., Hansen, C.R., Harcherik, D.F., Akkerhuis, G.W., & Cohen, D.J. (1985). Snout and visual rooting reflexes in infantile autism. *Journal of Autism and Developmental Disorders, 15*(4), 409–416.
14. Rutter, M., Bailey, A., Bolton, P., & Le Couteur, A. (1994). Autism and known medical conditions: Myth and substance. *Journal of Child Psychology and Psychiatry, 35*(2), 311–322.
15. Minshew, N.J., Sweeney, J.A., & Bauman, J.L. (1997). Neurological aspects of autism. In D.J. Cohen & F.R. Volkmar (Eds.), *Handbook of autism and pervasive developmental disorders* (pp. 344–369). New York: John Wiley & Sons.
16. Woodhouse, W., et al. (1996). Head circumference in autism and other pervasive developmental disorders. *Journal of Child Psychology and Psychiatry, 37*(6), 665–671.

17. Anderson, G.M., & Hoshiono, Y. (1997). Neurochemical studies of autism. In D.J. Cohen & F.R. Volkmar (Eds.), *Handbook of autism and pervasive developmental disorders* (pp. 325–343). New York: John Wiley & Sons.

18. McDougle, C.J. (1997). Psychopharmacology. In D.J. Cohen & F.R. Volkmar (Eds.), *Handbook of autism and pervasive developmental disorders* (pp. 707–729). New York: John Wiley & Sons.

19. Harris, S.L., & Handleman, J.S. (1997). Helping children with autism enter the mainstream. In D.J. Cohen & F.R. Volkmar (Eds.), *Handbook of autism and pervasive developmental disorders* (pp. 665–675). New York: John Wiley & Sons.

20. Rogers, S.J. (1996). Brief report: Early intervention in autism. *Journal of Autism and Developmental Disorders, 26*(2), 243–246.

21. Lord, C., & Paul, R. (1997). Language and communication in autism. In D.J. Cohen & F.R. Volkmar (Eds.), *Handbook of autism and pervasive developmental disorders* (pp. 195–225). New York: John Wiley & Sons.

22. Powers, M.D. (1997). Behavioral assessment of individuals with autism. In D.J. Cohen & F.R. Volkmar (Eds.), *Handbook of autism and pervasive developmental disorders* (pp. 448–459). New York: John Wiley & Sons.

23. Bregman, J.D., & Gerdtz, J. (1997). Behavioral interventions. In D.J. Cohen & F.R. Volkmar (Eds.), *Handbook of autism and pervasive developmental disorders* (pp. 606–630). New York: John Wiley & Sons.

24. Gray, C.A., & Garand, J.D. (1993). Social stories: Improving responses of students with autism with accurate social information. *Focus on Autistic Behavior, 8*(1), 1–10.

25. Siegel, B. (1997). Coping with the diagnosis of autism. In D.J. Cohen & F.R. Volkmar (Eds.), *Handbook of autism and pervasive developmental disorders* (pp. 745–766). New York: John Wiley & Sons.

26. Marcus, L.M., Kunce, L.J., & Schopler, E. (1997). Working with families. In D.J. Cohen & F.R. Volkmar (Eds.), *Handbook of autism and pervasive developmental disorders* (pp. 631–649). New York: John Wiley & Sons.

Acknowledgments

No words can fully express my gratitude to Sally A. Provence, M.D., Martha Leonard, M.D., and Mary McGarry, M.D. They gave me the benefit of their knowledge and skill in the fields of autism and of early childhood development, and generously of their valuable time. I thank Fred R. Volkmar, M.D., and the talented professionals of the Child Development Unit (known now as the Sally Provence–Irving B. Harris Child Development Center) of the Yale Child Study Center, who throughout many years have contributed to this project—one that often seemed to me just a pipe dream.

Many friends, notably Sally H. Levinson, Rena Gans, Ann Bliss, M.S.W., Betty Sword, current director of Ives School, and former teachers of Ives were an invaluable help to me. Encouragement and input came from these professionals in the areas of writing and editing: Mary Price; Gladys Topkis; Roberta Yerkes Blanshard; Richard Selzer, M.D.; Annabel Stehli; Maggie Scarf; Timothy Niedeman; and my friends from college years, Alice Gore King, Phyllis Feldkamp, and Geraldine Rhoads.

My research took me to many private special education schools and to special education departments of public school systems. The various professionals there were extraordinarily helpful either in discussing some of the individuals whose life stories appear in this book or in searching patiently for the appropriate files.

Starting in the mid-1970s, the parents of these individuals have given me their cooperation and warm encouragement to persevere. I deeply appreciate their friendship and their tolerance of the innumerable interviews and telephone calls required by the research for this book.

Sue Spight was instrumental in referring the manuscript to my original editor, Diantha Thorpe, who believed in *Fragile Success*. I am indebted to her for her editorial skill and expertise that shaped this book and to Sue Spight for her invaluable help.

The second edition has had much-needed editorial assistance from Louise FitzSimons. I would also like to thank the staff at Paul H. Brookes Publishing Co., who have been extraordinarily helpful and supportive throughout the process of getting out this second edition, particularly Editorial Director Elaine Niefeld and Production Editor Leslie K. Eckard.

Finally, I wish to thank Jean and Norvin Hein and Beverly and Robert Gregg for their invaluable help throughout both editions.

Introduction

In the 1960s, autism was a mysterious condition. It was poorly understood by physicians, and there was little concrete information available on its symptoms and treatment. From 1966 to 1972, the years that I was director of the Elizabeth Ives School for Special Children in New Haven, Connecticut, I often saw the painful frustration on the faces of the parents of the pupils at the school as they endured the confusion and emotional turmoil that went with raising a child with autism.

Soon after my retirement in 1972, I ran into an 11-year-old former Ives pupil and his mother in the aisle of a local supermarket. I had last seen the child when he was 7 or 8 years old. Sandy-haired, freckle-faced, and rangy in build, he beamed as he recognized me. Compared to the hyperactive, constantly chattering boy I had known, he seemed focused and in control. His mother told me proudly that her son was managing well in the special education program of his public school system. The change in him was really remarkable. She thanked me for the attention he had received at Ives, without which, she felt, he never would have come so far. In a flash of conviction and inspiration, it occurred to me that it could be beneficial to share with others, especially the parents of such children, some of the hard-won knowledge we at Ives had gained from working with children with autism.

Within a year, I began to collect data on the careers of 11 former pupils of Ives School. These children were chosen not because of their diagnosis but because I had a sound relationship with them and their parents. Geography defined the choices considerably, so they all lived within a manageable distance. Of these 11, I have included 9 stories of those whose original diagnosis was "autistic," "autistic-like," or "personality disorder with autistic overlay." Also, for this edition of the book I have added a tenth case in order to provide insights into another type of disorder falling in the autism spectrum, pervasive developmental disorder-not otherwise specified (PDD-NOS).

The parents gave me permission to obtain information from the various institutions and programs that had treated their children. The Yale Child Study Center in New Haven, Connecticut, which originally tested and diagnosed the 10 children profiled in this book, provided facts on their early toddlerhood, doctors' and social workers' analyses, accounts, interviews, test scores, and final diagnoses. (Doctors at the Center's Child Development Unit, specifically the late Dr. Sally Provence, Dr. Martha Leonard, and the late Dr. Mary McGarry, referred their most puzzling younger children to the Ives School from the school's inception. These three doctors also became consultants for the school.) Other information came from records at nursery schools, public school special education programs, state-funded programs, and private special education schools.

I compiled a full set of testing results for each child, from their earliest examinations through grade-level achievements and scores when each of the original nine turned 21 and "graduated" from high school. To help complete the profiles, seven of these children were retested as adults at the Yale Child Study Center.

I interviewed the children's teachers, social workers, and parents, and as the children got older I went to their graduations, workshops, group homes, and places of work. I took many of them out to lunch several times and kept interviewing them and their parents through 1999. At the time my research for the first edition was complete, the individuals' ages ranged from 23 to 30, and for the second edition, from 30 to 40. My original goal of discovering how these children would develop as adults has been accomplished. Nevertheless, I still keep in touch with all of them.

The 10 accounts in the following pages are the product of this work. It is now several decades since most of these children, now adults, attended Ives, and the study and treatment of autism has broadened and developed. Indeed, the opportunities open to individuals with autism—the programs for special children and the availability of special schools—are largely taken for granted. Readers may look on the description of these early years as a history of those who were among the first children to receive services designed specifically for individuals with autism. But the challenges faced by these children are not "history." Although many have learned, to some extent, how to cope with their disability, their needs and characteristics have not changed. Nor has the problem of diagnosis been solved: There are still many children all over this country and throughout the world whose behavior, whether diagnosed as autistic or atypical or even undiagnosed, confounds and disturbs their parents, doctors, and teachers. Such children present challenges to those who care for them that mirror the experiences of the people whose lives are recounted in these pages.

As the research grew, I questioned who would be the principal audience for this book. There were the pediatricians, who, in the early years of Ives, seemed largely unaware of childhood autism, now termed autism spectrum disorder. Then, there were the parents—fumbling, often despairing, and totally bewildered. They were constantly asking for guidance and reassurance or at least some predictions as to the future. Other medical specialists and social workers, too, were baffled by these children whose behavior can, on the surface, seem so strange. I wanted to address all three of these groups. During the 1960s and 1970s, we teachers of youngsters with autism were in a no-man's-land, where information, resources, and guidance were largely unavailable and where intuition and innovation were required daily tools of the trade. I wanted my book to record in an accessible manner what we learned, so others—whether doctors, teachers, or parents—could benefit from it. I also hoped to broaden the understanding of autism for various audiences, including employers and those in the community who deal with people with autism on a day-to-day basis. It is the kind of book I wish I had had when I taught at Ives School.

This book focuses on the stories of the adults themselves as they are shown maturing from infancy to adulthood in the year 2000 and their parents' accounts of raising a child with a developmental disability, including the effect this had on their own lives and the lives of their other children. The following chapters show who the very different children with autism are as adults—where they live, what work they do, what impairments have been moderated, and what disabilities remain unchanged. These individuals are dramatic examples of the wide range of autistic behaviors, and their stories demonstrate the kind of parental interventions and the medical, educational, vocational, and recreational services that played an important part in their growing up.

There is a secondary theme and hypothesis to this book as well: Early, concentrated intervention has led these 10 children to achieve comparative success in adulthood. Early diagnosis and medical and educational intervention were a tremendous benefit to each child. Without the unceasing dedication of parents, doctors, teachers, and other professionals, many, as adults, would be languishing at home or even in an institution. Like any other youngster, all of these people have talents that might well have been lost, totally blocked by their various disabilities. The effectiveness of our work at the Ives School was due largely to our firm belief that each child has his or her strengths and that, as with typically developing children, only by the discovery and use of their own individual talents can they really become strong and secure. Constant supportive guidance has helped all of the children in this book to use their talents and accomplish limited or, in a few cases, total independence.

For more or specialized information on a particular facet of autism, readers may turn to a list of resources at the end of this book.

To help the lay reader with the specialized terminology of psychology and special education, I have included a glossary, which appears at the end of this book after the appendices. In some of the older material, especially in quotes from researchers and studies before more person-centered terminology came into common usage, the children may be referred to as "handicapped," "autistic children" or "autistics." Of course, by this we mean children with disabilities or children with autism. To obscure the identities of the children (and families) discussed, names and birth dates have been changed; and permission has also been obtained for all material herein. The children, mothers, fathers, and siblings here stand as archetypes of those with developmental disabilities and their families across the country. The problems and solutions touched upon are universal.

Part I

Teaching the Child with Autism

1

Childhood Autism
and Related Disorders

Sally Provence, M.D.

Childhood autism, the clinical diagnosis assigned to the children in this book, is not a single disease with a single cause: Children diagnosed as autistic vary widely in intellectual ability, adaptive and defensive capabilities, general level of personality organization, severity of symptoms, and the extent to which they improve over time.

The term *autism* (or *infantile autism*) was first used in 1943 by Dr. Leo Kanner, professor of psychiatry at the Johns Hopkins School of Medicine, to describe a severe disturbance in social relatedness appearing in very young children and characterized by a profound withdrawal from contact with others.[1] Associated with autism were the absence of speech or the use of speech not intended for communication with others, an obsessive desire for sameness in the environment or pattern of the day, and panic reactions in which the child could not be comforted even by the best efforts of parents.

In the 1940s and 1950s, children with symptoms similar to Kanner's definition of autism were given a wide variety of diagnoses, among them childhood schizophrenia, infantile psychosis, primary personality disorder, atypical personality development, and severe deviational development. By the early 1950s, when the Yale Child

Study Center began its work with autistic and atypical children, there were two strongly divergent views about the cause of childhood psychoses, including autism. Many, citing Kanner's original report and the work of others such as L. Despert, B. Rank, M.G. Putnam, and S. Kaplan, assumed that psychogenic factors (i.e., deficits or noxious influences in the environment) were the principal cause of the disorder. Others favored a biological explanation.

The theory of a psychogenic origin of autism predominated in the 1950s and early 1960s, when the children portrayed in this book were first diagnosed. This school of thought held that the roots of autism could be found in the particular parent–child relationship: A deviant relationship between parent and child, due to the emotional coldness of the parent, caused the child not to be able to relate to other people normally. This view stereotyped the parents, especially the mother, as "cold" (the "mathematician" father and "librarian" mother were typical images of "cold" parents of the time). The stereotype arose from Kanner's observation that certain parents were unable to provide a warm emotional environment, and that many of the collateral kin were strongly preoccupied with abstractions of a scientific, literary, or artistic nature, with limited interest in people. Despert's extensive work with disturbed parents of schizophrenic children and with the children themselves led her to propose the terms *schizophrenogenic mother* or *frigid mother*.[2] Putnam, Rank, and Kaplan reported a number of children with severe personality disorders whose mothers had been depressed or otherwise psychologically unavailable to them during infancy and introduced the term *atypical personality development* to characterize these children.[3]

In contrast to the theory of psychogenic origin was the position of L. Bender, and others, who believed the disorder to be of biological origin.[4] Kanner himself, in a follow-up study published in 1971 of children in his group, attempted to clarify the misinterpretation of his theory, calling attention to a little-noted sentence in his original paper that stated that the children had been born with an innate inability to form the usual, biologically provided interest in people and social interchange.[5] He asserted that he did not assume a direct cause-and-effect relationship between parental personality characteristics and the autistic behavior of children.

Bender characterized autism as a childhood version of schizophrenia and based her conclusions on studies of more than 600 schizophrenic children between 1935 and 1952. Bender's definition went through various refinements and can be condensed as follows: Childhood schizophrenia (autism) is an emotional disturbance that reveals pathology in many areas of integration or patterning of the functions of the central nervous system. Interference in normal developmental patterns and regressive reactions are common. Severe, overwhelming anxiety is a prominent feature. Secondary to anxiety are withdrawal from human contact; regressions in behavior or, in some, panic states; temper tantrums; phobias and fears; and compulsions.

In Bender's childhood schizophrenia, the child expresses profound difficulty and confusion about personal identity, body image, orientation in time and space, and human relationships. There are disturbances in movement, appearing both as variability in motor skill and as stereotyped, often peculiar-looking body movements. Some childhood schizophrenics exhibit early and late patterns of maturation, or retarded and precocious behavior, simultaneously.

Margaret Mahler, a psychiatrist at the New York Psychoanalytic Institute and another backer of the biological origin theory, referred to similarly disturbed children as psychotic and described autistic and *symbiotic* types with at least two features in common: alienation or withdrawal from reality and a severe disturbance in the sense of self-identity.[6] Mahler's autistic type is descriptively similar to Kanner's, but Mahler considered autism as the mechanism through which the child shuts out the presumably unbearable sources of sensory stimuli in the outside world, especially those that demand social-emotional response. Mahler regarded symbiotic psychosis as a disturbance in the interaction between mother and infant in which the infant does not give clear signals of his or her needs and feeling states and the mother may have serious deficiencies in her ability to communicate with and nurture her infant.

Through the 1960s, the field of autism research and treatment was polarized by reports appearing to substantiate, or at least to emphasize, one or the other of the theories of psychogenic or biological origin. Gradually the theories advocating a totally psychogenic origin were discarded in favor of the practice of conducting diagnostic evaluations that included a careful look at both physical and mental factors in the child as well as conditions in the environment, particularly the family's contribution toward aggravating or alleviating the child's disturbance. Clinics and child study centers undertook studies to attempt to identify subgroups whose similarity might give clues to more targeted and selective treatment: genetics; neurological and neurochemical studies; methods of special education and speech/communication therapy; behavioral adaptation or conventional psychotherapy. Over time, a body of research has appeared ranging from neurochemical research to trials of various therapies and from cross-sectional examination to long-term follow-up studies.[7]

It is now fairly widely accepted that "the social disabilities of autistic persons are . . . recognized as a major if not *the* major defining characteristic of the syndrome . . . however, these factors have yet to be fully and adequately defined."[8] At present, "the autistic disorders are best understood as composing part of a spectrum in which multiple and interacting influences—biological and environmental—determine both the severity of impairment and variations in its form within the syndrome."[9]

What has been discovered is the strong tendency in autistic children for certain features or behaviors to cluster together. These are 1) absence or severe impairment of two-way social interaction, nonverbal communication, and imagination, and 2) a pattern of activities dominated by stereotyped routines. These symptoms are, by and large, characteristic of all autistic children to one degree or another.

In 1987, Lorna Wing, M.D., of the Institute of Psychiatry, and Anthony Attwood, Ph.D., of the Herefordshire Health Authority, both of England, suggested a clinically useful classification system to reduce some of the confusion engendered by the profusion of names of "new" syndromes that has arisen to describe the different combinations of features and behaviors exhibited by disturbed young children.[10] In this system, the major determinant of subclassification is the degree of impairment of social interaction. Autistic and atypical children are considered to belong to one of three groups: the "aloof" group, which consists of those who are most cut off from social contact; the "passive" group, which consists of those who do not make spontaneous social approaches except to obtain what they want or need; and the "active-but-odd" group, which consists of those who do make social approaches to others, but "in a peculiar, naive, and one-sided fashion."[11] This system does not totally solve the problem of classifying autistic disorders because of the variability in the additional findings in children in any one group (e.g., inborn errors of metabolism, lead encephalopathy, other central nervous system disorders).

The characteristics exhibited by the aloof group are those that most commonly come to mind when the word *autism* is used; they correspond fairly closely to the behavior that Kanner originally observed and defined as infantile autism. Most members of this group are severely retarded, though a few may test in the normal or near-normal IQ range. Aloofness commonly appears as indifference to the presence or actions of others. In infants, this appears as an absence of normal attachment behavior. There is a lack of demonstration of affection or bids for comfort when distressed. Some individuals will initiate contact, but only as a means to obtaining a specific need, such as food; once the need is filled, the child abruptly moves away to be by him- or herself again.

The aloof children are characterized by a lack of social communication, whether verbal or nonverbal. They will often not respond to direct speech and may appear deaf, except that they will react to other sounds that have meaning for them, such as a refrigerator door opening, a car driving by, and so forth. Aloof children who do speak often have a monotonous or otherwise abnormal voice quality and tend to exhibit other speech abnormalities such as *echolalia* (i.e., repetition of a phrase or sentence spoken by another person), pronoun reversal, excessive literalness in usage, and use of the minimum number of words necessary to carry meaning. Most important, aloof children do not use speech to communicate in the sense of an exchange for pleasure or comparison of ideas or interests. Speech is merely a tool to satisfy the individual's particular and immediate needs.

Aloof children tend to lack the capacity for imaginative play, although some may have highly developed manipulative skills. Instead of imaginative play, an aloof child may perform a single repetitive, stereotyped activity, and remain totally absorbed in that activity for hours on end. A child's attachment to one particular activity may persist for days or even years until another similar activity takes its place. To a certain extent, a child's level of intelligence will affect the nature of this type of activity as the child gets older. Children of low intelligence will continue to perform simple activities, such as flapping their arms, rocking, or other simple body movements. More capable children can, as they age, exhibit more complex repetitive behavior in the form of collecting objects or creating involved, rigid patterns of personal behavior, such as needing to take the same route to the store every time or needing to put clothes on in a certain order.

Wing and Attwood's second category, the passive group, tends to have a higher level of ability than the aloof group and to perform better on visuospatial tasks than in verbal skills. Members of this group with intelligence in the normal range can often manage in public school. Like those in the aloof group, members of this group tend not to make spontaneous social contact, but in general may be approached without resistance and may be led in games, although they are likely to remain in a passive role.

Although the facility for speech is better developed in members of the passive group than in the aloof group, the speech of passive children still shows the same sort of abnormalities. The main difference between the passive group and the aloof group is that, although members exhibit many of the same behaviors, the behaviors are less marked in the passive group. Because of their ability to respond to others, members of this group are often not diagnosed until they reach school age.

The third group, the active-but-odd group, possesses many of the abnormalities in language and behavior of the other two groups, with the major distinction of being able to initiate contact with other people, though in oddly mannered ways. The contact is not for real engagement and may be so persistent as to be disturbing to the other person addressed. Many children in this group speak late, although some, when they do begin to speak, are able immediately to use complete sentences and long words. Speech is still repetitive, long-winded, unnaturally formal, and over-literal. Nonverbal communication, interestingly, tends also to be impaired in this group with excessive or absent eye contact, odd or absent inflection, and odd body movements during conversation.

Active-but-odd children display characteristic autistic behaviors but may have more pronounced behavioral problems than passive and aloof children. Older active-but-odd children in particular may get into trouble through socially inappropriate behavior in public. Like the passive group, active-but-odd children are often not diagnosed until they are of school age.

There are ongoing efforts to develop systems of classifying the developmental and psychiatric disorders of infancy and early childhood based on research and accumulating experience with a variety of diagnostic and treatment methods. There is still much to be learned before the various disorders can be clearly distinguished from each other.

It was recognized in the 1950s at the Yale Child Study Center and other clinics that a comprehensive approach to understanding the child was necessary. Physical and neurological examinations, hearing tests, and laboratory tests for inborn errors of metabolism and other biochemical aberrations, though less refined than now, were much utilized by referring physicians and the clinic staff. Developmental and psychometric tests were part of the evaluation, as were play sessions with the child. It was usually difficult or impossible to perform complete standardized psychometric tests and arrive at an IQ score with meaning because of the unresponsiveness of the child or his or her inability to undertake the tasks. What one could usually do was to establish levels of functioning in various domains of development (e.g., motor skills, nonverbal problem solving, speech, social behavior, play behavior), and this, combined with the always-valuable information from parents, permitted a synthesis of findings.

In the early childhood years, based on the functional and behavioral picture presented by the child, it is possible to classify autistic children as mildly, moderately, or severely disturbed and to plan treatment accordingly. Nevertheless, this does not warrant a long-term prediction about the future development for an individual child, even though, as a group, most autistic children retain a degree of impairment ranging from relatively mild to severe.

As the case studies in this book illustrate, preschool-year global IQ scores often either cannot be established or are of no value in reaching a diagnosis. Marked scatter in test performance is common, and variations in symptoms and abilities are often extreme. Islets of unusual ability exist alongside deficits in abstract thinking. Some children exhibit remarkable musical, drawing, or sculpting abilities. Others demonstrate astonishing feats of memory or excel in such activities as block design and learning details of maps or subway systems. Beyond the difficulty in understanding these special abilities, such feats add to parents' perplexity about their child. In such instances, the social dysfunction and the major disturbances in communication—language as well as social communication—remain central and defining features of autistic disorders.

Given the severity of the conditions, their perplexing nature, and the relatively poor prognosis, it is not surprising that many treatments have been utilized.[12] Behavioral modification procedures may be helpful in increasing appropriate and decreasing inappropriate behavior. Psychotherapy is suitable only for a small percentage of autistic individuals. Medications, though they have not proved to be curative, may have a limited role in management of certain cases.

As Dr. Fred Volkmar of the Yale Child Study Center has indicated, the best available evidence suggests that early and continuous intervention—appropriate educational interventions to foster acquisition of basic social, communicative, and cognitive skills—is highly desirable.[13] Another very important development has been the realization in the professional community that not only must professionals inform parents of the need, over the long term, to be advocates for their autistic children in a variety of social and administrative settings, but that professionals must also be prepared to assist parents in this advocacy.

ENDNOTES

1. Kanner, L. (1943). Autistic disturbances of affective contact. *Nervous Child, 2*(2), 217–250.
2. Despert, L. (1951). Some considerations relating to the genesis of autistic behavior in children. *American Journal of Orthopsychiatry, 21,* 335–350; Putnam, M.G., Rank, B., & Kaplan, S. (1951). Notes on John I: A case of primal depression in an infant. In *Psychoanalytic Study of the Child* (Vol. 6, pp. 49–51). New York: International Universities Press; Putnam, M.G., Rank, B., Pavenstedt, E., Anderson, E.N., & Rawson, I. (1948). Round table, 1974, case study of an atypical two-and-a-half-year-old. *American Journal of Orthopsychiatry, 18,* 1–30; Rank, B. (1955). Intensive study and treatment of pre-school children who show marked personality deviations of 'a-typical development' and their parents. In *Emotional problems of early childhood* (pp. 491–501). New York: Basic Books.
3. Putnam et al., 1951, p. 49.
4. Bender, L. (1947). Childhood schizophrenia: A clinical study of 100 schizophrenic children. *American Journal of Orthopsychiatry, 17,* 40–56; Bender, L. (1956). Schizophrenia in childhood: Its recognition, description and treatment. *American Journal of Orthopsychiatry, 26*(3), 499–506.
5. Kanner, L. (1971). Follow-up study of eleven autistic children originally reported in 1943. *Journal of Autism and Childhood Schizophrenia, 1,* 119–145.
6. Mahler, M. (1952). On childhood psychosis and schizophrenia: Autistic and symbiotic infantile psychoses. In *Psychoanalytic study of the child* (Vol. 7, pp. 280–294). New York: International Universities Press; Mahler, M. (1968). *Our human symbioses and the vicissitudes of individuation.* New York: International Universities Press.

7. The Yale Child Study Center, to name one organization that studied autism, has produced for more than 40 years a variety of research papers and clinical studies on children with autism and atypical behaviors. See Ritvo, S., & Provence, S. (1953). Form perception and imitation in some autistic children: Diagnostic findings and their contextual interpretation. In *Psychoanalytic study of the child* (Vol. 8). New York: International Universities Press; Caparulo, B.K., & Cohen, D.J. (1983). Developmental language disorders in the neuropsychiatric disorders of childhood. In K.E. Nelson (Ed.), *Children's language*. New York: Gardner Press; Cohen, D.J., Caparulo, B.K., Shaguritz, B.A., & Bowers, M.B.J. (1977). Dopamine and serotonin metabolism in neuropsychiatrically disturbed children: CSF homovanillic acid and 5-hydroxyindolacetic acid. *Archives of General Psychiatry 34* 545–50; Dahl, E.K., Cohen, D.J., & Provence, S. (1986). Developmental disorders evaluated in early childhood: Clinical and multivariate approaches to nosology of PDD. *Journal of the American Academy of Child Psychiatry, 25,* 170–180; Provence, S., & Dahl, E.K. (1987). Disorders of atypical development: Diagnostic issues raised by a spectrum disorder. In D.J. Cohen & A.M. Donnellan (Eds.), *Handbook of autism and pervasive developmental disorders* (pp. 41, 60, 155–161). New York: John Wiley & Sons; Volkmar, F.R. (1987). Social development. Volkmar, F.R., Stier, D.M., & Cohen, D.J. (1985). Age of onset of pervasive developmental disorder. *American Journal of Psychiatry, 142,* 1450–1452; Sparrow, S., Rescorlo, L.A., Provence, S., Condon, S., Goudreau, D., & Cicchetti, D. (1986). Mild atypical children—preschool and follow-up. *Journal of the American Academy of Child Psychiatry, 26,* 181–185;

8. Cohen & Donnellan, 1987, p. 55; Volkmar, 1987.

9. Cohen & Donnellan, 1987, p. 677.

10. Cohen & Donnellan, 1987, p. 3.

11. Ibid., p. 9.

12. Volkmar, F.R. (1991). Autism and pervasive developmental disorders. In M. Lewis (Ed.), *Child and adolescent psychiatry: A comprehensive textbook* (p. 505). Philadelphia: Lippincott, Williams & Wilkins.

13. Ibid.

2

The World of the Ives School

With the exception of "Jane Thompson," the children in the case studies that follow all attended the Elizabeth Ives School for Special Children in New Haven, Connecticut, between 1963 and 1972. All came to the school as preschoolers after being diagnosed as "autistic" or "autistic-like" at the Yale Child Study Center in New Haven.

EDUCATING CHILDREN WITH DISABILITIES

Today, many opportunities exist for children with various types of abilities and disabilities, and public schools are much better prepared to provide services to all children. However, this was not the case when the Elizabeth Ives School was founded.

A Backdrop of Need

Well into the 1950s, American public education systems were not equipped to handle children whose educational needs differed greatly from those of typical children. Consequently, children who had physical, emotional, and intellectual disabilities were often regarded as unteachable. One of the first in the United States to assert that the public must take responsibility for the care and education of children with mental retardation and developmental disabilities was Dr. Arnold Gesell, a founder of the Clinic of Child Development (now known as the Yale Child Study Center), who crusaded for public understanding and acceptance of such atypical

conditions in children as minimal brain disorder, mental subnor-
mality, convulsive seizure disorders, autism, and infant psychoses.[1]
From 1913 through the 1950s, he campaigned for intelligence tests,
public school special education classes, special education training
for teachers, and, especially, developmental testing of infants in
order to permit early diagnosis by pediatricians and psychologists.

Nevertheless, by the mid-1950s there were still only isolated
responses to the needs of children with developmental disabilities
in the United States. Notable exceptions were the demonstration-
pilot study on the education of children with brain injury and
hyperactivity at the Montgomery County Public School System in
Rockville, Maryland,[2] and the day treatment center pioneered by
Carl Fenichel at the League School for Seriously Disturbed Children
in Brooklyn, New York.

The dearth of services for small children who were, at the time,
diagnosed as "autistic," "autistic-like," or otherwise "developmentally
handicapped" was typical not only of the United States but of Europe
as well. Organizations in Europe and the United States treating children with autism were typically child study centers, child development centers, or preschools for young children with hearing or visual
impairments, physical disabilities, cerebral palsy, or mental retardation. Children with a variety of development disabilities were often
lumped together with those who had mental retardation.

From the 1950s to the mid-1960s, several organizations in
Canada and England were among the pioneers of educational
methods for children with emotional and developmental disabilities other than mental retardation or what was then called mental
deficiency. Among these were the West End Crèche in Toronto,
Ontario, Canada, and, in England, the Clinic at Smith Hospital at
Henley-on-Thames; the Highwick Psychiatric Unit in St. Albans;
and the Abingdon Child Guidance Clinic and the Tesdale School,
both in Abingdon.[3] These schools within hospitals or clinics were
the prototypes of schools for autistic children, and wherever one
existed, it became the springboard from which separate nursery
schools, kindergartens, and public school classes came into being.

The Ealing School, one of the first English schools for children
with autism, was described this way:

> The Society for Autistic Children has opened a school at Ealing, the
> administrative arrangements of which have proved most satisfac-
> tory so that I will take them as a convenient model. The premises

were purchased and adapted by funds raised by the Society. The salaries and training costs were met from fees paid by the local authorities, but it is likely that there will be a deficiency each year to be covered by voluntary contributions. The school is open for the usual three terms a year. The hours are 9:30 A.M. to 4 P.M. . . . At the outset there were 10 children, most of whom I had previously taught in another school. . . . There were eight boys and two girls. More girls would have been accepted, but the applications were almost all for boys.[4]

The description of the Ealing School (with the exception of the financing) fits the Ives School at its inception.

IVES SCHOOL FILLS A VOID

In 1963, before the Ives School was founded, there was in the New Haven area no school for preschool-age children with autism, atypical personalities, or severe developmental disabilities. A special preschool at the Yale Child Study Center took children with developmental disabilities. One other private school took children with special needs, but at the elementary level only. To address this need, Elizabeth Ives, a teacher of children with neurological impairments, started what later became the Ives School in two Sunday school rooms at the church where her husband was minister. Together with doctors from the Yale Child Study Center and several parents whose children were being seen there, Ms. Ives developed a preschool program for young children with developmental disabilities. Ives's program was a pioneer in the field of education for preschoolers with autism.

Ms. Ives died suddenly within a year after the founding of the school; however, the parents, doctors, and educators involved with the school elected to continue its work. They reorganized the school under a new director and under the new name, the "Elizabeth Ives School for Special Children."

After 2 years, the school grew from 5 teachers and 10 children to 8 teachers and 14 children. Most of the children were referred to Ives through the Yale Child Study Center and other child development clinics. Some came from psychiatrists in private practice, and one or two were referred directly from public school systems. In 1965 and 1966, other private schools for children with developmental disabilities were started in the community. One of these schools was for children with severe autism. The other school was designed to educate older children and adolescents with a variety of moderate to severe developmental disabilities, those who would now be diagnosed as having pervasive developmental disorder-not otherwise specified (PDD-NOS).

The School Facility

The Ives School was set up in the church just like any other preschool. The two upstairs Sunday school rooms were equipped like preschool rooms, with corners for playing with dolls and blocks, painting and listening to music, and a place for books where children could sit and look at the illustrations. In each room there was a completely equipped play kitchen, which was very popular, and a place for water play. Various other centers of interest were set up around the room with dividers, creating cozy places where these children who were often distractible, often hyperactive, could find privacy and quiet. As the school grew, it expanded to rooms in the church's basement. One room was used for one-to-one teaching or to separate an unruly child from the group. (Some of the children called this room "the jail.")

The church also had a large, sunny playground equipped with climbing bars, a seesaw, a variety of sizes of swings, a glider, a sand pile, and various sizes of trucks and tricycles. Each spring, the faculty put together an order for new toys, games, and other teaching tools for the following September. There was also a large gymnasium in the church's basement, which was used often, particularly on rainy days. As the teachers' awareness of the children's needs grew, they began to use the gymnasium at the church more and added a swimming program in coordination with the YWCA. (This was particularly valuable for those children who needed to gain a better sense of their bodies.)

Personnel and Supports

The school hired a social worker (principally to work with parents), a speech therapist, and a physical education teacher. The faculty also began meeting on a biweekly basis with referring doctors who were specialists in the field of autism. Each of those sessions was devoted to a single child. The faculty found that consulting with someone who was clinically trained and not involved with the children was very supportive and helped increase their knowledge of autism and expertise in teaching the children.

The administrative setup of the Ives School was informal. Faculty meetings were held on Friday afternoons. They were group cooperatives in which the teachers collectively discussed schedules, new activities, needed changes, and teaching techniques to benefit one child or another. Faculty meetings were not only a means of planning programs and future curricula but were vitally important for mutual support. The teachers listened to each other's problems, discouragements, and sometimes moans of utter exhaustion. The collective sympathy, suggestions on "how to," and praise for each other's successes saw the staff through many difficult periods.

A board made up of the doctors, several interested members of the church in which the Ives School was lodged, parents, and the director was responsible for the business side of the school. Tuition at Ives was low, $400 yearly, largely because in the mid-1960s parents had to pay for their own child. Consequently, salaries also were comparatively low, approximately $1,200 to $1,800 a year. With the passage of the Elementary and Secondary Education Act of 1965 (PL 89-10),[5] and the amendment to this act in 1966 (PL 89-750),[6] the financial aspect of the school improved. The Elementary and Secondary Education Act of 1965 provided for federal assistance for programs to educate low-income children with disabilities, and its amendment created a Bureau for the Education of the Handicapped. This meant that the public school systems began to pay tuition for children attending schools such as Ives.

As mentioned, children were referred to the Ives School from the Yale Child Study Center and other sources: individual psychiatrists, pediatricians, general practitioners, and developmental pediatric specialists, as well as child development and pediatric clinics. Usually, a doctor or staff person contacted the director of Ives about a particular child, after which, with parental permission, the director and sometimes other staffers at Ives observed the child at play. They discussed the child's condition with the referring individuals and then decided if the Ives program was appropriate. Once Ives tentatively accepted the child, the parents came in to be interviewed. These admission interviews were held in the spring, and if all went well, the child entered the Ives program the next fall. Before the child came, all relevant material on him or her was forwarded to Ives from the referring source, and Ives staff members met with the child's social workers, teachers, and doctors. This helped the Ives staff obtain enough understanding of the particular child to prepare a tentative individualized program.

THE CHILDREN: PERPLEXED AND PERPLEXING

The children admitted to the Ives School were between the ages of 3 and 7 years, and as mentioned previously, all had been diagnosed as autistic, autistic-like, or atypical. They were impaired in their speech and understanding of language, and many were nonverbal or minimally verbal. Many had severe perceptual-motor and eye–hand control problems. Hyperactive, sometimes violent, and sometimes withdrawn, they were considered uneducable. They had been excluded from general preschools and frequently from special education services in the public schools.

When they arrived at Ives, all of the children had the air of being lost, with little sense of self. Most of them had no idea which side of their body was left or right; sometimes they seemed to have no understanding that they had a body at all. Many had compulsive, self-stimulating, stereotypic gestures such as aimless hand flailing, jumping up and down, turning one hand back and forth and looking at it as if mesmerized, walking on tiptoe, whirling around, and darting aimlessly about. A few ran headlong, usually out the door into the church hallways and once or twice even out into the street.

Wild, disoriented behavior; sudden, violent temper tantrums or hysterical crying spells; and catastrophic reactions to another child or to a change or to nothing readily identifiable—all were typical. A child might be intelligent and able to relate comparatively well to people and the environment and yet be subject to sudden, violent outbursts—screaming; racing around the room destroying everything; grabbing a teacher and mouthing or biting arms, shoulders, or breasts; swearing repetitively; or running out of the classroom.

Some were too quiet, and most of them seemed remote and unreachable. One little boy, new to the school, chose to sit in a chair, isolated in the middle of the room. He held himself together with such tension, staring as through a fog, that he gave the impression of total fragility. All of the children projected fearfulness, varying from remoteness, to shyness, to anxiety sometimes amounting to panic. They often felt acute or chronic discomfort in situations most young children would consider manageable or even interesting. Very seldom did any child exhibit signs of pleasure or enjoyment.

The children's expressions of their fearfulness were often peculiar. One child would back into the room with his eyes covered by his arm and then seat himself by backing up to a chair. He was never seen to miss. Another walked around with his eyes covered most of the time, one eye peeking under his arm. Many refused to look at others or seemed to look through them as though they did not exist. One child needed to hide in his teacher's coat when they went on walks. It took weeks for him to gather the courage to come out from under it.

The children very rarely used speech in social communication. Their speech was characterized by a variety of verbal expressions: babbling interspersed with meaningless shouts; superficial glibness interrupted by sudden hysterical crying and screaming; illogical nonstop chatter; swearing; loud, fast repetition of words; echolalia; speaking with a rising inflection so that every sentence sounded like a question; or using only three or four words as a sort of chant. Two of the greatest challenges the teachers at Ives faced were to discern what was behind the speech these children did use and to get them to speak meaningfully.

The most common and distinguishing characteristic of all these children was what one referring physician called their "imperviousness": that air of remoteness each displayed toward others. Each acted as though an invisible wall existed between him or her and everyone else. All of the children tended to treat other people, including their teachers, as objects of function only, as beings without recognizable personality. One little boy spent much of his time whirling aimlessly around the room. When he wanted to go from one room to the other, he would take his teacher's hand, place it on the doorknob, and twist the hand as a signal that he wanted to open the door. To him, the teacher was nothing more than a tool, some kind of human can opener.

Their inability to relate normally to others in no way meant that these children were unaware of their surroundings, however. One child who constantly stared ahead was given a demonstration by a teacher of how to do a three-piece puzzle. The teacher left the three pieces on the side for him to place. The child did not even look at the pieces, but when the teacher turned away momentarily, he did the puzzle in a flash—correctly. When the teacher turned around to look at him, he was again staring at the wall.

THE TEACHING METHODS AT THE IVES SCHOOL

In the early 1950s, several therapies emerged aimed at children with developmental disabilities. One was a method of play therapy advocated by Dr. Virginia Mae Axline of the School of Education at New York University, a student of "nondirective" therapist Dr. Carl Rogers; another was the system of behavior modification developed by Harvard psychologist B.F. Skinner, which is currently used by many schools; and yet another was the theory of muscular basis of behavior expounded by Newell C. Kephart, of Purdue University's department of psychology.[7] In addition, many special education classes in both private and public schools incorporated ideas on spatial orientation put forward by Dr. Ray Barsch, Professor of Special Education at Southern Connecticut State University.[8]

The underlying philosophy of school founder Elizabeth Ives was based on the work of Syracuse University Department of Education's William M. Cruickshank.[9] Ives used handmade teaching materials: red, blue, green, and yellow squares, triangles, and circles; block pattern designs, from simple designs to increasingly difficult block structures; pegboard patterns made with dots on tagboard to be copied by the child on the child's own pegboard; and two-, three-, and four-piece puzzles, usually magazine pictures cut in halves or thirds and mounted. Her method was an individualized, highly simplified, concrete form of teaching.

A Typical Week

The schedule at Ives was 8:30 A.M. to 2 P.M., Monday through Thursday. Because of the Friday afternoon faculty meetings, Friday was a short day, 9 A.M. to noon, and was totally taken up with the swimming program. When the children arrived each day, they hung up their coats and played for a while with whatever interested them. This was the settling-down period; it took about half an hour. Then came a work period. In the beginning, one teacher conducted the work period for several children while the other teacher supervised the remaining children at play. As the children adjusted to the routine and their behavior improved, each of the two teachers in the room was able to work with a child on a one-to-one basis while the other two or three children played.

The work period covered areas of specific needs. Given the children's different kinds of developmental disabilities in perception, eye–hand coordination, language and speech, and motor control, the teaching was tailored to meet each child's impairments, using strengths to help weaknesses, not "drilling" addressed to the deficits.

After the work period, there were games or some sort of collective activity, such as story reading, that got the children together and gave them the feeling of being part of a group. Then there was a juice break. Afterward, weather permitting, there was outside play. The teachers sometimes took them on trips and walks in a nearby park where there were slides, swings, and a sand pile.

Each teacher at Ives kept day-to-day records on each child in individual notebooks. Important as it is to keep individual accounts of children's progress in a general classroom, it was an absolute necessity to keep written notes on these children. There were no published guidelines for teaching children with autism, and no previous experience had prepared the teachers to handle the children's puzzling, sometimes shocking behavior. The teachers were therefore actually creating entirely new teaching strategies. Recording the specific instances of what had worked or not worked with one child helped teachers plan for that child's future and also permitted new techniques to be generalized or adapted to activities for other children. These notebooks offered an invaluable backlog of information. This was one of the ways the teachers at Ives learned how to teach children with atypical development, at least in the first 2 years. Later, the school shifted to more efficient record keeping.

Ives was a preschool only and stopped at the first- to second-grade level. Depending on the severity of their impairment, the children went from Ives to one of four or five external programs. The choice was the combined decision of the child's parents; their consulting physician; the director of the Ives School; a representative of the proposed school; and, after the public schools were required to provide funding, the child's public school social worker. Several individuals with the most severe impairments, many of whom were nonverbal, went to a private program for such children. Some students went to another private school that took them through the equivalent of high school. A few were able to attend general education classes at public school. A majority "graduated" into special education programs for students with developmental disabilities in public schools.

Legislation in 1966 had required Connecticut public schools to offer more varied classes for children with developmental disabilities. Programs, termed "service centers," were started under Connecticut Statute 10-66 and included a communication disorders program for children diagnosed as autistic and autistic-like. Children from Ives most often went to either the program for communication disorders or other types of special education classes.

Addressing Children's Social, Language, Emotional, and Perceptual Needs

The Ives preschool represented an effort to approximate as closely as possible regular nursery-school through first-grade programs and techniques. The curriculum and instructional materials were directed toward the specific perceptual, language, and comprehension impairments of the children. There was strong emphasis on social interaction and language and on the educational function of play, interwoven with some special education techniques.

Throughout the school day there was attention to language. The children had an acute need for inner, expressive, and receptive language. They were asked to perform basic exercises such as naming objects, then pictures; then they were asked to tell a simple, one-sentence story from a picture. The teachers also used puppetry, acting out nursery rhymes, creative rhythms to music, and nonobjective painting. Everything the children did—outdoor activities, games, trips, walks to the park—contributed in some way to purposeful language development.

To enable the children to name their feelings, teachers often started with simple pictures, naming them "sad," "happy," or "angry." Eventually the child was able to make a happy face or a sad face and would be shown his happy or sad face in a mirror. For the particular child he or she was working with one-to-one, a teacher would interpret other children's feelings as well. The teachers also tried to get the children to realize and articulate their own feelings. A teacher would say to a child who had become remote or who was distracted, "Tell me what you are thinking. It will help you keep your mind on your work."

There also were games: the hokey-pokey, "Here We Go 'Round the Mulberry Bush," Blind-Man's Bluff, Hide and Seek, and I Spy. Each one taught directionality, coordination, and teamwork. Each involved the child's seeing himself or herself as a person. Games also taught the children how to have fun, an unusual experience for most of them.

Of particular use were mirrors, tape recorders, puppets, and telephones. These tools, perhaps because of their impersonality, were very successful in teaching children with autism. Each one allowed the children to distance themselves from direct, face-to-face personal contact. One child, usually out of touch with people around him, talked freely on the telephone. Another, in the course of being retested as an adult, performed best when answering questions over the telephone.

The school's puppet theater functioned similarly. A real-looking stage with a backdrop, it stood on a table that was tall enough so first-graders could stand up behind it and yet be hidden by curtain skirts. Making scenery and furniture enchanted the children, and the impersonality of the theater encouraged them to talk.

Some children needed a great deal of time and repetition to grasp things. For example, the children played a game called "Postman" using flash cards of beginning reading vocabulary and their own names. One child was the postman. Another stood and asked, "Good morning. Do you have a letter for me?" The postman was supposed to reply, "What's your name?" and the other child would say his or her name. But one boy, playing the postman, parroted the other child by repeating, "Good morning. Do you have a letter for me?" The teacher had to lead him through the game and get him to repeat "What's your name?" after her. It took 2 months of endless drill for the boy to cease echoing and ask, "What's your name?" on his own.

The teachers worked on each child's body image in a variety of ways: naming the parts on a doll and matching these to the arms, legs, and other parts of the child's own body; using full-length mirrors; using paper dolls and pictures; and having the child crawl under or over a broomstick. Activities such as playing outdoors on the climber, seesaw, and glider swing; using a walking board; and swimming also improved children's body image.

Nearly all the children had perceptual confusions or problems with identifying objects and perceiving them in space. The difficulty with spatial relationships, part of the general perceptual impairment, was compounded by the children's general lack of a sense of their own bodies and self. To address perceptual problems, teachers first used real objects, later going to worksheets and pencil-and-paper exercises. Once the children could identify an object and its position in space, they were helped to understand and distinguish "in front of," "in back of," "beside," "above," "below," and so on.

The children also had difficulty with perceptual constancy, the ability to recognize shapes consistently (circle, triangle, square, and, later, oblong), not just in their simple forms but in other representations as well. The children learned the word "circle" along with the concept of "circleness." As a first exercise, they were to sort circles, squares, and triangles, at first by color and then by shape. This exercise was simple and unthreatening, and most of the children were willing to try it. (The ability to do this is part of typical public school first-grade reading readiness.) The perceptual constancy exercises progressed to where the children had to find a square in a house, a triangle in a sail or a tree, and so on.

Many of the children also had figure-ground discrimination problems: They were unable to distinguish foreground from back-ground, auditorily or visually. This problem showed in the dis-tractibility of the children; everything within their line of vision or hearing had equal importance to them. They needed training to be able to focus on one or two elements and block out the rest. Audi-tory figure-ground discrimination exercises were done with the speech therapist as well as with the teachers.

Often the children had impairments in their visual-motor skills (i.e., the coordination of vision with muscular movement and con-trol, sometimes called eye–hand control). Many could not draw a line on the chalkboard from the edge to a chalk dot in the middle or could not balance blocks. Or, if they could balance blocks, they could not balance the blocks in a pattern to make a block structure.

Even when they understood spatial ideas, severe perceptual-motor problems sometimes made it difficult for them to put one block "on top of" another. Some could not identify shapes or tex-tures by touch, cut with scissors following a line, or use a stencil. They often could not cut shapes in paper or put paste on a precut piece of paper. One student was 21 years old before she could cut out a valentine! Visual-motor difficulties had little or nothing to do with cognitive impairment, however, and often the children with the greatest intellectual impairments demonstrated good coordina-tion in fine motor skills.

The Importance of Intuition and Consistency

Because of the absence of firm guidelines for dealing with the problems of these children much of what the teachers did was necessarily intuitive, but this quite often turned into successful teaching. One child, for instance, could not separate from his mother. He had spent the first 2 years of his life apart from his mother, mostly in the hospital. In school, the minute she moved an inch away from him, he would honk with alarm like a baby elephant. Realizing the depth of his panic, the teacher decided to try separating the two very slowly. The mother first sat right next to him and then very slowly, under his teacher's instructions, inched her chair backwards day by day. It took a whole month for her to get from the play table, where he was playing, back to the wall of the room, but by that time he paid hardly any attention to the fact that his mother was not near him. The day of success came when, at the time for outdoor play, he got up and ran out of the room with the other children into the play yard without a backward glance at his mother. He had learned to leave her himself, certainly, but he had also been taught.

Successful teaching, of course, is relative. At Ives, each child had his or her own special teacher. The success of the teaching depended on the establishment of a consistent, unbroken relationship between child and teacher. For example, in using a color-matching exercise with an inattentive, withdrawn, or hyperactive young boy, the teacher might put down a red square, saying "red," and one blue square, saying "blue," and then carefully and slowly hand a blue cardboard square to the child. The color would catch the child's attention, and he would match it with the blue square. The teacher might have to say, "Where does this go? Blue goes on blue," or show him once. If the child performed the exercise successfully, it meant that his awareness had been captured and he had focused on the exercise, if only for a few seconds. This was the equivalent of getting a foot in a door; then the door could be pried farther open. The child's attention span could be stretched, under patient teaching, from seconds to minutes, with the child receiving constant praise from the teacher. As the child felt successful, he became less hyperactive, less withdrawn, and more attentive.

The educational approach required for these children and the goals that the Ives School's faculty tried to achieve in teaching each child were summed up by a referring specialist with regard to one little boy, Louis:

Louis is asking for a world that will control, limit, and organize him since he is not able to do it for himself. He seeks an environment that recognizes his difficulty in screening stimuli, in focusing in on a particular one. His need to control others, his discomfort with answers that only lead to more questions, his compulsive need to destroy things are calls for help in the fragile world in which he attempts to function.

To break through to a child with autism, teaching must be patient, unrelenting, and caring to enable the child to become engaged in learning and with people. This was the basic approach of teachers at Ives. The teaching at Ives was also informed: It was founded on sound knowledge of child development and general early childhood and elementary school educational techniques, and it was augmented by skilled medical and social work consultants.

Realities and Rewards

Despite the improvements in teaching children with special educational needs since Ives was founded, the basic truth remains that teaching children with autism and other special needs is a demanding, strenuous, and often frustrating job. Teachers are regularly exhausted and drained of energy at the end of the day. They are sometimes bitten, kicked, or slapped and are often put in awkward and embarrassing positions. One middle-age teacher at Ives was thrown onto the sidewalk and sat on by one of the larger Ives children who had exploded in a sudden temper tantrum. The teacher was only able to get up when a teenager from a local high school happened by and lifted the child off of her.

For those who work in this field, it is true that a 30-second breakthrough, the smallest lightning-flash of victory, counterbalances the exhaustion and sends the teacher home in a glow of success. Those who are committed to these children find this reward enough. Physical endurance, emotional stability, flexible responses, ability and willingness to improvise, and an intuitive "gut" feeling about a child—all of these are needed to work with children who have developmental disabilities.

This kind of teaching is not everyone's cup of tea. Between 1966 and 1972, three people at Ives were counseled to leave the field, one because she was afraid of physical violence and two others because they wanted "organized" classrooms. The Ives School staff evolved into a unique group of caring and informed people, each of whom brought to the job an enduring commitment to children with developmental disabilities.

A letter from the mother of a former Ives student, written on August 26, 1967, suggests the effect of the Ives program: "[A]ll the children (Frank's brothers and sisters) are looking forward to school starting, especially Frank, thanks to his former experiences under your tender care. We thank you again for all your time and loving concern for Frank. Good luck to you this year. May it be less hair-raising than the last!"

ENDNOTES

1. Ames, L.B. (1989). *Arnold Gesell: Themes of his work*. New York: Human Sciences Press.

2. Cruickshank, W.M., Bentzen, F.A., Ratzenburg, F.H., & Tannhauser, M.T. (1961). *Teaching method for brain-injured and hyperactive children: A demonstration pilot study*. New York: Syracuse University Press.

3. Weston, T.B. (Ed.). (1965). *Some approaches to teaching autistic children* (p. xxi). London: Pergamon Press.

4. Elgar, S. (1966). Teaching autistic children. In J.K. Wing (Ed.), *Early childhood autism* (pp. 224–225). London: Pergamon Press.

5. Elementary and Secondary Education Act of 1965, PL 89-10, 20 U.S.C. §§ 241 *et seq.*

6. Elementary and Secondary Education Act Amendments of 1966, PL 89-750, 80 Stat. 1191, U.S.C. §§ 873 241 *et seq.*

7. Kephart, N.C. (1960). *The slow learner in the classroom*. Columbus, OH: Charles E. Merrill.

8. Barsch, R.H. (1967). *Achieving perceptual-motor efficiency*. A space-oriented approach to learning: Vol. I. A perceptual motor curriculum. Seattle, WA: Special Child Publications. This book formed the basis for several college courses for teachers at the time.

9. Cruickshank et al., 1961.

Part II

Case Studies
in Autism

3

The Children and Their Parents

These are the stories of nine children who attended the Elizabeth Ives School for Special Children: Tom Brown, Jimmy Davis, Polly Daniels, Bill Kolinski, David Ellis, Karen Stanley, John Stark, Larry Perelli, and Eric Thomas—and a tenth, Jane Thompson, who has been added to provide further insights into the spectrum of disorders classified as autism. (Jane did not attend Ives School.) As children, they all were diagnosed as "out of touch," "impervious," "unaware of the environment," or with "inappropriate reactions to the environment." To a greater or lesser degree, these children illustrate the traits that define autism spectrum disorder: the concreteness of thought (all 10); inability to reason logically; speech patterns, whether articulate but odd (John, Polly), limited and echolalic (Tom, Karen), or totally lacking (Eric, Jimmy); eyes that refuse to look directly at you (all with the exception of Jane); stiff posture or ways of moving (David, Tom, Karen); compulsive gestures (Eric, Jimmy, Karen); fascination with repetitive movement (Karen, John, Tom); overwhelming anxiety communicated through posture; hair-trigger tantrums; and the need for sameness and structure (all 10). At the same time, these 10 stories demonstrate the great differences that exist among individuals with autism spectrum disorder.

In the stories that follow, it should be kept in mind that it is difficult to classify and diagnose each person exactly; the behavioral abnormalities found in the spectrum of autism disorders should not be regarded as rigid. Children can move from one group to another as they grow. Some, such as Polly, may have behavioral "overlays" associated with autism, but on the Autism Behavior Checklist (ABC; Krug, Arick, & Almond, 1980)[1] score "probably not autistic."

Each case study describes the child's educational interventions, from diagnosis to the present day, as well as the various types of schools they attended; family interactions; employment histories, if any; and living situations.

TESTING INFORMATION

At the end of seven of the case studies are the results of developmental testing performed in October 1987, when each individual was an adult and several years after each had finished his or her education. (Of the remaining three individuals, the parents of one opted not to have their child participate in testing, another individual had died in early adulthood, and one was not part of this original grouping.) The tests used were the Wechsler Adult Intelligence Scale–Revised (WAIS–R; Wechsler, 1981),[2] the Vineland Adaptive Behavior Scales (VABS; Sparrow, Balla, & Cicchetti, 1984),[3] and the ABC. In addition, another test was used, the Behavior Checklist for Identifying Severely Handicapped Individuals with High Level Autistic Behavior,[4] though data for this test are not given in the following case studies. Many factors—such as motivation, curiosity, creative talent, work habits, and achievement in particular academic subjects—are not measured by these or any other (intelligence) test, and that fact should be taken into account when interpreting these results.

The WAIS–R measures intellectual functioning. It has six subtests of language and verbal skills (the verbal IQ scale), and five subtests of perceptual motor or nonverbal solving ability (the performance IQ scale). IQ test scores reflect a sample of learning in several different skill areas, including actual knowledge, learned abilities, problem solving, memory, and attention. Therefore, these scores are generally good predictors of future learning, academic success, and other abilities, although intelligence in any individual with autism is blurred by the effect of the disability, which does affect cognitive functioning.[5]

There is a lack of integration in the senses that affects the input from the apparently normal eyes and ears of individuals with autism. Messages received by their brains do not convey a clear, understandable picture of what is seen and heard. The result of this deprivation is dramatic. If it is gross and prolonged, individuals may function as having mental retardation requiring extensive support. If they have potentially typical cognitive development, recovery tends to be rapid once the environment is adjusted.[6]

The VABS is a standardized instrument that, using interviews with a parent or primary caregiver, assesses a child's capacities for personal and social sufficiency in various areas (or domains) of functioning. These cover communication, daily living skills, socialization, and motor skills.

The ABC represents an attempt made in the early 1980s to provide a diagnostic instrument for autism. It contains 53 items relevant for the diagnosis of pervasive developmental disorders. These items elicit clinical information, in this case from teachers, from which it is possible to provide a score that corresponds to symptom severity. The validity of the ABC has been extensively studied at the Yale Child Study Center by Dr. Fred Volkmar and colleagues.[7] The weighted scores on the ABC can be used operationally to distinguish individuals with autism from those who do not have autism, although a clinical evaluation is necessary before a firm diagnosis of autism can be reached. Individuals with an ABC score of 67 or higher have a high probability of having autism; those with scores in the 53 to 67 range possibly have autism; and those with scores lower than 53 are unlikely to have autism.

The October 1987 testing cited throughout this book was performed at the Yale Child Study Center under the supervision of Dr. Sara S. Sparrow, Associate Professor of Psychology at the Yale Medical School and Chief Psychologist at the Yale Child Study Center. The testing itself was done by Alice Carter, Ph.D., Assistant Professor of Psychology, and Fred Volkmar, M.D., Director of the Sally Provence–Irving B. Harris Child Development Center and Assistant Professor of Psychiatry and Pediatrics at Yale Medical School. The ABC was rated in September 1987 by me, Virginia W. Sperry, retired director of the Ives School, on seven of the children as they were at ages 4–8 years.

THE VOICES OF PARENTS

Immediately following six of the case studies presented are the parents' stories. These personal accounts, taken from taped interviews and written accounts in 1994, convey what it was like for each parent to discover that his or her child had autism; what the parents did when they found out; and how they are coping as their children have grown into maturity. As each child is different, so are the parents, although the general characteristics of autism spectrum disorders provide a basis for similarities. For most parents, talking about themselves and their children was difficult—not because they didn't have a lot to say, but because it was hard for them to expose and re-experience the painful emotions that have accompanied each stage of their child's life.

Many of these parents were angry and embittered when their children were first diagnosed. A few were resigned. One was thankful for her child as he was. And some lived day to day, still fearing that their child might close up and become unreachable or, to use one mother's words, "back off the edge of the earth and never return." But, happily, when this edition of this book was published the attitude of every parent—without exception—had changed. All are proud and happy with their children. In short, they have come to accept their children's limitations and are pleased with their achievements.

ENDNOTES

1. Krug, D.A., Arick, J.R., & Almond, P.J. (1980). *Autism Behavior Checklist. Autism Screening Instrument for Educational Planning (ASIEP).* Portland, OR: ASIEP.
2. Wechsler, D. (1981). *Wechsler Adult Intelligence Scale–Revised.* New York: The Psychological Corporation.
3. Sparrow, S., Balla, D., & Cicchetti, D. (1984). *Vineland Adaptive Behavior Scales (VABS).* Circle Pines, MN: American Guidance Service.
4. Denckla, M.B. (1986). New diagnostic criteria for autism and related behavioral disorders: Guidelines for research protocol. *Journal of the American Academy of Child Psychiatry 21* (2), 221–224.
5. Wing, L., & Attwood, A. (1987). Syndromes of autism and atypical development. In D.J. Cohen & A.M. Donnellan (Eds.), *Handbook of autism and pervasive developmental disorders* (p. 4). New York: John Wiley & Sons.
6. Ibid.
7. Volkmar, F.R., Cicchetti, D., Dykens, E., Sparrow, S., Leckman, J.F., & Cohen, D.J. (1988). An evaluation of the Autism Behavior Checklist. *Journal of Autism and Developmental Disorders 18*(1), 83.

4

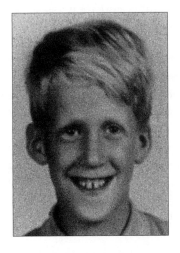

Tom Brown

Essentially Isolated

born February 4, 1960

When Tom came to Ives, he was 5 years old and only whispered in two- or three-word sentences. He had been diagnosed at the Yale Child Study Center as having slow general development and an atypical (autistic) personality disorder. The physician who examined him at Yale noted that Tom had been an irritable, difficult-to-comfort infant who cried a great deal and could only be quieted by being rocked. He spoke no words until age 2 and had delayed motor development as well. On the developmental evaluation, he showed mildly uncoordinated motor functions but did well with structured materials, showing relatively good form perception. He could discriminate size and follow a pattern. Number concepts and motor control were his weakest areas. Language was a year below age, at a 4-year-old level, and reasoning ability was at a 3-year-old level. He appeared to have a neurological disability that affected his body image and general perception of the world around him.

Tom's parents were described in teacher reports as well-educated, professional, and sensitive, and their concern for him had perhaps exaggerated his dependence. His clinging but oddly impersonal relationship with his mother was noteworthy. He was unusually sensitive to temperatures, sounds, and smells. He was especially vulnerable to anxiety and had difficulty in forming close relationships with others. He had problems in logical thinking and in differentiating reality from fantasy. He was considered more hindered by his personality disorder than by his mild mental retardation. His parents were advised to enroll him in special education to address his social and emotional problems, as well as his cognitive delays. Shortly after undergoing this evaluation, Tom was referred to Ives, and he entered in the following fall.

Tom attended the Ives School for 3 years. In his first 2 months, he was quite passive and seemed content to follow his teacher's suggestions. He showed considerable diligence in the pursuit of his activities, often to the point of *perseveration*, and frequently, regardless of the task, he would stay at something until the teacher moved him to something new. Yet, he displayed a lack of feeling about the results, showing neither pride nor pleasure nor anger. His conversation was limited to "What?," "No," and "Yes," and he was passive in the face of the aggressive acts of other children.

In the spring of his first year at Ives, Tom began to show signs of gradual gains. He became more negative to teachers' guidance and said "No" to any and all activities. The teachers were encouraged and felt that this "No" was at least the beginning of something other than an absence of recognizable reaction. Tom also made other progress. He began to move his chair away from an aggressor and react when displeased by spitting.

During this year, Tom used the most words while he was involved in doll or water play—to the doll he would say, "You're a bad girl," or to himself while washing doll dishes, "This is wet," or "That's a mess." His direct conversation with teachers consisted of "No" or naming objects in pictures. Otherwise, he did not use words. At snack time, he pointed to what he wanted, and although he enjoyed the game of Lotto, he would reach for a card without saying the appropriate words. Although he would listen intently to stories read aloud, his facial expression remained dull, and unlike the other children, he never commented on the stories.

Tom had good form perception and was good with fairly difficult puzzles. But, he seemed to have some visual-motor problems:
He found it nearly impossible to stack one block on another in order
or to follow a block model, and he had difficulty thinking logically.
Though he recognized color, he would not use it as a clue to proper
placement of the blocks, and he could match colors but could not
use them to follow a block pattern. In painting and drawing, he
would color circles or primitive stick figures and immediately
blacken out the picture.

By the end of his third year, Tom, at age 8, was ready to go back
to special education classes in public school. He was then reading
in a preprimer. He was very distractible and still made compulsive
flailing motions with his hands, but he played with other children,
one at a time, and could talk audibly. He still had to be taught on a
one-to-one basis.

Tom was seriously hampered by his bland *affect*. People tended
to treat him as a cipher. But, the teachers at Ives concluded that Tom
knew more and felt more than he was able to express (a feeling
shared by many who have come to know Tom).

An Ives School teacher's report dated in the spring of Tom's
departure provided this description of him:

> Tom still does not really interact with other children. Although there
> is considerably more direct contact between Tom and other children
> and also more direct conversation, nevertheless most of the time the
> contact remains indirect and experimental. In playing house, for
> instance, he plays with the teacher. Outdoors, he is much more likely
> to appear to be playing with a child as they ride on bikes together.
> Indoors, the times that he has played with classmates, involving
> reciprocal conversation, have been rare and usually have revolved
> around trucks and blocks. Tom is an imitator, picking up other chil-
> dren's provocative ways. He makes lots of noise with the sticks of the
> Lincoln Logs (banging them on the table) or raising up the radiator
> cover and letting it fall with a bang, or (slyly) moving the large air-
> plane close to the radiator and turning the propeller against the radi-
> ator. He has never hit or struck out at another child. He will flail at
> the air with his hands, or he'll sometimes touch a child saying, "Stop
> that" or "That's not nice," or "Shut up!" He will sometimes footnote
> this in an aside to the teacher saying, "Hey, Jimmy's hitting me." His
> calling out of toilet words is much less frequent this year. When Tom
> does get really physically hurt, he gets very upset, reddening and
> tensing up, with tears in his eyes, looking hurt resentful, and frus-
> trated. He hardly ever verbalizes his feelings. If you do this for him,

such as "That really hurt you, Tom, and it makes you very mad, doesn't it?," he sometimes acknowledges this with a lessening of the tension, a direct look in your eyes, and a little half smile. When Tom makes a direct protest, it is done timidly and in a bland voice.

Physically and emotionally, Tom is hard for an adult to get close to. Many people, in first dealing with him, tend almost to forget his presence in the room. After long acquaintance, at least two of his teachers feel real affection, warmth, and understanding for him. Tom in this area, too, is making slowly improving attempts at direct personal contact. One day, he concentrated on one teacher with abusive language and lots of loud nonsense talk. This was on the playground. She had to leave to go into the room and invited Tom to come help. He started to follow her in but then would only yell at her, "Shut up, shut up." Just as she was getting to the door, she heard him say sweetly, "I'll be waiting for you." She was out the next Monday, and on Tuesday, Tom said softly to her, "We missed you yesterday."

Mrs. Brown and Tom's good-byes to each other are usually shy with Tom normally turning his back but always taking a peek at her as she leaves. He runs to her gladly at the end of the school hours; however, there is never direct warmth. On her part, Mrs. Brown's caring for Tom, though undemonstrative, appears so deep and her feelings are so disturbing to her that one wonders how much of her anxiety Tom feels.

It is next to impossible for Tom to stay on a walking board or a balance board. In joining in a circle game, his gait is shambling and awkward. He does not skip yet and has trouble hopping. He is now working with another child in reading and enjoys the competition. He has a funny streak of stubbornness and on some days refuses to say vocabulary words aloud which he knows and you know he knows. This would tie in with the kind of uncooperative behavior he demonstrated toward the speech therapist at the Rehab Center. He many times refused to say things and told his mother later, "I didn't talk."

The report also discussed another difficult aspect of his personality:

Anyone who deals with Tom should be on the alert for his desire for special consideration and his hostility if this is not forthcoming. This quality may not be immediately apparent but runs deep. It means he has keen feelings about one person relating consistently with him. In a teaching situation, this seems to be of primary importance.

On the subject of his stubbornness and quiet hostility, his mother, many years later, wrote, "I always felt that Tom's hesitancy to answer was his way of getting back. No one could make him talk. He always needed to be first."

When Tom was 13 years and 7 months old, he was given a psychological evaluation by his local school system at the request of his parents. On the Wechsler Intelligence Scale for Children–Revised (Wechsler, 1967), he had an IQ score of 55. He failed every item on the Bender Visual Motor Gestalt Test (Bender, 1942).

Tom spent 2 years in the special education class in his public school system. At that point, his family moved, and he transferred to another school system where he again was in elementary special education classes. After elementary school, he moved on to the special education vocational high school. According to his parents, Tom received excellent treatment at this school. The teachers were professional in their approach to the teaching of children with special needs. Tom learned many life skills, such as how to use a savings account and how to deposit his salary. Tom learned how to cook and read simple recipes, how to shop for groceries and add up the bill, and how to handle a telephone. He also learned to read simple maps.

In high school, he was mainstreamed for sports, music, and art. Although he was still quite inarticulate, he nevertheless handled himself well with typically developing children and was well liked by the teenagers in these classes.

During summers and afternoons in the winter, Tom went to Saltaire, a Department of Mental Retardation regional center, for practical job training in work skills and for specific vocational courses such as dishwashing. On weekends, he worked as a dishwasher in a small local restaurant, a job he still holds, miraculously, decades later.

Tom seemed to have considerable ability. Although throughout high school he continued to have trouble speaking directly and audibly and thinking logically, he always gave other people, including his teachers, the impression that he had more ability than he was able to demonstrate. His guidance counselor at Saltaire also said, "He can do more than just wash dishes."

At age 20, Tom graduated from his vocational training class in high school. After graduation, he continued to work in the restaurant as a dishwasher from noon to 5 P.M. each afternoon. His employer was very pleased with the way he worked; in one of her reports she said, "We do not have enough business to use Tom for longer hours, but he clearly hates to leave the restaurant, so he deliberately slows down on his dishwashing!"

At Saltaire, Tom developed socially. Through the center, he became involved in several recreational events. He bowled every Saturday and was good at it; he even had his own bowling ball. He went square dancing with a group sponsored by the local Association for Retarded Citizens (the national organization that is now called The Arc of the United States), and was a skillful dancer. There were frequent summer picnics and winter parties. Tom's mother reported that though he spoke infrequently, he was liked by everyone, and at school he always had a friendly group around him. Tom enjoyed staying overnight occasionally at the summer camp run by Saltaire, allowing his family to take short vacations.

As a young man, Tom's independence had its trouble spots, however. He startled his mother by twice leaving the house and disappearing for several hours. Each time, he went on his bicycle to Saltaire to see his friends and from there went straight to work, on time. Still, he did not understand that he needed to communicate his whereabouts to his mother.

Though Saltaire had helped him become more social, Tom was still a loner and most of the time he stayed at home. There, he spent a lot of time in his room listening to records, and he used to spend hours playing with computer games. He had an audiotape recorder and talked into it a great deal. His mother never listened to the tapes. He watched a lot of television. Although he had developed comparative autonomy, Tom still followed the pattern of his late teenage years. He did chores at home and cooked for himself. He still had no peer companionship, other than people he saw during any of his structured social activities, such as bowling and square dancing. He did not go to friends' houses, nor did any friends come to his.

At this point in his life one of Tom's main problems in making and maintaining relationships with others was his lack of social initiative. A good example of his level of social interaction occurred one summer at a picnic. He took his parents to meet his friend, a 40-year-old woman with mental retardation with whom he had been bowling. After the introductions had been made, Tom ignored his parents and stood beside his friend most of the evening, neither one of them talking.

His interaction with his family remained a matter of everyday routine. He talked very little and, unless forced, avoided all eye contact. This has been quite difficult for his parents over time. His mother once said bitterly that children with mental retardation are supposed to be rewarding and affectionate, but neither she nor her husband has ever felt that Tom is fond of them. Mrs. Brown is a tall, gentle person who has resilience, strength, and a good sense of humor. Intelligent and decisive, she had difficulty with Tom's disability when he was young and often cried, but over time she gradually acquired self-confidence in dealing with the issues involved.

Although autism creates walls around those who have it, raising a child with autism has often been socially difficult for families as well. While Tom was living at home, if his parents went to a party where he could "fit" in, they took him. He tended to spend such evenings sitting, smiling occasionally, talking to no one unless spoken to, apparently content in his isolation. Mrs. Brown found introducing him gracefully an insoluble problem. As she said, "I can't say 'This is Tom, my retarded son.'" Both parents are keenly aware that people meeting Tom are thinking, "What is wrong with him?"

Social interactions were a bit easier for Tom's sister, who has mild mental retardation. She worked at a big supermarket and could carry on a conversation with some give-and-take, which was almost impossible for Tom. She had two good friends, with whom she went to movies and to programs at the nearby Center for the Developmentally Disabled. The dilemma for Tom's parents was that although it was a temptation to ask his sister to include him on her outings, they felt it would be unfair to do so.

Though a lonely one, Tom's life was fairly contented. In the summer, his family vacationed at a lake, where Tom swam and fished. His family went out to dinner frequently both at home and on vacations, and this contributed to Tom's social experience. Nevertheless, despite Tom's apparent stability in his job and other routines, his family, especially his mother, continued to experience the strain and frequent distress that came with having to care for two adults with special needs.

As Tom matured, his parents knew that their son, being as independent as he was, needed some basic sex education. Tom's mother once attended a lecture on sex education for individuals with mental retardation and enrolled him in a 23-week Planned Parenthood class on sex education. Although he was not sexually active, Tom was aware of sex; he spent a lot of time in the bathroom, "masturbating, probably," according to his mother.

Tom's degree of autonomy posed some other critical questions for Tom's parents, too. How could he have sensible independence and yet still be looked after? When Tom turned 21, a legal guardian was supposed to be appointed for him in the case of his parents' deaths, but this wasn't done until 10 years later, in part because his parents did not know where to seek the proper legal advice. (At that time there were fewer lawyers who handled such concerns.) They were continually concerned about Tom's "aloneness." One solution they seriously considered was to buy a condominium for him and his sister. After some consideration, the Browns decided not to put the responsibility for Tom onto his sister's shoulders. They realized that he should be living in a group home or some supervised apartment-type living arrangement. As a result of the deinstitutionalization movement, however, most of those individuals leaving institutions were placed in alternative living arrangements ahead of those who were already living in good homes, and so, at that time, new living opportunities for Tom had not opened up.

Plans to place Tom in a group home were postponed when he had a seizure at the age of 28. He was at home in the kitchen when it happened, causing him to fall, unconscious and face downward into a sink full of dirty dishes, his long arms extending over the counters on either side. Both parents came running and carefully picked him up and stretched him out on the floor. Tom regained consciousness within 5 minutes but remembered nothing. He went back to work the next day and seemed fully recovered. (A complete neurological examination disclosed no abnormality that would explain the seizure, and there has never been a recurrence.) Despite their concerns for his health, the Browns renewed their commitment to finding an answer that would ameliorate Tom's isolation and allow him more companionship with peers.

When it came to his job, Tom had proven to be quite an independent and responsible adult. He traveled to work on his bicycle. He deposited all of his salary, at first with help from his parents, who aided him in filling out deposit and withdrawal slips. By age 20, he had saved $2,000. When he was approximately 21 years old, Tom increased his hours from part time to full time. At 30, he had saved $15,000. He bought his own clothes, magazines, and record albums. His supervisor and his co-workers all viewed him with affectionate understanding and were supportive, yet firm. The seizure did not seem to have affected his work at all. He was able to function independently, with all of the people in the restaurant around him, without getting flustered or withdrawing. One example of this was that he was able to select his own lunch from the multitude of choices.

For almost 6 years, from ages 30 to 35, Tom was in a research group at a local mental health center. A year after he had joined this research group, Tom was diagnosed as having fragile X syndrome, a syndrome sometimes associated with autism. Tom was put on Luvox, a commercial brand of fluvoxamine. His social awareness and ability to focus became much improved.

When I went to lunch with Tom in 1997, he shook my hand and said, "I liked your book"; then he told the waitress proudly, "She wrote a book about *me*." I found him a far cry from the bland, hard-to-reach little boy who came to Ives School some 30 years before.

Tom stood 6 feet 3 inches tall and was still quite blond. He had a newly acquired sense of self-confidence and a directness of communication that he did not possess while in his twenties or even early thirties.

Tom's original diagnosis of atypical personality disorder was one of several broad terms used in the 1960s to define autism. He was described by the referring specialist as "Bland, slow in all developmental landmarks." This is still true of Tom at age 39, but the blandness has developed into an advantage. During his high school years it was perceived as amiability and is in fact just that today. The stubbornness he showed as a child has translated into determination.

This conviction can be seen in the progress he has made despite what his test results might have indicated when he was 27 years old. At that time, Tom's scores placed him in the mild range of mental retardation. But, his VABS Daily Living and Socialization scores, which were 80 and 83, were astonishingly high in view of the general picture presented by his IQ and Communication scores and the fact that he has a pervasive development disorder. This shows that testing, no matter how accurate, cannot define that intangible quality called "personality." In Tom's case, his stubborn determination and responsiveness to teaching meant that he was open to and took advantage of every educational opportunity. Recently, Tom's mother said that the situation had pretty much stabilized for him. He continues taking Luvox, which appears to have improved his attitude generally, helping him live independently.

Tom's social life today consists of different activities planned by the local Arc, usually on Friday nights. The Arc sends out a schedule listing weekly events and Tom signs up for those that interest him, usually swing dancing or going to a ball game or movie or, as his mother describes it, "getting together in small groups." He also joins his family for a summer vacation in the west where, at their cabin by the lake, he still enjoys fishing.

Another landmark in Tom's life is his living arrangement. During the course of his 20-year work history, he had accumulated a $25,000 savings account. With these funds, and with his father's help in researching places to live, Tom helped his parents achieve their dream of independence for him when he bought a two-bedroom condominium in a pleasant area approximately 2 miles from his parents' home. There, he receives assistance from the Eastern Community Development Corporation (ECDC), an organization that provides people such as Tom with a supportive network of caseworkers, social workers, transportation, and general supervision in daily living tasks. He is now able to live comparatively independently and has done so successfully for several years. Comparative independence means 3–4 hours daily of staff support from ECDC and the state Department of Mental Retardation as well as hands-on parental oversight. Individuals from these organizations help Tom with his bill paying, meal planning and grocery shopping (the emphasis is on less snack food and more fruits and vegetables) house cleaning, and keeping up with his various appointments. Tom also is driven by a case worker or staff aide to various appointments, though he continues to ride his bike to work. Although he does not talk about it himself, it has been reported to his parents that he is seen riding his bike around the seaside community where he lives, apparently content to move around the area and find his own way back home.

Although his parents had at first envisioned Tom living with a roommate, finding someone to share the condo presented problems. Rosie—a middle-age woman with mild mental retardation—moved in, but she left to get married, much to Tom's distress. His anxiety was such that at a staff meeting that included his case manager, caseworker, social worker, parents, and others, the group members unanimously agreed that it would help Tom to see a psychotherapist to help his understanding of relationships. Tom is now driven by a staff person to see his counselor once a week, but the staff member does not participate in these sessions. Many issues are discussed with Tom participating fully; he seems to enjoy each session.

Tom now lives alone by choice. In mid-1999, according to his mother, his case workers introduced him to a possible roommate as a replacement for Rosie. They tried to get Tom to say whether or not he liked this young man. Did he really want a condo-mate? The effort to get him to express his wishes was to no avail. He would *not* tell them. Finally, his mother asked Tom to write her a note saying whether or not he wanted a person to share the condo. Wonder of wonders, Tom wrote his mother saying emphatically that he did *not* want a roommate. He wanted to live alone. So, the roommate issue was settled. But, his ability to express himself in writing illustrates the autistic trait of difficulty with personal interactions. He could write his opinions but could not express his feelings during direct social contact.

It is worth noting that throughout his work career Tom has been commended for being a valued and popular employee. He still manages the dishwasher but now also takes care of the food storage, putting away items that have been ordered and bringing down what is needed from the stock room to the kitchen.

When it was suggested to the restaurant owner that Tom was lucky to have found such support and understanding at his place of work, the owner retorted, "It's quite the reverse. *We* are lucky to have found Tom!"

Because Tom earns minimum wage at his restaurant job, he had to reduce his work week to 4 days when the minimum wage increased in 1997 so that he would continue to qualify for Medicare and Medicaid. Otherwise, his income would have been too high for him to continue to receive the services that enable him to live in the community and to be essentially self-supporting financially. Like most people with disabilities, his medical condition makes him uninsurable privately.

His father has been very interested to learn of the recent government decision to raise the income limits under which individuals with disabilities can retain the right to Medicare. Because of this change, it is expected that Tom will soon be able to resume working full time.

In the summer of 1999, I met with Tom's mother for lunch on the open upper deck of the restaurant where he works. It was a brilliantly clear, late August day, and the sun glinted off the sailboats moored at the edge of the bay.

On his lunch break, Tom brought up his plate of pasta and salad. Maturity had changed Tom's appearance. He was heavier than when I last saw him and, as he walked into the restaurant dining room, he seemed to tower over the other occupants.

His original evaluation spoke of "mildly uncoordinated motor functions," and he still moved awkwardly. He had hurt his right leg in a fall "in the stockroom," he said. Luckily, he had not broken anything; he'd only suffered muscle strains. His limp added to the awkwardness of his gait, however.

Facially, his lean, lantern-jawed look had filled out. He was wearing glasses, a new development. Behind the glasses, his eyes seemed more aware. He wore jeans, a T-shirt with a "green trees" logo that he had purchased during the summer vacation, heavy work shoes, and a white restaurant apron. In many ways, however, he reminded me of the little 5-year-old boy who came to Ives School. While we were talking, he looked away, usually to the left. His conversational skills still seemed limited. When I asked him, "What did you do on vacation, Tom?," his echolalic response was, "Yes, I did fish . . . did fish . . .yes, I did . . . ," and then he drifted off into muttering.

His mother remarked, "He talks to everyone but me."

This was quite apparent during lunch. The more she asked questions, trying to get a response, the more Tom was evasive and unintelligible. When his mother wanted him to tell what fruit he and his sister had picked when they were on vacation, it took many repetitions of the question and many hints before Tom said "blueberries," hesitantly but clearly. It is possible that, had I been alone with Tom, he would have talked more freely.

Tom's parents say that they are "content" with his situation as it is today. They are now in their late sixties and, with no younger family member able to take on the role, they are considering the problem of how to provide for his guardianship in their wills.

There is no doubt that Tom constitutes something of a triumph over the disabilities of autism in that he has achieved comparative independence. Tom is grounded enough in reality to take pride in

doing a job well, and he has a well-
developed sense of responsibility. He,
of course, still has the characteristic
traits of autism, but he has developed
a great deal from the almost nonverbal little boy who first came to Ives.

                               *   *   *

In June 1981, at the age of 21, Tom received psychological and vocational testing. He was neatly and appropriately dressed. His behavior during testing was exemplary. The psychologist, who considered the test a valid measure of Tom's ability, reported:

> Tom presented himself for testing as a quiet but friendly 21-year-old young man. During testing, he exhibited a sustained level of concentration and attention throughout. He approached each task with an air of confidence.

> Tom's current level of intellectual functioning falls in the upper limits of the Mentally Deficient range. There is no significant difference between verbal and performance abilities.

> In the verbal areas, Tom's strength is his ability in abstract reasoning or logical thinking, which is average. His word knowledge is borderline, while his abilities in general; judgment and common sense, arithmetic skills, and short-term memory for numbers; are very deficient. . . .

> On the Bender Gestalt, a measure of visual motor coordination, Tom' performance is indicative of an individual having serious visual motor difficulties which suggest organicity. . . .

> Tom's academic achievement as measured by the Peabody Individual Achievement Test [Dunn & Markwardt, 1970] is at a grade three level for overall achievement. His ability in mathematics, which is his lowest academic area, is limited to counting items from 1 to 20; simple addition and subtraction of whole numbers up to 6; number recognition at least to 30; and knowledge of the idea of what an object that has been cut in half looks like. In word recognition, Tom's highest academic area, Tom's ability is at a mid-grade four level. Reading Comprehension is at a grade three level. . . . Tom's fund of general knowledge is equal to individuals functioning at a high grade three level.

The report then discussed the results of Tom's vocational testing:

> Individuals with abilities in this range (upper extended level of competency), such as Tom, have the verbal-cognitive ability to understand simple concepts and analogies and can superficially relate these to their environment. These individuals often do not internalize concepts and therefore have difficulty generalizing from one set of circumstances to another.

The report went on to say that although Tom showed mild motor impairments that would ordinarily indicate a sheltered workshop environment, he had proved that he could work successfully in the community. His motor abilities "are sufficiently developed to allow for safe operation of some air-powered and motor-driven equipment under close supervision. Tasks requiring a 15- to 30-minute time period for completion can be performed by Tom."

In summarizing his impressions of Tom and the test results, the psychologist depicted Tom as a pleasant young man who appeared shy but confident of his abilities. He described him as being unable to initiate conversation and incapable of understanding or relating to the emotional needs of others. He had difficulty in gaining meaning from his experiences and had shallow contact with the environment. During testing, Tom made little if any eye contact with the examiner. The report concluded,

> Although [Tom] seems content with himself, he expresses the desire to be smarter. There seems to be some insight, although limited, into the fact that his abilities are limited. On the surface, these feelings of inadequacy are not readily apparent. There is an internal disappointment in the gap between aspiration and the ability to achieve.
>
> Tom appears to have some behavioral strengths. Patience, high frustration tolerance, persistence in performing work tasks, good concentration, a cooperative nature, and pleasant personality. . . .
>
> Behaviorally, Tom has many emotional and coping skills that he utilizes to his benefit. His limitations in this area are socialization and his inability to understand the impact of his behavior on others. . . . Tom seems to be able to perform at a slightly higher level than test results indicate. . . .

Tom was 27 in October 1987, when he was again tested at the Yale Child Study Center. Tom's scores follow.

TEST SCORES

WAIS–R
Verbal IQ score: 64
Performance IQ score: 69
Full-Scale IQ score: 65

VABS

Domain	Standard score	Adaptive level	Age equivalent
Communication	38	Weak	7 years 11 months
Daily Living	80	Moderate–low	13 years 9 months
Socialization	83	Moderate–low	15 years 6 months
Adaptive Behavior Composite	62	Low	12 years 5 months

ABC

107: Quite autistic

"It takes endurance
to stand up for your child..."

by Pat Brown

1994

Tom was just over a year old when we moved to Connecticut. I was then pregnant, expecting our daughter Jennifer, and moving was traumatic. We moved in February, and maybe it was the new situation, but Tom just seemed to feel very uncomfortable. He cried all the time. I felt that something was wrong with him. He didn't appear to be developing properly, and he was so easily upset by people. He just cried and cried, which was very frustrating. Our pediatrician reassured me that Tom did not have anything wrong with him, that he was a middle child, and that his being a middle child might explain his being socially upset.

Tom didn't like to be with other people. I can remember sitting outside with other women and children. He would climb onto me to be away from them, but he couldn't settle down even then and kept fidgeting. He didn't walk until late, and he didn't want to feed himself. He was very interested in things that spun and in any toys that moved. He would watch the wind in the trees, waving his arms and flapping his hands. He used to flap his hands when the automatic garage door closed. (As an adult, he still likes to watch the garage door close.)

I think Tom must have been 2 when the pediatrician finally sent me to the Yale Child Study Center. There, they didn't give any specific diagnosis; they just said he was atypical with autistic tendencies. All they gave me was oral information, nothing in writing. That was their policy at the time. They would write letters to school, but they would not give a parent a written diagnosis. I didn't get a written diagnosis until Tom was 21.

I don't know when we learned he was autistic. It was probably when he was about 4, when I went to register him for nursery school. The people at the school said that he was not the sort of child they could take. We had him tested [at the Yale Child Study Center], and the results showed that he was mildly retarded. They said he had "autistic tendencies" and was "mildly retarded," but they never said that he was an autistic child. They never had a definite reason for Tom's problems. We never knew until just within the past year what caused it.

Finally, last year, Tom was diagnosed as fragile X positive. It's helpful finally to have a definite diagnosis. My husband, Steve, definitely found it a help, and it's now very plain that Tom's sister, Jennifer, has the same thing. Evidently, it's a genetic abnormality on my side of the family, which bothered me, but I can't think of anyone in my family, except perhaps one uncle, who might also have had it. They said sometimes several generations pass without it showing up. They also told me that one of the signs of being a carrier is crying all the time for no reason. I do that.

Tom attended Ives, and after Ives he went to public school, which worked out very well. Tom's special education teachers did a lot for Tom, and I was very pleased with what they did. I also admired their patience. The only difficulty I had with the public schools occurred when we moved, a few years after Tom started the special education program. I spoke to the head of special education at the public school in the town we were moving to and arranged for Tom's schooling there. I told her about Tom and gave her all his records, but when September came, they hadn't done anything. They weren't sure where they were going to place him at all. They thought they might put him in the same class as his sister. I got quite upset, because I had always tried to keep the two apart in school. The school system ended up putting Tom in a junior high special education program at the last minute.

Ultimately, the public school special education programs were very good for Tom. He got a lot of help, and his teachers worked with the state Department of Mental Retardation to get him job training after he left high school. He trained at the local regional center to learn dishwashing.

We had more difficulty from the public schools with Jennifer. After having failed kindergarten, her psychologist at the Yale Child Study Center recommended that she go to a certain special school, which had a good learning-disabled program. Everything was arranged when the public school system, which is responsible for paying the tuition for such special schools, up and decided that because the Yale Child Study Center had merely suggested that this would be good for her, not insisted on it, the school system was not going to pay the $1,200-per-year tuition. Eight years later, we finally sent Jennifer to a private residential school that cost $13,000 a year, which, of course, the public school system ended up having to pay for anyway.

In dealing with all of the administrative issues that come up when you have a special child, it's very difficult if you don't have a lawyer working for you. Money is always the issue, and although I think things have improved because now there are more laws requiring that public school money be spent on special children, it still takes a lot of endurance and gumption to stand up and fight for your child. For me it did.

Since 1979, when he left high school, Tom has had the same job, which he got through the regional training center. He washes dishes and does some cleaning. He has picked up some other skills, such as peeling and washing potatoes. He goes to his job 5 days a week, and he's always there ahead of time after a 4-mile ride on his bicycle.

Jennifer has an apartment with a roommate, but Tom still lives at home. He doesn't relate much to us. He talks to his sister on the phone and they seem to have wonderful conversations. I don't know why, but he talks to other people much more than he talks to us. I think somehow we inhibit him. We've always controlled him, and he has the need to be in charge of the situation.

He performs his jobs around the house promptly without being reminded—things like emptying the trash and the dishwasher or helping to cook. He seems to enjoy basic cooking and will probably learn more. He understands how to use the dishwasher, washing machine, dryer, stove, and microwave, although he usually needs help deciphering directions for the microwave.

He uses the telephone well. He remembers numbers: his social security number, bank account, telephone numbers. He goes to the bank by himself to deposit his check and make withdrawals, but he needs help balancing his checkbook. He loves to buy things, but he never asks to buy anything or wants to buy anything on his own. For the last 10 years, he's had the same things on his Christmas list. He goes to the barber shop by himself when he is reminded. He seems to read the newspapers but never comments on what he reads.

Tom has always been interested in plants and keeps track of the temperature and barometric pressure in the house. Once I was concerned about his losing weight, so now he weighs himself every week and writes it on the chart. He has a cassette recorder and listens to the same tapes over and over again. When he's watching television, if people come up and say "hello," he doesn't say "hello" out loud. He just sits there and bows.

He enjoys social activities with people his own age, but he has no close friends and doesn't make any contacts on his own. He likes sports and has become a very good bowler. He has also become very good at playing a number of computer games. These involve a good deal of manual dexterity, and he has a good memory for them.

He does require help with money arrangements of any kind, with hygiene, such as when to shave, and, at times, with appropriate dress. He doesn't know how to use public transportation either, but I think he could probably learn.

He is somewhat of a mystery, and I think he is capable of doing much more than he does, particularly with things that do not require judgment and logic. Tom can learn to do many things perfectly. He runs machines really well. His only difficulty comes if something goes wrong. He isn't able to ask for help. Once he broke the aquarium in his room and tried to soak up the water with bath towels. We found out about it when we noticed that the downstairs ceiling was damp. He couldn't explain why he hadn't told us about it, but that is his normal way of dealing with problems. You have to be sensitive to the nonverbal clues to find out that something is wrong, since he will never volunteer the information, even though he needs your help to fix the problem.

Sometimes, Tom just doesn't seem to deal with reality. One weekend, we asked if he wanted to go to ceramics or golf, and he said ceramics. I said, "Do you know what ceramics is?" And he said, "No." And so I explained. "Oh yeah," he said. "That sounds really great." But, when I mentioned taking golf lessons, he said, "Golf?" as if he didn't know what it was. And his father plays golf all the time.

You are never really sure if he quite understands. And sometimes when we're doing things, you can see he's just confused. He doesn't know which way to turn sometimes. When we're walking down the street or going somewhere, he's sometimes not quite there. You can see this look in his eyes.

Tom has never yelled or shouted or gotten angry in a way I could tell by the sound of his voice. He will throw or break things when he's frustrated, though, and we explain to him that we know he's angry because he broke something. I think he doesn't know how to express his frustration in words.

I think that autistic people are very aware of everything, but they just don't or can't admit or express it. They can almost reach into your minds at times, as if they know what you are going to do next, even before you do. It's as if they pick up on a signal that you give out. I think Tom is this way. He seems to know everything I'm going to do, and he always will. If I'm going to get up out of a chair, he'll get up first. I talked to some other relatives of autistic people down at Yale, and they said similar things.

Recently, we finally acquired a guardianship for Tom through the probate court. We asked for a full guardianship, but they said they very rarely give them because they like the handicapped person to be able to make some decisions for him- or herself. So, Tom and I went to a meeting with the Department of Mental Retardation. Unfortunately, I started crying, as usual, and I think that influenced the department's decision. I didn't really want the representative to change her mind because of that; I wanted to convince her of the merits of my position. As a compromise, she asked if Tom could be allowed to make decisions about his living situation. I said of course he could, but that at the moment we couldn't find anything available. They ended up recommending that we get full guardianship, and I felt a bit guilty because I thought I changed their minds by crying.

Recently, we also got Tom into a Planned Parenthood class on sex education, which goes on for 23 weeks. He has gone twice. It's not only sex education but also how to behave in the community, proper hygiene, and such things. Someone from the Department of Mental Retardation is there to work with the Planned Parenthood people. I tried to ask Tom what they talked about in class. He finally said, "Where babies come from." I said, "Well, where do babies come from?" And he said, "I don't know." I had been concerned about Tom's sexual awareness because when we filled out a form about his bowling, he wrote something on a piece of paper and stuck it on the outside of the envelope. It said something about watching a woman teacher—the one the envelope was going to—walking around the street with no clothes on. The teacher called and told us about it. We talked to Tom about this incident and said that it's not appropriate. You can think these things, but you can't write them in letters.

Tom should be in a group home, but I think that putting him in one would be very traumatic for him. It's also hard to find a job and a live-in situation that are close enough together. I've turned down a couple of options because they were too far away from his job. A group home would be much better for Tom because he sort of isolates himself at home. He's protected here, but he doesn't have much communication with my husband and me or with other people.

Tom's sister, Jennifer, lives in a condominium we bought for her. Since Tom has saved a good deal of money, it might be possible for him to buy into some kind of apartment or live-in situation. Tom's caseworker at the Department of Mental Retardation has been talking about apartments. But, although Tom could very well take care of himself, an apartment, and cooking if someone came in each day, I would still be concerned about his isolation, even if he had a roommate. He takes no initiative with his social life. He loves to go out if someone else plans something, but he doesn't make any plans himself. I can see Tom sitting in his apartment, going to work, going dancing on Friday (because he does that every Friday), but not ever telling his roommate or neighbors what he does. Jennifer's roommate organizes all kinds of things, and that's great for Jennifer. What Tom really needs is some sort of warm atmosphere where he can be with a group of people. That would give him something to do and people to relate to. We have had Tom's caseworker get him on the list for a group home.

There is one place I know near here where they have a number of apartments in one building and 24-hour supervision. I'm thinking about trying to get Tom in there. There's always a long list for placement, but that's the kind of thing I'm thinking of. It's very similar to what we did with Jennifer. She's getting services through the Department of Mental Retardation, and in case something did happen with us—if we moved, for instance—she is settled. If we ever moved, we would not take Tom or Jennifer with us.

Another thing that has put Tom's living situation on hold is the proposed state budget cuts for the handicapped. Cuts are hitting the recreation programs, too. The entire recreation staff in our district was laid off for a while. The Department of Mental Retardation recreation program has provided Tom with most of his outside activities. They have had a lot of their own programs and they ran all the Special Olympics programs, which they don't do in most of the state. The recreation people got their jobs back, but their transportation budget has been cut, so they aren't doing as much as they did. They have come up with a program on Thursday nights, which unfortunately is the night my husband and I go down to New Haven to attend a meeting for parents of adult autistics at the Connecticut Mental Health Center. The recreation staff used to have a party or other social event once a month, but they don't anymore.

They had a party once this winter, but parents had to bring their kids themselves. They came up with the idea of taxi vouchers, which they sold for $1.60, so the kids could take a taxi. Jennifer and her roommate have used those a lot. Tom's never taken a taxi, so he didn't use the vouchers himself. We were going to the theater that night, so we drove Jennifer, her roommate, and Tom to the party. The girls took Tom to their condominium in the taxi after the party, and we picked him up from there when we got out of the theater.

We go with Tom to the autism clinic at the Connecticut Mental Health Center in New Haven, and I think it's good for him to go there. I feel at least there's someone I can go to if I need help. They're willing to deal with any sort of problem, and they can point us in the right direction. I've had a lot of help from the Department of Mental Retardation and our caseworker. I've learned to use them much more within the past 3 or 4 years. It's good to know there is someone who is aware of Tom, who knows that he's looking for a place to live and knows what my intentions are for Tom. I now feel I have some control over his situation.

The way the system works is this: The public schools legally provide funding and services, so they are in control. Once Tom was school age, he was involved in that. Today you'd be involved even early on through the early intervention programs, but at the time Tom was young, it was just the school system. We went to Yale, had Tom diagnosed, and sent him to the Ives School without anyone really helping us. Only when Tom was enrolled in the public school system was there a single bureaucracy interested in his welfare and his future.

The system works well until the kids get out of the school system when they are 21. Then, the parents are back almost on their own. You are supposed to go to the Department of Mental Retardation for help, but it's up to the parents to know all this. Every year, the parents have to make arrangements and figure out what's going to happen in that year. And each year you find out that this program's stopping, or this person says your child should be going here, or that person says he should be going there. It seems like you go to one place and they deal with a certain problem, and then you go somewhere else and start all over again explaining the whole thing. There's no coordination. So, you're supposed to deal with all of these different support systems. There's really no one single place you can go. No one actually is in charge except the parent.

It is frustrating to deal with all of the different agencies and doctors. It's just up to the parents, and it gets to be kind of a drag. I'm tired of thinking about Tom. Sometimes it seems that's all I do. Every time there's someone new; the professional people come and go. And then you're back to square one. A better system of coordinating the agencies must be developed.

Postscript

Much has improved for Tom. He is living in a condo on his own. He cooks, cleans, does his laundry, and enjoys his independence.

This has come about with the help of many people. Tom's father has taken on the highly challenging job of deciphering the bureaucratic maze that enables Tom to pay his way. Our Department of Mental Retardation case manager is always ready to address any problems. A DMR Self-Determination Grant pays for a supported living provider, which means a daily morning visit to check on Tom's readiness for work, help with shopping, bill paying, banking, transportation, and medical appointments. Tom's employers for the past 20 years have treated him as family. The restaurant is Tom's home away from home.

I no longer feel that Tom's welfare depends only on me. Learning to give up some responsibility has led to this successful transition. I'm still Tom's mother. I worry about the little things. Housekeeping is perhaps not up to my standards. I have concerns about Tom's inability to express his wants and feelings. Talk he does, but he has difficulty making important decisions or relaying information to those who work with him. Everyone finds this frustrating. I would prefer he have a live-in companion, but he has turned down several.

I believe Tom is satisfied with his life. We will continue to assist him in every way we can to live his life to the fullest.

5

Jimmy Davis

Living with a Profound Communication Disorder

born September 22, 1962

At the age of 3, because of a delay in his speech development, Jimmy Davis was referred to the Connecticut Department of Health's New Haven Evaluation and Counseling Program for Retarded Children. The physical and neurological examinations he received there did not reveal a cause for the delay: His hearing was normal, and he already wore glasses for nearsightedness. The testing did find, however, that his mental development was at the 2-year-old level. The physician at the speech and hearing clinic said, "Jimmy closes people out." Subsequently, a public health nurse who visited his home described him as seeming to live "in a world of his own," but permitting brief periods of interpersonal contact.

Between the ages of 3 and 4, Jimmy attended a small preschool, but the experience was unsuccessful. The school's report on Jimmy stated:

> The only way in which Jimmy could be present at group activities was by the teacher holding him on her lap. This he liked. He enjoyed water play but had to be watched closely at it. One day he tried to push the tub that contained the water; he became frustrated because he could not move it and had a tantrum that frightened the other children. He jumped, kicked, screamed, bit, and hit his head with his hands very hard.

During the time he attended this school, Jimmy was evaluated by several clinics at Yale-New Haven Hospital and also by the local state-run rehabilitation center. Each evaluation gave a similar diagnosis: organic brain damage and mental retardation. His parents were a bit confused by this, as Jimmy appeared intelligent and was responsible for caring for himself at home. The pediatric specialist at Yale–New Haven's child development unit explained that although in all probability Jimmy had some brain impairment, he was, above all, disabled by his emotional disturbance, which left him afraid, angry, very upset, and puzzled. With no ability to talk out his problems, the physician said Jimmy would behave as if he had mental retardation and would have the same needs as such a child.

At 4½ years old, Jimmy was diagnosed at the Yale Child Study Center as emotionally disturbed with conspicuous autistic symptoms. His maturational age was 2 years. He was described as a nice-looking, robust child who was clearly aware of others but who often avoided social contact. His speech remained markedly delayed and garbled (in fact, he has remained basically nonverbal all his life), and his parents were concerned about hyperactivity as well.

Jimmy's erratic response to formal testing made it impossible to assign a global developmental level. A series of individual sessions over several months at the Yale Child Study Center helped to clarify the disabling nature of his autistic personality. Jimmy responded positively to the individual sessions with a teacher, and on the basis of that he was referred to the Ives School that summer.

During Jimmy's first weeks at Ives, he behaved like a madman. He pinched, scratched, and screamed. He liked to butt people in the stomach, and he bit children and teachers. He was totally self-absorbed, keeping his head down and his eyes covered with one hand, successfully avoiding having to look at anyone. Outdoors, he sat in the sand pile and poured sand on his head or ate it. He walked around the play yard protected by the arm of a teacher, again shading his eyes as though he was unbearably afraid of the world. During the fall and winter, on outings to the park, he insisted on walking buttoned up inside his teacher's coat, which created the rather strange apparition of a person with one head, a very fat stomach, two large feet, and two small ones.

By October, Jimmy was putting sand in containers and eating less of it. He had learned to use the slide, had climbed two rungs on the jungle gym, and used both the glider—a swing with two seats—and the single swings. Using the glider meant that Jimmy had to work with another child, an important step out of his self-imposed isolation. Indoors, he began putting together puzzles and snap beads, but he had no tolerance for failure. One mistake brought on a tantrum. He could be moody and withdrawn. Often, in those weeks, he worked in a room alone with one teacher. Because he still sometimes resorted to scratching, butting, and biting, one of the staff members checked frequently to be sure that his teacher was surviving.

In June, at the end of that first year, Jimmy, then almost 6 years old, held up his head and looked at people. He smiled and laughed. On walks that spring, Jimmy ran ahead with the other children. He still did not talk, but he clearly understood what he was told, enjoyed listening to stories, and followed instructions if he happened to be in a cooperative mood.

Although Jimmy improved in his first year at the preschool, he regressed the second year. He became increasingly belligerent and by February could tolerate being with only two children. He often had to go back to the one-room, one-teacher routine. The February report said, "Jimmy is a pathetic little boy, scared, insecure, with a poor self-image." As spring advanced, he resisted doing puzzles, coloring, and all of the other nursery school activities he had enjoyed. Outdoors, he sat on the edge of the sand pile, his head buried in his teacher's lap. He appeared to have become overwhelmingly afraid again of the outside world and to feel safe only when protected by his self-isolation.

Gradually, it became clear that it would be impossible to keep Jimmy at Ives. There were some difficulties at his home between his father and mother, and the teachers at Ives felt that this accounted for the change in his behavior. There was no other available school at the time, so the doctor at the Yale Child Study Center decided residential care was the best solution. Mrs. Davis consented, and she cooperated with the doctor in finding an appropriate environment.

The final report from Ives to the Yale Child Study Center and the public school system said, "Jimmy has the knack of finding his way into your affections. We are all devoted to him and have been fighting for him to the best of our abilities. He can be charming and appealing. He obviously has deep feelings blocked completely by his lack of ability to talk." The letter ended by saying, "We remain convinced that there is real potential here, and all of us hate to 'give up' on him."

From Ives, Jimmy went to a regional residential school for individuals with emotional disturbances and mental retardation located in a nearby town. This school had a wide spread in the age range of its residents, from preschoolers to 40-year-old adults. Jimmy stayed there for 5 years, but it ultimately was an unsuccessful experience. Some of his clothes were stolen, and he was overmedicated because of inadequate supervision. Consequently, his mother began to insist that he come back to live at home. She had divorced Jimmy's father, and guided by the Ives School social worker, had been able to improve her home situation. She wanted to take total responsibility for Jimmy and felt she could create a more stable and supportive environment for him.

At that time, the Connecticut State Department of Education began funding a communication disorders program specifically for children with severe developmental disabilities. Jimmy transferred to this program when he was 11 years old, and because the public school in his hometown had started a facility under this program, he was able to return home to live. The program was well run, and parents received reports on the progress of their children and met monthly with the teachers. When Jimmy entered the program, he was aggressive, phobic about animals, and hyperactive. After intensive work by his teachers, this behavior lessened, and he began to calm down as he developed a little self-confidence.

The major accomplishment in these years was helping Jimmy improve his ability to communicate, achieved by teaching him to use sign language. At first, the learning method used for Jimmy consisted of having him wear hearing aids in each ear and listen to cassettes. The teacher showed him a picture, and a voice on the cassette said the name of the object pictured. The teacher made the appropriate sign, and Jimmy copied this signing. Once he possessed an adequate signing vocabulary his intelligence was liberated, and his drive to achieve motivated and activated his learning. He made rapid progress and was soon moved to a higher functioning group in the program. In this group the ratio of teachers to students was two to six. Jimmy's potential was obvious to everyone from the beginning. He was aware of other people, and he became more responsive and continued to progress rapidly.

By the time Jimmy was 17 years old, his mother had gone to business school and had remarried. Jimmy was then in his second year of high school. His mother and her new husband worked, she as a secretary at the hospital and he in business. Because of this, Jimmy was alone for 45 minutes or so when he came home from school. He managed very well. He took the school bus, had his own key, and was quite self-sufficient. His ability to care for himself was considerable. He was particular about putting out his own clothes and being sure that they matched. He cooked simple things such as eggs and hamburgers. He went to church every Sunday and was able to follow the service correctly. He could safely stay home alone if his parents went out in the evening. He enjoyed his stereo and television.

When Jimmy was 21 years old, he graduated from high school and entered a vocational training program. During the first year, he blossomed, learning among other things, how to sort bolts and screws quickly and accurately. His instructor felt that Jimmy could be successful in a supervised vocational program or workshop, although his problem with teasing would make supervision tougher. (Although he would tease others, he could not stand to be teased himself.)

The instructor's estimation of Jimmy's work potential came true: For a year, he worked in the same sheltered workshop. His boss, when interviewed, stressed Jimmy's determination, ability, and sense of responsibility. Soon after this, Jimmy was written up in the workshop's newsletter, with his picture, as Worker of the Month.

Jimmy's success at the workshop did not translate elsewhere, however. Because there was a push by both the federal and state departments of mental retardation to get people who were working in "sheltered workshops" out into the community, when Jimmy was in his late twenties he made the transition to a shipping company as part of a janitorial crew, cleaning bathrooms and toilets. He hated this and soon returned to his sheltered workshop.

Subsequently, he was accepted into a research program at a local mental health center because he had become uncharacteristically aggressive. This was the same research group attended by Tom (discussed in Chapter 4) and Karen (discussed in Chapter 9). At that time, Jimmy was put on Risperdal (risperidone), which temporarily lessened his aggressiveness. Jimmy's mother, his social worker, and the head of the workshop were delighted.

But, a very recent visit with Jimmy and his mother made clear that the medication's side effects had increased his hyperactivity and his "bizarre behavior," in his mother's words. Before going on the medication Jimmy rarely left his yard. Instead, he would sit in his mother's car "reading" or play with his dog. Once he started taking Risperdal he would run out of his yard, laughing or making strange noises, crossing the street and then running back. He went into the neighbor's yard and tore all the laundry off the clothes line and threw it on the ground. His mother told me, "I took him off the medicine then and there. He's been *fine* ever since."

Jimmy was expected eventually to be able to enter a group home, although his instructor felt that for him to adapt well, the supervision would have to be very skilled and specialized, and the number of residents limited to four or five. As predicted he did get accepted into a group home, however, his parents requested that he continue to live at home, as he does today.

Now, as an adult in his mid-thirties, Jimmy is a 6-foot-tall, broad-shouldered man who stoops slightly. He dresses well and wears thick glasses and, often, a mischievous smile. He is only slightly verbal but is able to communicate with simple words, such as "food." He is able to express himself also through gestures and guttural sounds. He has shown great drive to succeed and to please, and in general he has done well.

Perhaps this is the time to note that Jimmy was blessed with an appealing personality. From his first day at school, he charmed all of his teachers. This quality, as well as his sense of humor, his awareness of people, and his quickness to learn—as shown by his rapid and eager acquisition of sign language—has certainly determined who he is today: an attractive, rather dignified young man.

During my most recent visit with Jimmy and his mother, the major aspects of his current life were discussed. First, the whole system of "private providers" has changed dramatically. Private providers are organizations that, under contract to the state Department of Mental Retardation, take care of adults with special needs who are older than 21. Each organization has an identifying name such as Eastern Community Development Corporation or Association for Community Organization and Resource Development. Previously, they only took care of adults in group homes; however, they now place each person individually in a day program, allowing both the adult and the parents to make the choice of programs.

In Jimmy's case, after his sheltered workshop had closed, the first day program he attended was disastrous. According to his mother, "They just did puzzles and played games." Jimmy and his mother were given a choice of two or three other organizations and chose a large one that includes varied activities. Jimmy is now being given on-the-job training as a gardener. He was delighted to bring home a $56 paycheck recently.

Interestingly enough, through this same provider he also works for Meals on Wheels, helping deliver to shut-ins. He is happy, as is his mother, with his current placement. His instructors, according to his mother, "are wonderful." Recently, they took Jimmy to the Motor Vehicle Department to get him a picture ID. They are also working to help him learn how to cross the street independently.

Jimmy's mother works in a clerical position in a city hospital, and she is also a minister. Jimmy is very involved in her church and serves as a junior deacon. On Wednesdays, Fridays, and Sundays, he sets up chairs and other equipment for the service, and he cleans up afterward. All of this he does efficiently and on his own initiative.

At home, he helps with chores such as the laundry and cooking. His specialties are pancakes, sausages, and spaghetti. He helps clean the house, and takes care of their dog, whom Jimmy named "Choo-choo" because a train was passing by as he was choosing it. Jimmy's affection for his childhood dog Mr. Bobo and now for Choo-choo is noteworthy in itself, considering his animal phobia when he was younger.

Always a finicky dresser from childhood, Jimmy goes to the store with his mother and chooses his own clothes. They have to match, and they are always conservative in color and style. On Saturdays, his shopping day, he buys magazines and sits for long periods of time looking at them. His mother believes that he can read basic vocabulary.

It is evident Jimmy has been taught by his mother to be polite. On a previous visit, there was an occasion when his mother said sharply, "Jimmy, remember you are a gentleman." When I reminded her about this a year later, she exclaimed, "Oh, yes. He holds the door open for me and has very good manners." In some subtle way, this training shows in Jimmy's dignified manner and bearing.

One touching incident occurred during my most recent visit. The telephone rang, and Jimmy answered with rather loud guttural sounds. His mother prompted him to say, "Hello, Jimmy." By the inflection and tone of his voice, one could sense how hard he was trying. How tragic it is for Jimmy to have this frustrating neurological disability combined with intelligence and no way to communicate easily.

Still, Jimmy has increased his ability to use sign language, even to the point of teaching and correcting his mother. One hopes with his new, very caring instructors, this charming young man will find sign language to be the communication outlet that verbal speech can never be.

*   *   *

In 1987, at age 25, Jimmy was given a formal communication evaluation to determine whether his communication could be improved. His workshop supervisor felt that a testing program at the local teachers' college might give a clearer diagnosis of Jimmy's basic abilities. The clinician there described Jimmy as a pleasant young man, very cooperative, who concentrated for the entire hour-long testing session. He was responsible for communicating in short and simply phrased questions or statements but could not follow anything more complex. He exhibited his frustration at his inability to understand by loud, vocal outbursts and waving; or by persistent, protesting actions of his arms and hands. Testers noted that Jimmy exhibited occasional stereotypic arm movements including frequent turning back and forth of his clenched left fist and looking at it with his head bent and one eye as close as possible to his fist.

The evaluation concluded that Jimmy had a profound communication disorder secondary to his mental retardation. The prognosis for any significant improvement in his verbal communication was poor, due to his neurological dysfunction. Nevertheless, the prognosis was good for further development of his communication skills through sign language. His excellent fine motor skills, his ability to pay attention, his strong long-term memory, and his improved social interaction skills, as well as his supportive family, made it likely that he would be successful in developing a good sign-language vocabulary. Unfortunately, at that time because both his mother and his stepfather worked, no one could take Jimmy to the communication center at the teachers' college for lessons in sign language. No WAIS-R, VABS, or ABC scores are available. Jimmy's mother withdrew her permission for the October 1987 testing because she felt the strange surroundings and change of routine would be too upsetting for him.

"I thank God every day for Jimmy. . ."

by Victoria Davis

1994

Jimmy is now 29, and he still works at the workshop. He has been doing pretty well; on one task, they said he is the only one who could do it because he's so fast with his hands. He is a very good worker and has found favor with the people in the workshop. I just talked with Lisa, his social worker, whom I meet with once a year. She said he's doing well, no problem at all.

Once he had an outside job at the shipyard, but it didn't last. When he was working on the boats it was all right. He was good at the carpentry and things, but part of his job was to clean the bathrooms, and he didn't like that, although he did a good job. He began to behave inappropriately, especially with his laughter, so I said they should bring him back to the workshop. Maybe he was just not ready to get out there with so many people.

Now, he goes to workshop Monday to Thursday. Jimmy gets up about 6 A.M., washes, and dresses himself. Then, he goes downstairs and usually eats his breakfast before he goes to work. The bus picks him up at 8:15 or 8:30 A.M., and he gets back to the house about 3 P.M., except on Wednesday, when he gets home at 1 P.M.

He has a key and lets himself in. When he comes home, he puts his stuff away and then walks the dog. Usually, he and my nephew walk the dog together, but if Jimmy is alone and has to walk the dog by himself, it is all right. He is able to cross the street by himself. After he finishes walking the dog, he lies down in bed and waits for me to come home from work. When it's time to cook dinner, he stays in the kitchen and, sometimes with my help, makes spaghetti or something simple. After dinner, usually either he watches television or we sit around talking or popping popcorn. That's his daily routine.

Jimmy earns money at the workshop and is paid each week. The amount varies a lot depending on his work. Sometimes he brings home $2, sometimes $3, sometimes $30 or $40. I think his biggest pay was when he was working at the shipyard, when he brought home about $78 a week. Of course, he uses his money and knows its value. He buys the paper, and he goes shopping and gets haircuts on Saturday. He reads the paper every day. He reads all the time. He gets four or five magazines a week. He has always loved books, too. When we go shopping he looks at *The Enquirer*.

Saturday is our shopping day. We always go shopping once a week. We used to go to Sears, but now we go to Caldor's or the mall. He likes to go to the amusement area in the basement of the mall and to the miniature sports car track outside. You should see him. Once he drove off the course, hit a tree, turned around, and kept going. He loves it.

On Sunday, we go to church. We have our own church now and I am the pastor. It's the Holiness Church of Jesus Christ Incorporated. We started it after my second husband, Jimmy's stepfather, passed away. He and I were going to do it together. It was something my husband dreamed of. After he passed, we got busy, and it was a challenge. Jimmy helps move the tables and carry the equipment. He sets up the instruments and takes up and blesses the altar.

Jimmy was very, very hurt when my husband passed. My husband had a heart attack, and Jimmy was there when he died. I was at work at the hospital. When I came home, I ran up the steps. Jimmy ran behind me and saw how my husband was laid down in the bathroom. Later, he kept trying to tell me to get my coat to go, because he thought my husband had been taken to the hospital. He kept looking and looking for him. He sat on the stairs and stayed there all night, so he knew something was different. Then, the house was so full of people, and it was clear he knew something had happened. He kept looking out the window. That was sad. The people at church kept saying, "We're praying for Jim, because we know how attached he was to him." Now, Jim understands when we go to the graveyard. He goes to the grave, and he says, "Daddy." I was very lucky to marry such a wonderful man the second time around. He was very good to Jimmy.

The only problem I have with Jimmy is that sometimes he has restless nights. That's because he comes home from work and takes a nap. After that, he's up half the night. Sometimes, he's up until 3 A.M. watching television. When he goes to bed, he shuts the TV off, turns off the lights, and covers the birds—he has two birds: a cockatiel and a peach tree lovebird, which he feeds and takes care of.

One of the things that happened this year was television. Jimmy never used to pay attention to television. We bought a new television for Christmas, and now he sits there with the remote control. You can't get it away from him. He hides it. He takes it when he goes to the bathroom. I don't even get a chance to watch it. So, I watch television in my own room now.

He likes the Spanish station. He watches it so much I call him "Mr. Rodriguez," which makes him laugh. I notice that the Spanish station has a lot of festivities and Spanish girls dancing. He also likes the wildlife shows with the different animals. He watches that off and on and the programs where they're making things like cabinets. He watches a variety of things.

Jimmy's at the age where he observes women. At church or wherever we go, sometimes he is very aware of the opposite sex. He's fascinated by women's hair and by women with big busts, maybe because I'm heavy-busted. I think there are times he desires a woman, because I think that part of him is normal and has that normal urge. Once he got into trouble because he masturbated on the bus. I think he still does, but he does it at home discreetly. I've told him to go in his room and close his door if he has to because that's private, and he seems able to do that.

Jimmy sometimes acts up around women. Once he acted up so much on the bus that he got kicked off, and I think his getting overexcited about women was one of the things that caused that. But now, at home at least, he keeps his fooling under control. About 2 weeks ago, he was fooling around before he went to work. So I talked with him, and my sister talked with him, and she stayed with him until he got on the bus to cool him down a bit.

Jimmy is a snappy dresser. He goes to Sears and picks out his own clothes. He has very good taste in clothes and likes expensive clothes. He has about seven or eight suits for going to church. I'm proud of him because he does look really very good when he's dressed up.

He still doesn't go to any social gatherings by himself. He spends time with my nephews, and his godmother takes him places, but most of the time he's with me. Since my husband died, he does not want to be too far away from me. It's been a year now, so we're hoping that will ease off and that I can go someplace myself occasionally.

When Jimmy was a little boy, he was shy, and he kept his hands over his eyes all the time. Every now and then, he still does that, but most of the time he observes. He is very much aware of what goes on, very aware of what's going on with the church, when we're supposed to be devotional, when we're supposed to take up the altar. He's very aware of everything in the house, too, and where everything is. If you want to know where something is, Jimmy will show you. Even when he and I get groceries, he knows what I get, what I buy. He's pretty much on top of things. I really thank God he's as well as he is.

Jimmy has been a tremendous help to me in the house. He cleans, and he picks up anything that's out of place in the kitchen. When we're through with dinner, he puts the dishes in the sink and cleans them up. He does not like his house to be messy. He takes the clothes downstairs to the washer for me. He vacuums. He rakes leaves in the yard. He's very good.

I think things are pretty good for Jimmy. I don't have too many problems managing him. He's a big muscular man, but underneath all those muscles, he's really a pussycat. He loves me, respects me, and obeys me, and I don't have any trouble.

As long as I'm living, Jimmy will be living at home. As long as I'm in my right mind, as long as I'm able to, Jimmy will always be home. Home is very important to Jim. He has his own room. He has an apartment, which I call "up in the attic," where he took a lot of things and where he spends a lot of time with his books.

He still has his dog. We call him "Mr. Bobo." Mr. Bobo has been with us since Jimmy was a little boy. We got him when Jimmy came back home from his residential school. He was afraid of dogs and was afraid to go outside, and so to help him, we found a dog at the church boarding home. In the beginning, Jimmy used to get up on the table to get away from the dog, but after a while he got to know Mr. Bobo, and now he loves him, and the dog loves him back. Jimmy takes him for walks, feeds him, and washes him. Mr. Bobo is a part of our life. He won Jimmy over, and now Jimmy is not afraid of dogs.

The only thing I find an obstacle in our life is that Jimmy still does not talk. If he could talk, I think it would be amazing what this boy could do.

I thank God for Jimmy. I really do. He has been a great help to me. He's always been there for me. When my husband died, he was still there for me, and we have a very beautiful relationship, mother and son. When he comes home from work, I always hug and kiss him and ask him how his day was. Before we leave we always hug one another, and I say, "Have a good day."

Jimmy has come a very, very long way. Somebody asked, "Who do you owe it to?" Well, I'll tell you. Being a religious person, being a minister, and being a servant of the most high God, I realize that my help comes from God, and I've realized through the years it was the Lord who brought me Jimmy. I thank God that I feel that I'm a good mother to Jim. There are times when I have lost patience, especially when he gets so overexcited, but through it all, I feel that I've been a good mother. And Jim has been a good son to me, as good as an autistic child can be. And I thank God because I find that he is much better. I've seen many autistic children, and I think Jim has really come a long way. He does everything. I don't have to do anything for him but to take care of him and love him.

6

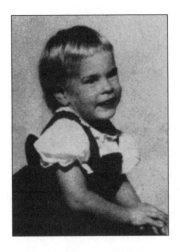

Polly Daniels

A Frenetic Perfectionist

born October 16, 1959

As an infant, Polly was placid and lovely—a blessing to her mother, who already had active young sons. As time went on, however, her parents were troubled by her behavior. Polly was unusually passive and uncomplaining, watchful, and excessively quiet. She did not speak at all until she was 2½ years old, and despite the optimism of Polly's doctors, her mother became increasingly disconcerted. When Polly was 3½, virtually overnight she began to talk in non-stop sentences. She also began to show extreme fear, often amounting to panic, in response to a variety of noises.

Between the ages of 3½ and 5, Polly increasingly displayed symptoms of a severe emotional disturbance: multiple irrational fears, temper tantrums, and an inability to play with others or to modulate and control her emotions. There were times during which she appeared to have psychotic episodes. On top of this, when she was 4 years old, she had an extremely traumatic hospital experience related to a tonsillectomy.

At the age of 4, Polly was treated at a local clinic and then later at the outpatient clinic of the Department of Mental Health, where she was diagnosed as schizophrenic. Shortly afterward, she was referred to the Yale Child Study Center, where an attempt at a more precise diagnosis was made. Polly's diagnosis was not clear, however, because along with a personality disturbance with autistic tendencies she was found to have perceptual problems that only heightened her confusion about her orientation to time, space, and reality. A treatment plan was developed at the Yale Child Study Center under which Polly would receive psychotherapy and attend a preschool group at the center. There would also be social work counseling sessions for Mrs. Daniels to help her cope with the difficulties of daily living with Polly. It was hoped that this would not only help Polly and her family but would further clarify the diagnosis and identify what kinds of continuing services she might need.

Two years later, when Polly was 6 years old, she had made little improvement. She remained perplexing to all who knew her. At the nursery school, she would scream, overturn furniture, and throw toys and juice cups. The teacher would try to help her regain control but had little success. Her specialist at Yale recommended continued psychotherapy and placement in a therapeutic educational program. At age 6, Polly was referred to the Ives School by her physician at the Yale Child Development Unit and her nursery school teacher. The teacher's report from the nursery school said in part:

> Polly, originally referred to our clinic as a behavior problem, is a mixture of lovableness and exasperation to all who work with her. Her behavior ranges from angelic to impossible and even when she is being angelic, one wonders when she will next explode, for her anxiety is tremendous and her impulse control extremely poor. She is plagued by various physical problems, particularly a skin condition that causes her to itch. A perceptual problem adds to Polly's emotional and physical difficulties, and this is an obvious interference in Polly's learning ability.

The report further described Polly as an appealing, attractive child who, although small, was physically strong. It also called her a "frenetic child." It concluded that "she is left-handed and is more skillful with the left side of her body." It recommended that a teacher "work with Polly on an individual basis" and that the teacher genuinely like Polly in order to help her like herself.

When Polly came to Ives School at age 6, she had the vocabulary of a typically developing 6-year-old, unlike the majority of the students. On the surface, she behaved with social appropriateness. She learned the kindergarten and first-grade academics fairly easily and was determined to succeed. But her acute perceptual impairments, particularly her lack of depth perception, certainly added to her emotional unpredictability. At first Polly appeared a dainty, exquisitely dressed little lady. She was punctiliously obedient and eager to do everything her teacher suggested, almost before the fact.

But this was illusory: The petite charmer was a walking time bomb in a tense struggle to maintain control over herself. Her anxiety was apparent in the tenseness of her movement, her excited speech mixed with stuttering, and her often-repeated gesture of smoothing her blonde hair—left hand, left side; right hand, right side. And, if Polly was tense, so were her teachers, who waited apprehensively for the explosion. It finally came after 4 months at Ives. Polly remained controllable until the week before Christmas, when she began to slap people, throw things, yell, and kick. Neither her social worker at the Yale Child Study Center nor her teacher at Ives could explain what set it off. It might have been a visit to Santa Claus: Polly had been terrified of his beard and bushy hair. Whatever the cause, Polly could no longer maintain control and, under what must have been unbearable pressure, had fallen apart.

The difficulty was what to do about her outbursts. Physically, her teachers could not sustain $2\frac{1}{2}$ hours daily of volcanic behavior—hitting, kicking, upsetting the preschool table, biting, and screaming all of the time. Even two teachers working together had trouble holding her.

Polly's psychiatrist, social worker, and teacher (with advice from the rest of the Ives staff) collectively arrived at a decision. They felt that Polly had been at Ives long enough to know that the teachers there cared about her. To the extent that she could feel safe, she felt safe with the people at Ives. They decided, in essence, to take a risk. They would try sending her home at the first hint of misbehavior and see if this produced a positive reaction. Polly's mother agreed, even though she had to make an hour-long round trip between her home and the school, and there was now the possibility that Polly would remain in school for only 15 minutes. Mrs. Daniels was willing to do it on the chance of helping Polly internalize some control.

The first day of this experiment, Polly's teachers told her repeatedly, "We care for you, but we don't like your behavior." That day she was sent home after she had been at school for only a half an hour. Her mother reported that Polly, much upset at being sent home, covered up by pretending she had been at school the right amount of time. She was sent home three or four times at most. By the end of the week, her teachers knew, just by her demeanor when she entered the school, that she had made a decision. From that time on, she remained in control about three fourths of the time, frequently responding when other children teased or provoked her, "I will behave."

With Polly's improvement in behavior came improvements academically and in handling the equipment in the play yard. The teachers worked to increase her control and to reduce some of her anxiety. They worked particularly on her perceptual impairments, specifically her lack of depth perception. Her behavior at home also improved. By the time she was $7\frac{1}{2}$, after one school year at Ives, the staff at Ives and Polly's parents felt that Polly was ready to attend public school. After conferring with her teachers at Ives and her parents, the director of pupil personnel at the public school placed Polly in a class for younger children with learning disabilities. She was to attend on a half-day basis.

By the time Polly left Ives, she had improved vastly. She could work a half hour at a time at a table behind a screen (which was used to provide privacy in the classroom) in the company of up to three other children, as long as at least one teacher was there. She seemed to know most of her ABCs and had finished one story in a preprimer. She could "match" words (e.g., recognize that the word *dog* on a flash card was the same as the word *dog* on another flash card), and from this she had built a minimal vocabulary. Her retention of a word had to be as a whole word. Using phonetics was impossible for her. Whether her problems stemmed from perceptual impairments or the aggravated anxiety that accompanied them or whether there was a problem with long-term recall was unclear at that time.

It was certain that Polly had severe perceptual impairments, some in the area of depth perception. There were several clues to this: Polly could not master a balance toy known as "Bill Ding," which consisted of perhaps eight 3-inch-tall wooden men, colored green or yellow, blue or red. The trick was to balance them one on top of the other, each standing on the shoulders of the one beneath. Polly could not place one man's feet squarely on the other's shoulders. She would turn the man sideways so that his feet would be in the air, and he would fall, knocking over the first man. Polly showed extreme frustration at her failure to master this game. Her therapist also said that she could not make a coordinated design with colored shapes. He commented that it was extraordinary how poor her performance was when she was left to herself and how difficult it was for her to learn from instruction.

Polly recognized that something was wrong with her, and her frustration increased. Her behavior in the play yard illustrated this. When she first came to Ives, she froze in terror on the bottom rung of the climber, but by the end of the year she could climb to the top. Nevertheless, when she attempted to lie flat on a slanted board used in balance training, which required her to lean onto the inclined board, she was terrified. It was as if the board simply were not there. She would grasp the board with both hands, but her body would miss the board entirely, and she would fall flat on the ground. Then, aware of and disturbed by her failure, she would get up and run off to the swings.

Even at age 5 years, Polly could only manage stairs by crawling up each step, and she went through doorways as if she were blind, her hands outstretched to feel the emptiness.

Nevertheless, Polly had some real strengths. She had a good voice, and she sang on key and in rhythm. She loved music and dancing. Although she was a bit bossy with her peers, she had real leadership qualities. She was also determined to succeed and put great energy into all of her efforts at school. She was delighted with praise when she was successful and correspondingly downcast and angered by her failures.

In September, when Polly went to public school for the first time, she spent 1 year in the class for children with perceptual disabilities. During that year she was given the Stanford-Binet Intelligence Scale (Terman & Merrill, 1960) and achieved an IQ score of 67. According to the test, at age 8 years, 3 months, she had a mental age of 5 years, 9 months. Polly was consequently transferred to a class for the "educable mentally retarded," where she remained until she graduated.

Polly made good progress at school with only one major period of setbacks when she was 12 years old. At that time, Polly suffered two traumatic events. One occured when her grandparents went on a 6-month trip to Arizona. Polly was very close to them, and she projected her sense of loss by angry, disruptive behavior and constant talking, regressing to her earlier pattern. At the same time, her junior high school class for students with mental retardation was mainstreamed for some academic classes, such as math, science, and English. This meant that the adolescents with developmental disabilities could take part in classes for typically developing children. Academic mainstreaming was a bad plan for Polly. She could not adjust to the higher behavioral and academic expectations of the teacher. She was treated for 2 years by a pediatrician and a psychiatrist to help her adjust, but in the end her behavior in class and at home became so intolerable that her doctors asked that she be removed from academic inclusion. She stayed in general classes for physical education, choir, home economics, and music, however, where she was able to do well and was pleased and satisfied with herself.

Until Polly reached her middle teens, she continued to suffer from incidents of violent behavior, although these were never as extreme as the ones she had experienced earlier. She received psychotherapy during two periods in her life, as a young child and between the ages of 12 and 14 years. She was on several medications until the age of 15, but then was taken off medication entirely.

Polly made the transition from the self-contained junior high classroom for children with mental retardation into the special education section of the high school. This meant that she now had to negotiate corridors, stairways, and doors all day as she went from class to class. The toughest part in learning her way around the big building was the adjustment to an individual program. She could not rely on a group to help her between classes. The program she was in varied: Mondays, Wednesdays, and Fridays for certain classes; Tuesdays and Thursdays for others. On top of the physical difficulties, she and her classmates with developmental disabilities had to learn to adhere to a schedule and be responsible for themselves in every way. Polly's teacher said that she went over this for 4 or 5 weeks with the whole class each morning. Polly reacted to the change with only moderately anxious behavior—whining, crying, constant talking—and within 3 weeks she had mastered both the building and her schedule. Her excessive talking moderated within 2 months, and by the second year she was much more comfortable.

At the high school, Polly's academic performance did not change. She continued to perform between a second- and third-grade level. She did well in music and cooking but could do little if any sewing. The school's overall goal was to equip the students who had developmental disabilities with the skills for basic survival, to get them to read on at least a functional level, and to teach them simple, job-related math. These students were also introduced to vocational training of local greenhouse and tearoom at the Connecticut Association for Retarded Adults (CARA).

Polly's greatest talents and strengths showed up in the area of her job. By graduation, she was working daily as a waitress in the tearoom. Here, Polly astonished many people by her success: Her abilities in handling responsibility and, usually, in remaining calm under pressure were surprising and remarkable. She was efficient and a good organizer. In addition to her waitressing duties she occasionally worked at the cash register (under supervision) and did well at it.

Polly was also successful in another unexpected area: athletics. She developed her athletic ability late but applied herself well and won a gold medal in the 100-yard dash and a silver medal in the girls' relay in the Connecticut Special Olympics. She was one of their best swimmers and baseball pitchers.

Polly graduated from high school in June 1979 at age 20. After graduation, she and four others from her class were taken on a trip to Washington, D.C. Later that summer, she was one of five from her class chosen for training for a community job sponsored by CARA. The training took place at a special summer camp for individuals with impairments. At the end of the summer, Polly started work in a popular local restaurant, which employed some individuals with disabilities. There, she was in charge of making salads.

Polly was a good worker and, by and large, retained control of herself. Nevertheless, as with many people with developmental disabilities, she lost control at times. Once, for instance, in a kitchen aisle she found her pathway blocked by two employees, who, busy talking, did not move to one side. After saying, "Excuse me" once or twice, Polly walked past, unintentionally shoving one of the employees. When she was reprimanded for this rudeness, Polly exploded and threw herself backward onto the red-hot stovetop

grill. She was saved from being severely burned by the other terrified employees, but it took them a half hour to calm her hysterics.

Later, Polly worked in another restaurant as a waitress. Her
boss there was very pleased and regarded her as quick, capable, and
responsible. The customers apparently liked her friendliness and
her serving skills. At this restaurant, Polly also was in charge of food
preparation for the following day. She was responsible for getting
out the big cans of basic ingredients for the soups on the day's menu
and getting the elements for various salads ready and placed in the
refrigerator. She was given more accountability and independence
at this restaurant than at her previous job, and she responded well
to the challenge. She appeared to perform better in a smaller, more
individually run organization, working with only four or five others, than in the large restaurant sponsored by the CARA.

Originally, just after graduation from high school, Polly's intention (and that of her family) was for her to live in a group home.
After 5 years of waiting, however, she still had not been placed in
one. At one point Mrs. Daniels was notified that there was an opening for Polly to share an apartment with a young man, who was in
a wheelchair because of spina bifida. To discuss this possibility, a
meeting was held, attended by Mr. and Mrs. Daniels, other parents
of girls also being considered for the opening, and the professionals
in Polly's provider organizations, including her program supervisor, her case worker, and others. However, the apartment was geo-
graphically too far away from Polly's job, and she also lacked the
training for independent living (grocery shopping, managing a
checkbook, and so forth) that is usually obtained by living in a
group home first. The state had overlooked this essential step. Fur-
thermore, Polly and her family were aghast at the thought of a male
roommate.

Polly insisted on sharing living space only with another
woman. Mr. and Mrs. Daniels explained both obstacles: Polly loved
her job and did not want to change it, and she was frightened of
sharing an apartment with a young man. The Danielses felt encouraged that "this time" (Mrs. Daniels's words) the professionals heard
their needs and understood the family situation.

At this time of her life, Polly's future seemed somewhat unsure.
Of all the children described in this book, Polly's developmental
course remained the most perplexing to the professionals who
worked with her. Had Polly's pervasive developmental disorder

been more clearly defined 30 years ago and the work with her and her parents started earlier, professionals believed she might have advanced farther than she had. Over the years, many mental health professionals and teachers who have known her have come to believe that she had an unrealized potential for growth and adaptation.

This is the dichotomy in Polly's case, and perhaps the tragedy, too. She has been more adaptable than expected; that is, she has always been able to accommodate herself to new people and surroundings. And, perhaps most poignant, she is very aware of her situation and refers to herself as "retarded." When asked how she feels about this, she says, "It makes me sad. I get very angry sometimes because I can't do things. I cry a lot. I cry when I see my friends cry, too."

When I visited the Daniels' home in 1992, her situation was unchanged. Polly continued to work happily (and successfully) at the same restaurant. She still lived at home. Mrs. Daniels said that she accepted that Polly would probably never have the opportunity to live in either a group home or a supervised apartment. She described herself as angry and embittered, but resigned. Still, Mrs. Daniels managed to achieve some life of her own. Always musical, she had a small organ at home, as well as a portable organ. For many years she has operated a business of providing music, accompanied by a guitarist, at parties and restaurants. This was certainly an outlet, allowing her some time away from home and Polly's constant demands.

Then, that same year, Polly was told that she should be in a group home within a year. This seemed optimistic in view of the pressure group homes were under to accept deinstitutionalized individuals first. If Polly got into a group home, it was expected that she would stay there 1 or 2 years and then—if all went well— move into a supervised apartment. As for work, her ability to advance in her job was understandably limited, but based on her past job performance and her proven efficiency, it was believed she might be able to become an assistant manager in a restaurant.

Mrs. Daniels was still fearful of leaving Polly alone, and justifiably so. One time, Polly was at home while Mrs. Daniels took one of her dogs to the veterinarian, thinking she would be gone from the house only an hour. During this hour, a severe, unexpected storm with thunder and lightning developed. When Mrs. Daniels arrived home and called out, "Polly, we're home," there was no answer. In a state of panic, she ran to Polly's room to find Polly curled up in a fetal position, as if she were frozen. Mrs. Daniels soothed her and comforted her but to no avail. Only after several hours did Polly come out of this state of petrified fear and finally talk about the storm. It was this sort of situation Mrs. Daniels had in mind when she said her daughter might go over the edge of the earth and never come back, and the possibility that this type of thing might occur again kept her virtually chained to her home and to Polly.

Fortunately, things have changed for the better for Polly and her family. In the mid-1990s, Polly moved into a supervised condominium that she shares with another woman who has mental retardation. Polly successfully manages her commute to work and her checkbook, banking, and daily living. She has held jobs in an eyeglasses factory and as a salesperson at a popular department store, and, currently, she is working part time at a biomedical factory. For several years, she has taken the public bus to get to work, an accomplishment her family thought she never would be able to do. She is well-liked by her supervisor. Ironically, Polly has come up against the same problem as Tom in that her salary is threatening her Medicare benefits. Her employer was so distressed that he was unable to give her the raise he feels she deserves that he supplements her income with gifts (e.g., a year's worth of movie passes).

When I met with Polly in March of 1997, she commented excitedly to me on how much she loves being independent. The reader will remember that Polly has always called herself "retarded." Dr. Sally Provence, who edited all of the original case studies in this book, commented, "Polly had such potential that had she had the advantage of current-day medical knowledge and current treatment technology, she would today be realizing more fully her abilities." Polly's comparative independence, today, supports the assessment held by all who worked with her that she did, indeed, have a great deal of potential.

Two years after that meeting, on a beautiful summer day in 1999, Polly and I met again for a luncheon date. Polly, all smiles, was waiting in the door of her condominium and came running out to the car.

"Hi," she exclaimed. "How are you?" We exchanged assurances of "fine" and "wonderful" and discussed where to go for lunch. We agreed on Vic's, one of her favorite restaurants.

Polly had changed markedly in several ways since I had last seen her. She still had the exquisitely pretty face, chiseled features, blue eyes, and blonde hair. However, she had gained a great deal of weight—almost 20 pounds. Polly immediately announced that she had something very exciting to say. She was going on vacation to Wisconsin with her parents to visit her brother. She would see her nephew. She had never gone on a vacation with her family before as an adult, so this was a big event for her.

In the midst of this conversation, she added that she was still working at the biomedical factory. She enjoyed reporting on her hours: She gets up early and takes the bus to work, then she is through around lunchtime. And yes, it is a paying job.

Suddenly, interrupting herself, she asked "Oh, how is your husband?" I was surprised and said, "Polly, you remembered that he had been in an accident 2 years ago. How amazing!"

"Yes," she replied. "So, how is he?"

We arrived at Vic's, found a booth, and ordered. Polly commented that she wasn't "used to lobster, so I'll have a hamburger, fries, and a Coke."

Despite noise from a children's birthday party, we managed to cover her current schedule. On weekdays, she gets up at 5:30 A.M., catches the bus, and gets to work by 7:00 A.M. She returns home by 1:00 P.M. In the afternoon, she and her roommate sometimes walk to the center of the small town where they live and "hang out" at the mall or the stores on the green. They can walk to the movies, but their caseworker takes them bowling, to pizza parties, and on sightseeing trips, and helps them with shopping and other chores that require a car.

Though Polly was once a Special Olympics medal winner, she said she had stopped competing in athletics many years ago. She still swims regularly for the YWCA and planned to swim at her brother's home in Wisconsin.

Her excitement at going on this trip with her family seemed out of proportion compared with what most people feel at the thought of going on a simple vacation. It brought to mind how unpredictable she had been growing up—too difficult perhaps to take on trips. So, for Polly, traveling with her family was a new and exciting experience.

As an adult, Polly is one of the most independent of the individuals featured in this book. In terms of living on her own and holding down a job, she is able to function almost completely on her own except that she does not drive a car, and she was one of the few who could legally sign the authorization form needed to publish her updated study and her picture included in this book.

There is an interesting difference in today's Polly from the Polly of the past, however. She seems more reserved; a subtle wall now exists between Polly and the rest of the world. It is as if she has been embittered by a silent acknowledgment of her inability to "be the best." One could conjecture that because she is so aware of her limitations while at the same time so motivated "to be first," she has become discouraged and in some things has given up, raising this protective wall against what she sees as the more "normal" world.

She parted with me affectionately, though not demonstratively (no hugs or kisses), and she promised to meet with me after her vacation to have her picture taken and to tell me about the trip.

True to our mutual agreement, I met Polly for a picture-taking session when she returned from her trip. She was waiting at the door of her condominium, and came out smiling warmly, saying "Hello! Hi! How are you?" In the same breath, she announced, "This weekend is my *fortieth* birthday!" There were many exclamations of "Congratulations!"

Polly posed for several pictures in front of the condominium and then accompanied me to lunch, again ordering a hamburger, fries, and a soda.

The visit to Wisconsin had been a big success. She had stayed with her brother and sister-in-law, had seen her nieces and nephews, and had gone swimming. Most exciting of all, she had gone to a large fair; I had the impression it was her first. "I loved it," she said decisively.

Despite her enthusiasm, again, I was struck by the impression that, although Polly had always been emphatic in her judgments and feelings, she was more serious and subdued. As the interview continued, my feeling became a conviction. I felt that something had happened this summer that had redoubled her sensitivity to being "different." Her drive to be "best," to be "first," was very much a motivating force, combined with the increased awareness of a disability that she was struggling to understand.

Polly turned to me and asked, "Doesn't the Child Study Center have a new building?" When asked how she knew that, she explained that her psychiatrist had an office there.

It was clear that Polly and her doctor were working on a better understanding of her disabilities. In discussing the staff who help her balance her checkbook, count out her daily medication doses, keep house, and shop for groceries, Polly announced firmly, "I told Susie (Polly's case worker) that I *must* take my medication myself, and I *must* learn to balance my checkbook myself!" Again, she gave that decisive shake of the head. She appeared determined to learn to take more responsibility for herself.

Polly also talked about some of the activities she shared with her roommate who, she added matter-of-factly, "has Down syndrome." That evening, they were going to a play at the local high school. She also bowls regularly and participates in tournaments and sometimes goes dancing and to the movies. Staff provide transportation and accompany their clients to these activities.

The following week, Polly was going to spend Thanksgiving and the weekend with her parents. "Oh," she said, "Mom's going to have a back operation, and did I tell you, Dad is doing his watercolors again?"

Perhaps it was the arrival of her fortieth birthday that prompted her, but, in addition to her determination, there was another element to her mood that day: pride.

"I look at my life. . . . I say to myself, 'I have a job, and I go there by myself. I have a nice place to live in my condo with my roommate. I have staff to help me do things. I have friends. I go places with my family and my friends. . . . I have accomplished a lot!'"

*   *   *

In October 1987, when Polly was tested at the Yale Child Study Center, she was 28. The psychologist described her as extremely cooperative and appropriate in her range of affects. She told the psychologist spontaneously about her job, and asked if the psychologist had met one of her friends, who was also being evaluated. It was interesting that she appeared to have some difficulty descending a ramp to the testing room, and perhaps this is a continuing indication of a degree of perceptual disability.

A Communication score of 36 on the VABS illustrated that mysterious inability of autistic individuals to pick up general social cues. Her high Daily Living score of 85, thus, is all the more surprising; but here test scores can sometimes *reflect* personality. Driven to succeed, Polly has always wanted to be "in charge," or to be "the best." The ABC score may add some understanding: Dr. Volkmar rated her score of 49 as more atypical, probably *not* autistic. Putting all of the scores together explains her ability to travel on buses independently; to work as a salesperson (certainly a socialized skill astonishing for someone described in early years as having autistic tendencies); and, now, to work happily and successfully, she says, in a biomedical factory.

TEST SCORES

WAIS–R
Verbal IQ score: 63
Performance IQ score: 62
Full-Scale IQ score: 61

VABS

Domain	Standard score	Adaptive level	Age equivalent
Communication	36	Low	7 years 7 months
Daily Living	85	Adequate	14 years 9 months
Socialization	59	Low	10 years 4 months
Adaptive Behavior Composite	55	Low	10 years 11 months

ABC
49: Probably not autistic

On the WAIS-R, Polly achieved a Full-Scale IQ score of 61, which would place her as having mild mental retardation. Within her Performance IQ score of 62, she showed relative strength on a test for the ability to copy symbols paired with numbers, demonstrating an aptitude for learning unfamiliar tasks. Polly has speed and accuracy in visual motor coordination.

On the VABS, Polly's composite score, including communication, daily living skills, and socialization, was 55. This was in the low range compared to all the adults in her peer group. She showed weakness in communication and strength in daily living skills. But, compared with adults with mental retardation in nonresidential facilities, Polly's score was in the above-average range. Her maladaptive behaviors included biting her nails, being extremely anxious, having tic-like movements, and having difficulty with concentration and attention.

One of the psychologists at the Yale Child Study Center, Alice Carter, had this to say about Polly's VABS scores:

> It is striking that she continues to have difficulty in communication skills. She is on a fourth-grade level in reading, alphabetizing, and writing. In socialization, she is functioning in the mild deficit range. This is good adaptation comparatively. Her daily living skills are in the adequate range compared to her normal peers.

"I spent all day trying to restrain her …"

by Jane Daniels

1994

At 3:30 each afternoon, a blonde whirlwind enters our home. Her exuberance is overwhelming. She's so full of news that she's fairly bursting. At 5 feet 2 inches tall, she's about 10 pounds overweight—10 pounds of solid muscle. Her figure is full-blown, a fact that makes her quite self-conscious. Her blue eyes sparkle, twinkle, and miss absolutely nothing. As she starts filling me in, in minute detail, about her fascinating day, I recall those uneasy first few years of Polly's life.

Childhood to 1976

Polly was born October 16, 1959. After a calm and uneventful pregnancy, her easy birth, with little or no labor, came as no surprise. She was a lovely, compact baby, the delight of the hospital nursery. She weighed 7 pounds 2 ounces and was just 18 inches long. I must admit that Tom and I were delighted to have such an adorable, placid infant. My son, Jim, at 3 years old, was hell on wheels. And Danny, at just a year, took up most of my time.

Polly's first year was routine and uneventful. She turned over, sat up, crawled, and walked on the same timetable as the boys. However, there was one huge difference: She made not a sound. No, that's not quite accurate. She cried or softly wept. But the cooings, gurglings, and normal attempts at sounds were strangely absent. By the time she was 2 years old, I was constantly questioning her physician about her silence. His answer was always the same: "Why should she talk with four people to wait on her?" Polly's silence was accompanied by the most passive behavior I've ever seen. She never objected when Jimmy or Danny took her toys, or if she was trampled in play. In fact, she never objected to anything. She remained perfectly calm, quiet, and unruffled, perfectly willing to be a spectator, always sitting in her stroller or on a lap and watching.

By the time Polly was 2½, I was distraught. She still had made no attempts at speech, not even a "da-da." Because of her silence, we were forced to play dangerous guessing games when illness struck, and Polly was plagued by colds and earaches. It was becoming frightening. I instinctively knew something was very wrong, but still her doctors laughed at my concern.

One spring morning, when Polly was 3½ years old, I was awoken by a tap on the forehead (Polly's favorite method of awakening us), and a small, totally unfamiliar voice said, "I'm thirsty. May I have a drink?" I was stunned. Here she stood, 30 inches high, speaking for the first time, and in a sentence. I can still recall how excited we all were. Grandparents, friends, and neighbors were called, and everyone breathed a sigh of relief. We were all sure that the doctors were right. Polly hadn't spoken simply because she had no reason to.

Our excitement and pleasure lasted for about 1 week. It became quickly evident that Polly had gone to the opposite end of the spectrum. For 3 years we had despaired of ever hearing her voice, and now we heard little else. Where or how Polly found her voice we'll never know, but once found, it's never been lost. Perhaps, in her innermost mind, she's afraid that if she does stop talking, her voice will disappear again. For whatever reason, Polly talks day and night, awake and asleep, right through television programs, school, workshop, movies, records, and church—Polly TALKS!

The one constant thing we've all asked of Polly is to please be quiet. And, it's the one thing she cannot do. Isn't it ironic that 3 years of worry and prayer should have turned out like this?

It became evident, at the same time, that Polly had learned something else along with speech. And that was fear. It became an integral part of Polly's character. She was terrified of noises. She even heard noises no one else did. A fire siren would send her screaming with her hands over her ears. The 12 o'clock whistle was a daily trauma. A dog barking would make her scream. A truck coming near on a street would make her freeze in her tracks. She could not maneuver steps without crawling up them on her hands and knees. Approaching a doorway, she gave the impression of being blind, and she'd put her hands out in front of her to feel the emptiness. If she ran, she fell. So, with the sudden freedom of speech came terror.

When she was almost 5, it became suddenly evident that Polly had lost her hearing, and for once the doctors agreed. They say it never rains but it pours—well, it sure poured all over us. Polly was due at the hospital for a tonsillectomy on May 10. On May 5, she became very ill with strep throat. On May 7, we were told she had scarlet fever. She was given massive doses of penicillin, and she responded well. At 7 o'clock on the evening of May 9, Polly's dad became violently ill, so ill, in fact, that he was put to bed for 3 weeks with an acute gall bladder infection and ordered not to get up.

Polly and I left at noon on Thursday, May 10, to register her at the hospital for a series of misadventures not to be believed. The first problem was simple—no bed. A small child had been waiting for 6 hours to be picked up and brought home. And no one had come. Polly and I waited in the playroom. By 8 o'clock that night Polly was in her room and becoming more and more apprehensive (which always increases her perseveration).

I stayed with Polly until she fell asleep, and then, on the advice of her doctor, I left for home and my sick husband. The other two mothers in the room offered to look after Polly should she awaken during the night. Her doctor said Polly was scheduled for surgery at 8 A.M., and he would call me at home by 11 A.M. and tell me when I could see her.

I'll never forget how the minutes crawled by the next day. When the phone remained silent until afternoon, I nearly lost my mind. At 2 A.M. they called to tell me that she was just out of surgery and in recovery. It seems they had prepped and medicated her for surgery at 6:30 A.M., then someone realized that they hadn't done a blood-clotting time. Surgery was delayed until 11 A.M., but no further medication was given.

The mothers in her room filled me in about Polly's terrified screaming and fantastic attempts to run away. They told me that orderlies and interns had to come from all over the hospital to restrain her. Polly was carried screaming into surgery. I heard all of this with a sinking heart, not knowing what would come down from the recovery room. It was more than an hour before they brought her down to me, a tiny, pathetic waif covered from head to toe with blood. They "allowed" me to clean her up.

When Polly was completely out from under the effects of the anesthesia, she tried, even though her throat ached, to talk. It was awful. The stuttering and stammering startled us both. I took Polly home as soon as possible and tried to comfort her, reassure her, and love her—to try in every way to erase the painful memories the hospital had left.

Polly's behavior for the next year was impossible. Her pent-up fury spilled over everywhere. Her nonstop talking irritated everyone. Her perseveration became so overwhelming that I counted the same question asked 45 times in 60 minutes. Through all this she continued to stutter and stammer. However, her fears seemed to vanish in the face of this rage.

When Polly was 5, we were advised by her doctors not to have any guests in our home, not even relatives. This went on for 2 years, and then the grandparents were finally allowed to visit. But for 2 more years no friends of the boys or of ours were allowed in our home. Polly's whole sense of being and security was tied up in me and our home. She became very threatened when someone outside of our family entered, or at least this is what we were told.

How detrimental this has been to us all! It became a habit always to be alone. It was unhealthy and cruel, to say the least. It has been difficult for both Tom and me to combat the feelings of frustration and disappointment we experienced when our friends forgot us. I find, even now, that Tom is cynical in his approach to people. He tends to embrace such solitary hobbies as painting and sailing.

It took quite a few years to convince our boys that they could bring friends home. I had to devote my absolute attention to Polly while any stranger was in our home. But it was worth it to know the boys' friends were welcome.

When Polly was 6, we were finally referred to the local hospital's child psychiatric unit on a 6-week emergency treatment basis. Because of the uniqueness of Polly's problems, she continued to be treated there for 3 years. She spent the last year in a special nursery class where she could be observed. During all 3 years, she was seen twice a week by a leading child psychiatrist. Unfortunately, this doctor could not or would not have any dealing with the parents. Therefore, I was again ignored when I expressed alarm over the new and destructive behavior I was seeing at home. I spent my time with a social worker trying to learn how to live and cope with Polly.

Her tantrums were becoming more and more violent. It is horrifying for a mother to watch an adorable, petite (at 6 years old, Polly was barely 3 feet tall) child attempt to strangle a beloved pet or deliberately pull the wings off flies and butterflies. We listened to her plead with us to hurt her, and we listened to the terrified screams all night from nightmares she couldn't or wouldn't remember.

It was heartbreaking to hear Jim and Danny beg me each morning to protect their dog from Polly and not let her hurt me either. We sent Jim and Danny away each weekend to stay with their grandparents to give them some relief from the continual screaming, kicking, and throwing things. This tiny, adorable child was destroying my home right under my eyes, and I was powerless to stop her.

A climax came in June of that year. Danny and Jim left on Friday afternoon to stay with Grandma, and Tom was away working the whole weekend. I was left alone with Polly. She had lost all control. She broke two windows, three lamps, a table, and many odds and ends. She then tried to get scissors or a knife to use on herself. I spent all of Saturday and Saturday evening fighting to restrain her. Both she and I fell asleep on the floor from sheer exhaustion, but at 3:30 Sunday morning, I heard her muttering and found her again trying to get something with which to hurt herself. I spent Sunday morning restraining what was now a small, furious, soiled, screaming animal.

By knocking the phone off the hook, I managed to call the operator, and she contacted the doctor. Within half an hour, both the pediatrician and Polly's psychiatrist were at the house. Polly was given a shot to knock her out and was stripped, bathed, and put to bed. The pediatrician and I had furious words with the psychiatrist, who admitted he had seen this breakdown coming and, in fact, had promoted it. He had allowed and encouraged these episodes because he thought they were the only way to break through the wall Polly had erected. He obviously did not believe in considering the effects his therapy might have on the rest of the family. The consequences of what he had done were disastrous.

I would not allow them to take Polly to the hospital, although I now realize that I was in no condition to make any decision at all. Polly was given massive doses of Thorazine [chlorpromazine] daily. I lost 15 pounds in 2 weeks, and her brothers were nervous and frightened. The whole episode seemed to break something within Polly, and she, seemingly overnight, reverted to a confused, frightened, insecure little waif.

At the time this was happening, Jim was 9 years old and Danny was 7. Danny is very quiet, shy, and almost withdrawn. Jim is quick, aggressive, and slightly hostile. Danny's stuttering and Jim's asthma may or may not be attributed to Polly, but the fact remains that both boys were severely affected and needed professional help. My husband was sick over money, and so was I. Financially, we were sunk. Polly's expenses had been appalling. Her doctors, special nursery schools, and medications had come close to ruining us. I could not work because I had to drive Polly to the Ives preschool and back each morning. Add all of this to the burden of worry we carried, and it's a wonder we survived.

But survive we did. Jim and Danny's relationships with Polly have never been good. Now that they are adults, they have told me that they lived in constant fear that Polly would physically harm me or that I would crack up under the strain—a fearful way to grow up.

Then things began to change for the better. Polly entered the Ives preschool for special children when she was 6 and stayed just over a year, until she had turned 8. The hours were 9–11 each morning. Polly spent school time with four patient and understanding teachers at the Ives preschool. At this point in her life, her gross motor control was fair; her fine motor control was horrible. She had no depth perception. Her spatial relationships were poor, her sense of self nil, and so on. The head teacher gave Polly her first taste of classroom structure and discipline. I made many trips to the school to pick up Polly and bring her home in the middle of the morning when she was dismissed early for being overly disruptive. The teacher would give her three chances to behave, then call me. I never needed to say a word to Polly. In her eyes, being sent home from school was the worst punishment ever. And she improved quickly. At 8, Polly was allowed to join the public school system and spent half-days in a class for children with learning disabilities. When she was 9, our town decided to try her in an all-day educable mentally retarded class.

The years between 9 and 12 were relatively uneventful. Polly adjusted well to the educable mentally retarded class, although her relationships with peers were poor then and are not much better now. However, she related beautifully to her teachers. This has been a pattern with Polly.

But when Polly was 12, she had two setbacks. Just as she entered puberty, her paternal grandparents retired to Arizona for 6 months of every year. She was very close to them. She had spent much time with them and loved them dearly, and she reacted to their absence much as a small child reacts to a death in the family. Her feelings of anger and rejection spilled over everywhere. Her behavior started to break down at an appalling rate—there seemed to be little we could do to help her.

At the same time, Polly became caught up in a new and, for her, tragic mess at school called "mainstreaming." For some academic subjects, she was put in the same class as "normal" children her age. It was hard to believe that any professional could expect a child with an IQ score of 61 and a second-grade performance level to be comfortable in an eighth-grade math class. I repeatedly tried to convince the authorities that Polly was breaking down under the strain caused by academic mainstreaming, but it wasn't until the fall of the year she was 14 that her classroom behavior became as intolerable as her behavior at home.

We took Polly to a very expensive child psychiatrist out of sheer desperation. At 14, Polly was 5 feet 2 inches tall and weighed about 115 pounds. When she threw a tantrum or, worse, pulled down that invisible curtain that shut out sight and sound, I had to subdue her physically. It was becoming nearly impossible. The constant battle was wearing us all down. Again, Jim and Danny became very concerned about me, and we were torn about the real possibility that Polly might have to be put in a residential school.

The prescription from this child psychiatrist was that Polly *must* be removed from regular classroom academics and only mainstreamed in nonacademic subjects. The following year she went to the high school educable mentally retarded class with some mainstreaming in the morning and an area services workshop in the afternoon. The remainder of that first year was a nightmare, but Polly responded, and the next year was worth waiting for.

Things began to stabilize a bit. Jim, Danny, and I spent a year examining our feelings at a counseling center. It helped us all tremendously. Polly adored the high school, and she was so relaxed at home it was like having a different child around. She was very successful at the workshop and loved going. She was trained in food services that spring and afterward worked as a waitress in a tearoom operated by the workshop. She was very proud of her paycheck and knew she had earned every cent of it.

When our eldest son decided to get married, he became very concerned about having children. I felt that this was a realistic concern, and we spent 6 months going to a genetic clinic. I'm afraid their results were not as definite as I would have liked. The conclusion was that Polly was mildly retarded; she was classified as "moderately educable mentally retarded." The results also described her as severely learning disabled, and no genetic reason could be found for either condition. We decided that Jim and Danny had every bit as good a chance of having normal babies as anyone else.

By 17, Polly had leveled off intellectually. As a parent, it's hard to accept the fact that your daughter will never progress beyond the second-grade performance level she achieved at that age (she was tested every year), but as an educator I'm thankful she had 17 years before reaching that plateau.

Polly spent 3 years at the high school with half days in her educable mentally retarded class and half days at the workshop. When she was through at the high school, she was 20. She remained at the workshop facility and trained to have a simple job in the community while she worked there. By the time she was 24 or 25, we hoped there would be group housing available for the retarded in our community. I wanted to see Polly living and working as independently as is possible for her. Perhaps then we could begin to live without tension and dread hanging over our heads.

Ten years later, Tom and I are now in our mid-fifties and Polly is 27. The changes in Polly's life, and therefore in ours, can only be measured in inches since she graduated from high school.

Polly is now an attractive, slender young woman—tense, nervous, obviously unsure of herself in any new situation. She still relates poorly to her age group but very well to very young children or elderly people.

She is still home with us, but her brothers no longer live at home. Jim is married and has a child; Danny is single and lives alone, but both boys have chosen "helping" professions: one is in social work; the other is a teacher. Interesting that the siblings of so many handicapped people choose to devote their lives to helping others.

Polly has been at the head of a waiting list for a group home for 6 years. However, because federal and state funding for group homes is being cut year after year, applicants are chosen on the basis of need. As it stands now, one of us or both of us would have to die, or in some way abuse Polly, in order for her to be considered for a group home.

Change. That word looms very large in my mind. Polly reacts to, resents, and resists change in any form—changes in people, places, and jobs. Even changes in furniture or draperies upset her. The changes that normally take place in a family cannot take place in the family of an autistic adult. The freedom that Tom and I should be experiencing now, after raising our family, is not there. We must always plan around Polly's schedule. We must always take her with us on trips, because she cannot stay alone. We have no quiet time to reflect and discuss things because she is always there. And, she talks and talks and talks.

Polly still works in the restaurant owned by the area sheltered workshop. She has had success as a waitress and now as an assistant cook. Until recently, her work hours were the same as her father's. Now she works from 2 P.M. to 10 P.M., which leaves us time alone in the evening, and I do appreciate that. But, like most things to do with Polly, we take two steps forward and one step backward. This new schedule also means that I have Polly alone with me all day, every day. And ironically, while I now have a few hours alone with Tom, I'm so exhausted from spending my days with Polly's anxieties and constant perseveration that I can barely function.

Polly's new hours now include Friday and Saturday nights. Do I tell Tom I can't go camping weekends because I must wait for Polly to get home from work? Or, do I go camping, hand Polly a key, and say, "See you in 3 days. Good luck"? How can I leave her alone when I know full well that an emergency, no matter how small, will send her right over the edge, and that small, persistent voice inside me asks, "Will that be the time she can't come back?"

Privacy in our home is at a premium. A quiet request, asking Polly to leave us alone for a few minutes, is viewed by her as rejection. She insists on staying in the room for any and all telephone calls.

Somehow, although none of these behaviors is new, all seem harder and harder for me to deal with. I enjoyed raising my children, but I did look forward to the day they'd be out on their own, and Tom and I would again be a couple. By and large, however, for most of us with handicapped children, the natural course of events—children growing up and leaving home—will not take place. Perhaps, someday, this will be addressed by the professionals. There is a need—*I* have a need.

7

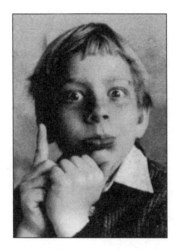

Bill Kolinski

The Child Fantasist

born January 17, 1963

Bill came to Ives from a public school kindergarten. According to his school's social worker, Bill had been in trouble from his first day at school because of his behavior, which was so disruptive that his teacher could no longer manage him and still teach 20 other children. A teacher from Ives was asked to observe Bill in class to see if the Ives program would be appropriate for him.

Bill would walk up and down the aisles, and sometimes he ran all around the room. He often babbled nonsense syllables. Even when he talked understandably, he would suddenly break off and chant. As he made his way up and down the aisles, he would lightly tap a classmate with his hand or, occasionally, a workbook. He sat down when told to by the teacher but was soon up again, wandering once more. There were angry, protesting murmurs from the other children, but Bill appeared as unconnected with the reality of the classroom around him as a cloud floating by. It was easy to see why he could not be contained in a public school setting and to understand why the children teased him unmercifully.

The teacher reported that Bill was hard to manage in many other ways. When he was willing to stay in his seat, he refused to follow any general classroom instructions unless convinced by the teacher that it was important. At home, if Bill misbehaved, he was so sensitive that a look of disapproval from his mother was sufficient to discipline him. Sensitive and shy, he would also run away and hide, or at least refuse to speak, if there were visitors who came to the house.

Ives accepted Bill into its program provided that he be evaluated first by the consulting specialist at the Yale Child Study Center. Like most parents who have sustained the shock of discovering their child is "different," Bill's parents had not yet come to terms with his condition. They came to visit Ives, bringing Bill along. His father, a chemical engineer, was a reticent man, but he listened with intelligent and concerned interest to the discussion of the school. Bill's mother, in contrast, was outgoing. She smiled warmly, and she asked most of the questions. Both parents explained Bill's strange behavior by saying, "Bill marches to his own tune. He does not join in the children's playing because he is too bright and grown-up."

Their visit to Ives only half-persuaded them that Bill might benefit from the change, and reluctantly they signed the consent form for him to undergo developmental and psychometric testing at the Yale Child Study Center.

Bill was almost 7 years old when he was tested. His mother had told him that the testing was important, so he was cooperative. His performance on the Stanford-Binet Intelligence Scale (Terman & Merrill, 1960) yielded an IQ score of 94, which placed him in the low-average range. He did very well on rote learning and memory items, scoring as high as the 9-year-old level. This suggested that through special help in dealing with his short attention span, his problems with distinguishing fantasy from reality, and his difficulty with logical thinking, he could function intellectually at a typical level. He had some additional symptoms, however. He showed considerable discomfort in social interaction, he was very difficult to reassure and calm down when he was upset, and his speech evinced substantial problems in social and emotional development and functioning. Bill was often withdrawn and apparently preoccupied with ideas and fantasies that impelled him to bizarre behavior. Yale diagnosed him as having an atypical personality with autistic features.

The test results convinced Bill's parents that he needed different schooling, with small classes and more individual attention, and they chose to send Bill to the Ives preschool. He stayed 3 years.

During Bill's first year at Ives, he was withdrawn, physically awkward, rigid, and fearful. When he joined in play, he was a follower. He had trouble choosing which toys, which art materials, and which pieces of outdoor equipment to use, but he liked to ride on the large toy trucks. His speech held many odd sounds, like "Boom!" "Bang!" and other sounds or words that appeared to have no reference to anything. Rather than answer a question directly, he would answer with an association that made sense to him but seemed far-fetched or improbable to others. He could not distinguish between reality and fantasy. When he pretended to be a rabbit or an elephant in rhythm games or in acting out a story, he became so involved that he lost his awareness of the game and seemed to believe that he *was* the animal he was imitating.

The teachers at Ives worked with his illogical thought processes in many ways. They spent a good deal of time patiently untangling his confusion, for example, over how to see similarities in two different things, such as a plum and a peach. They showed him pictures of stuffed toys or, when possible, of real animals, saying, "This is a rabbit [or 'an elephant'], but you are Bill." At the same time they showed him in a full-length mirror that he was a boy, not an animal.

By the end of the first year, he had improved. His speech was more direct and meaningful. He was beginning to distinguish more clearly between what was real and what was fantasy. He liked outdoor play with one or two children at school, and he was playing at home with the neighborhood children.

By the end of his third year at Ives, Bill had improved dramatically. His bizarre behavior had almost disappeared. He was enthusiastic about physical activities, running relays, doing handstands, and playing circle games. This new involvement and comfort showed in his swimming. Instead of clinging to a teacher or the side of the pool, he was swimming freely. He liked to bounce in the water, to put his head under the water, to sit-jump into the pool, and to be involved in races and chasing games with one child and a teacher.

Despite this improvement, however, Bill retained some fearfulness. He hated being splashed, was afraid of the water gushing from the side of the pool, and in general showed his sensitivity to and fear of the unknown. This was borne out in his social relationships. He approached cautiously new or different situations or people, asked a great many questions, and was only satisfied with a concrete answer or reassurance.

By the time he was 9, Bill met first-grade standards in all school subjects. He had developed writing ability in both stories and plays. He loved to draw maps of the streets in his town. He now walked, ran, jumped, and hopped more easily than he had before and seemed to have lost some of his prior awkwardness and clumsiness. His doctor thought that there had been some improvement in Bill's neuromotor organization. The specialist at the Yale Child Study Center, the Ives staff, and Mr. and Mrs. Kolinski agreed that Bill was ready to return gradually to public school.

At this time, Bill also was retested at the Yale Child Study Center. The testing confirmed the improvement in Bill's functioning on the Stanford-Binet Scale (he scored an IQ of 99), as well as the even more dramatic changes in his personality and behavior. The evaluation described him as less withdrawn, much less lost in fantasy, and much more in touch with everyday events and people. His thinking was less rigid, his responsiveness to people more personalized, and his general behavior less stereotypic than it was at age 7. Although there remained some tendency to bottle up his feelings and, as his mother put it, "to cry inwardly," Bill had grown in his ability to say how he felt and to respond to efforts to help him.

He still retained some literal-mindedness and a relative inflexibility, which showed itself in his failure to get the point of pranks, jokes, and incongruities. He expected things always to be logical and predictable and became confused when they were not. But unlike many children with autistic traits, he was not attached to certain toys or books. The evaluators noted that he had a few obsessive preoccupations (such as mapmaking), but that these were not as absorbing as they had been earlier and could now be used as vehicles for learning. He continued to need help with adapting to social groups and his relationships with his peers.

Starting in the spring of 1972, when he was 9, Bill attended the Ives preschool in the mornings and a general third-grade class in the afternoons. At first one of the Ives teachers went with him, but as Bill became comfortable in his new setting, this stopped. That fall, he entered general fourth grade. On the advice of Bill's public school social worker, one of his teachers at Ives visited his class several times during that fall to facilitate the transition for his teacher, Bill, and the rest of the class. This succeeded, and Bill was soon accepted by his classmates and was doing well in all subjects.

Years later, Bill reflected on his experience at Ives and the transition back to public school: "I didn't know that [Ives] was a special school. I liked it because there weren't many children, and I got a lot of attention. . . . I minded going back to third grade in public school because there were so many children."

Throughout public school, Bill did well, and he graduated at the age of 18. He had been particularly involved in the drama club. He still could not talk about his feelings easily, and, at one point, his social worker had recommended that he see a psychiatrist. Bill, with his family's cooperation, had tried this but felt that therapy had not helped. His own comment on the experience, made several years later, was "I didn't know how to use it. I could use it now."

After high school, Bill enrolled in a local teachers' college. He planned to major in drama with an emphasis on acting, but also took courses in chemistry, English, psychology, math, and speech and theater. He performed very well academically, making As and Bs. He lived in a house with young men on one floor and young women on another. They all took turns cooking, which Bill enjoyed, and had a good deal of fun together. But hospitable and friendly as he was, there was still a sensitive, wary, cautious quality in his approach to people.

Bill graduated from college in June 1985 at the age of 22. That summer, he went abroad with a student group and had a wonderful time, yet at home he had no friends his own age. He had majored, finally, in journalism, and minored in drama. He worried, however, that the field of journalism was so competitive he would have a hard time starting a career.

After college, he worked in a fast-food restaurant and went to classes in library science at night. After receiving some job counseling, he changed his career goals and entered an out-of-state culinary institute.

Between his first and second years at the culinary institute Bill once again traveled abroad, some of the time with a group. He visited his Polish relatives in Warsaw and attended the university there. During the trip, he met an attractive American girl who invited him to visit her in the Midwest, which he did some time later.

In summer 1987, Bill had three job offers from local restaurants and chose the one with the busy lunch trade because of its favorable downtown location. He became responsible for the salad bar and used his mother's Polish salad recipes. His potato salad was considered special, as were his artistic decorations of the salad bar. He left this restaurant to go back to his last year of school with a letter of recommendation from his employer for a job well done.

By the fall of 1988, Bill was making the dean's list in school. He had a friend as a roommate, and they joined a church group that sponsored a senior citizens' camp. Bill and his friend went there on weekends to cook. He also had a part-time job in the cafeteria of the institute.

At age 25, Bill had matured. The tentative, shy, and hesitant quality of his speech and manner had been replaced by a self-confident directness. His voice was deeper, and although he occasionally seemed to hesitate over certain words, he spoke with assurance and decisiveness. Bill's strength lay in his verbal ability. He beat everyone at games such as Trivial Pursuit. According to his mother, "He seems to know it all," but she remained concerned that his slow, deliberate approach to problems or to work might hinder him.

As an adult, Bill has achieved a degree of independence rare among people with autism. He started out with several advantages: a basic intelligence, good health, and parents who supported and encouraged him at every stage. The one-to-one teaching he received from ages 6 to 9 at Ives gave him a sound academic first- through second-grade foundation and helped him overcome his confusion between fantasy and reality. Last, but far from least, it enhanced his ability to relate both to adults and to peers so that he could return to public school.

By the time he was in his mid-thirties, Bill felt that he had "grown out" of autism. (Unlike the other individuals portrayed here, he is able to regard himself and assess his life, often eloquently.) About this time Bill took a job at Disney World in Florida. He had been nervous at first about moving, but he found a nice apartment and bought a used car—responsibilities many high-functioning adults with autism cannot handle. He sent a postcard of "Main Street, U.S.A." to one of his old teachers, describing his new job working "for the Mouse" (as he put it). His boyhood physician at Yale read this postcard with a smile, saying, "How nice! He's really succeeding, isn't he?"

Bill joined a church, and became very involved in all church-related activities. It was here that he met his future wife. When he heard that his case was going to be described in the first edition of this book, he asked to write an essay for it, which is included as Appendix A: "Growing In and Out of an Autistic Mind." Bill said that he was proud of the way he had "overcome" autism.

For 5 or 6 years, Bill worked in a Disney World restaurant. Though he was trained as a chef he found he could not stand the pace of a big kitchen. He asked his boss to let him be in charge of ordering restaurant supplies, instead. His supervisor agreed, and provided him with his own office and computer. Later he was offered a position in the largest gift shop in Disney World. Here once again he was in charge of computer ordering. He was subsequently asked to be one of the gift shop's floor managers. So, wonder of wonders, several days a week, dressed in his best clothes, he acted as a "greeter"—his word—to the would-be customers. Bill's last job at Disney World was in its own way an indicator of his astonishing development, for he worked for a time in the *sales* department. He had to learn a new computer system, but had no trouble in mastering it.

Bill married in the mid-1990s. His wife, Peggy, has a visual impairment and uses a Seeing Eye dog. They moved to a small town near Orlando, where Peggy could be near her supportive family. They have a young son and daughter. Bill is now working in a repair department of an electronics company.

Peggy says that a desire to serve others, based on her own experiences as a person with a disability, led her to work at a camp for children with special needs, including several children with autism. Bill had explained his early diagnosis of autism when they met. She felt their disabilities balanced each other.

As their family grew, Bill and Peggy found their apartment too small for them, so they applied for a Habitat for Humanity house. Bill spent every spare moment working on other Habitat houses as part of the contract with Habitat, and in anticipation of getting their own house. Peggy says Bill has gotten so much out of the Habitat for Humanity experience because the others working on the projects teach him new skills.

Another quality of Bill's that is worth noting is his remarkable sense of direction. As a little boy, one of his favorite occupations was to draw maps, and according to his mother, today he does not even need a map to find almost any place. He had, and has to this day, an uncanny ability to know in which direction to go. This illustrates the mysterious abilities sometimes possessed by those with an autism spectrum disorder.

Despite all of these obvious successes in his life, traces of Bill's sense of social awkwardness still remain. Peggy has remarked that although Bill has made great strides in his personal development, there are still instances of his innocence of social cues. On hearing this, I immediately thought of one of the first times when Bill was to meet me for lunch. I found him waiting, not inside, but outside, sitting on a bench, looking unsure of himself and isolated.

His mother recalled another instance: During Bill's senior year in college, he told her he was going to a party with his friends after the football game. But several hours later, he showed up at his parents' house looking puzzled and disappointed.

"There wasn't any party," he complained. "All the guys and girls did was lounge around drinking beer and eating pretzels . . . things like that!"

His mother said laughingly that, for Bill, parties meant a table with a fancy tablecloth, flowers, candles, and nice food, just like he had seen at home.

Bill's mother recently visited Bill and his family in Florida, and went with them to a pre-Thanksgiving dinner held by his church's social group.

"There were lots of people," explained his mother. "And Bill was always the center of the group, talking and laughing!" She added proudly, "Oh, he is *so* much improved!"

Bill's wife feels their marriage is a match arranged in heaven because of the way they complement each other. She says, with a chuckle, that when they were married, she was the "talker," the leader, and the decision-maker. She is amazed at his continuing development. He now acts as the decision-maker more often and is becoming more of a leader. For instance, in the church groups with whom they meet, Bill is one of the leaders. He knows all the books of the Bible, and astonishes the group by the variety and depth of his knowledge.

In view of Bill's former "shyness," Peggy believes that these new
developments are "totally surprising." In fact, he never ceases to
astonish her with his achievements.

*   *   *

At the age of 24, Bill achieved the following scores during the October 1987 testing at Yale Child Study Center. Bill's mother answered the questions on the VABS.

TEST SCORES

WAIS–R
Verbal IQ score: 103
Performance IQ Score: 85
Full-Scale IQ score: 94

VABS

Domain	Standard score	Adaptive level	Age equivalent
Communication	97	Adequate	17 years 9 months
Daily Living	108	Adequate	18 years 11 months
Socialization	74	Moderately low	13 years 9 months
Adaptive Behavior Composite	90	Low	12 years 5 months

ABC
63: Possibly autistic

The following is a discussion of the results abstracted from the report of testing:

> Behaviorally, Bill appeared extremely anxious, clearing his throat and stuttering; his face was flushed. During the Object Assembly task, he manipulated one puzzle piece for 3 minutes unsuccessfully. He achieved a score in the superior range on a verbal task administered in a subsequent session (because of the shortage of time) *over the telephone.* The psychologist commented: "It is unclear whether or not the interpersonal distance of the telephone minimized Bill's anxiety and enhanced his performance."

On the WAIS–R, Bill's Full-Scale IQ score was 94, in the average range of intellectual functioning. There was a significant difference of 18 points between his verbal scale score of 103 and his performance scale score of 85. Bill, in short, is stronger in verbal expression and comprehension than in nonverbal visual-spatial tasks. He showed relative strength in abstract verbal reasoning (similarities) (e.g., How are a dog and a cat alike?).

On the VABS, Bill obtained a composite score of 90. This covered communication, daily living skills, and socialization. He is in the average range when compared to typical adults in his peer group. He showed significant strengths in daily living skills and weakness in socialization. Maladaptive behaviors included poor eye control, occasional anxiety, overdependency (i.e., relying on other people for initiatives), and difficulty with concentration.

While Bill's composite score of 90 places him in the average range of his typically developing peers, it is evident that he is stronger in daily living skills than in socialization, and this shows today in a certain shyness and diffidence of manner. Yet, his job as floor manager was an extraordinary responsibility for someone once diagnosed as autistic. I was reminded of what a specialist once said to his Ives School teachers about Bill long ago: that his IQ scores of 94 at ages 6 and 24 were a *minimal* estimate of his intelligence. Because of Bill's difficulties with testing, this specialist believed, no one will ever be able to accurately gauge his intelligence, which is probably higher. His later development and achievements surely bear this out.

"He wrote a book himself…"

by Fran Kolinski

1994

Bill lives in Orlando, Florida, now. He went to a culinary institute in Rhode Island, and when he graduated, he was offered a job at Disney World. He has a new apartment and is very friendly with some people there who are almost like second parents to him. He bought a car, and he seems to enjoy himself.

Bill was going to be a chef when he went there, but they thought he was too slow for that, so he was made assistant chef. He helps the chef by preparing salad, dessert, and hors d'oeuvres. He's also partly responsible for ordering food. He has to keep a list of what they need, and he has to store it and make sure the supplies are all there. I think it bothers him that he is not a full chef yet, but he really doesn't know what to do about it.

Bill surprised us at Christmas with a book he wrote himself—a history of our family entitled *The Branches of a Proud Tree*. He gave every member of our family a copy. In it he talks a lot about himself and a lot about his brother Steve, who is his idol. Bill has done many things in his life just to prove that he could do the same things Steve did. His brother went to Europe; Bill went to Europe. Steve learned to ski; Bill went skiing. Bill is very honest in what he writes, for instance, that Steve was successful in school and that he, Bill, was not that good. He doesn't try to make himself look good, and he writes exactly what he feels.

In Florida, Bill has joined a church group and has mentioned something about being born again. They seem to have a nice group of young people, and they help Bill a lot. Just before Christmas this year they put on a play, which they performed at several different churches. Bill had a small role, but he gave so much emotion to his part that people came up to him and asked him if he was interested in performing professionally. I think he likes acting so much because on stage he can forget that he is Bill Kolinski and be somebody else.

I can't remember when I first heard the word "autistic." Bill was having trouble in kindergarten. My husband and I met with his teachers, and they advised us to try a special school for Bill. At the meeting my husband got kind of upset. He said, "There's nothing wrong with Bill." But they explained their concerns to us, and we realized that there was more to it than Bill's being just a little shy, different, or slow in maturing. He did things that were different from what other kids did. For instance, when Bill was 4 or 5, he started touching people. Without any reason, at kindergarten and at home, he would get up when everyone else was sitting down. If he didn't feel like sitting down, he would get up and start touching people. We would say, "Bill, don't do that." Then he would get a kind of stupid grin on his face. We never asked anyone about it because we didn't really think there was anything wrong. He also would sit in front of a record player just watching the turntable going around and around. He could sit for an hour and just stare at that. A normal child would never do that. After Bill started school at Ives, we were told autistic children are fascinated by movement.

He's better now, but even when he comes home for a visit, if I ask him the wrong question, a little too close to what he doesn't want to talk about, he won't answer or say anything; he'll just stare away into space. Now I just walk away and say, "It doesn't make any difference," and after 2 minutes he's normal again.

In his book, Bill writes about Ives. He states that he asked me once when he started school why he went there, and I said, "Bill, you were kind of silly and bothered the kids in the other school and they didn't like that, and you do better in a smaller group." He writes that he needed a one-to-one situation where a teacher could concentrate on him. That must still be what he believes; it was also true, and Ives made a great deal of difference in Bill's education. When he left Ives for the [public school's] third grade, he never missed a class.

Bill tests as a perfectly normal person, and throughout school he always made at least Bs and Cs. He still has autistic behaviors, though, and they reach into his performance. It's hard to describe; he's almost normal. But something always seems to be there to hold him back.

Compared to "normal" kids growing up—getting fresh, disobeying parents, not having any respect—Bill was always a pleasure to be with. He was a little bit slow and a little bit strange sometimes, but he was always a joy. He was loving, in his own way. He never came out and put his arms around us, but we never had any feeling that he was unaffectionate.

Bill is shy. Even now, I think he gets lost in a big group. You have to address him personally; otherwise, he is not a person to come up to you. When someone wants to hug him, he used to put a stop to it, but now he is much better. I was surprised when I visited him in Florida. We went to a restaurant, and he said to me, "I'm always telling you about this girl. I want you to meet her. She's coming over, and she's having a cup of coffee with us." The girl was a very outgoing person. She came in the restaurant and said, "Oh, hi, Bill." And she hugged him and kissed him right in front of everybody, and he did the same thing, and I thought, "Oh, look at that!"

Our grandson, Robert, is only a few years younger than Bill, and they went to culinary school together. Robert arrived from high school and took the full 4 years to finish. Bill had gone to college and so was able to graduate in 2 years. I don't think Robert realizes that there is anything "wrong" with Bill. Just once in a while he gets impatient that Bill's not fast enough. Robert is kind of like the brother from the movie *Rain Man*. He likes money—that type. They see each other at Christmas, and he will tell Bill, "C'mon, you have to complain to your boss that you want a raise." And then Bill gets kind of scared and insecure. He doesn't really know what to answer. In one way he probably thinks that Robert is right, but he realizes that for him that's not the right thing to do.

Bill and I saw *Rain Man* together. I liked it, and he loved it. Many of the things that Dustin Hoffman did remind me of Bill, like the way he looked when people talked to him and he was day-dreaming. All of a sudden he wasn't there. I asked Bill if he had heard of autism. After he saw *Rain Man*, I asked him what he thought of it. He said, "Oh, that was a fantastic film." But he never said anything to suggest that he thought he was perhaps a little bit like that. I wondered if he ever had any suspicion that he was autistic. Even when he was at Ives, he always seemed to think that he wasn't really like the other children. He was more interested in what the people did who worked there. He once said to me, "I think when I grow up I would like to be a counselor like Mrs. Sperry to help these children."

Of course, we are proud of him and happy for him. His happiness is most important. He is not that successful, but it's good enough for him. If lack of success made him unhappy, I would be concerned, but he does well enough and realizes that he cannot do more. And he is content enough. In general, I don't worry about him. We always think about the time when we are not here anymore, when he will have to take care of himself, but so far he is doing a good job.

Bill has never given us a reason to be angry with him. He has always been obedient and loving. It's almost like God giving us a special child to take care of, and it's a privilege for us to be able to do that.

8

David Ellis

Lacking Spontaneity

born April 16, 1965

David was referred to Ives School in the spring of 1969 at age 4. He had been regarded as perfectly typical until about age 2, when his slow motor development and lack of speech began to concern his parents and pediatrician. He had asthma and recurrent ear infections, and often he had to be taken to the emergency room because of acute asthma and bronchitis attacks. Consequently, he was closely monitored by a pediatric team at the Yale-New Haven Hospital, where he was given a thorough physical. No physical findings, however, explained his delay and "differentness."

Before Ives, David was tested at the Yale Child Study Center. The evaluation showed that he had mild mental retardation and possibly suffered from *aphasia*, a brain disorder in which the ability to use language is affected and sometimes totally absent or lost. But it was difficult to test his developmental level. He had some success with nonverbal items at a 3-year-old level. His language was the most delayed and consisted only of five words: "ball," "cookie," "key," "car," and "water." He also had superficial relationships with people and difficulty in coping with anxiety. His major impairments were thought to be his social and verbal communication disorders. He also had difficulty with tasks requiring reasoning and visual-motor coordination.

The doctor who tested David said that he could not be induced to use more than a few of the test materials. Outdoors, he ran around chasing other children but never playing with them. At times, he appeared to try to cooperate during the session, but the doctor was never sure David understood words, although he was alert to sounds and followed a few directions when they were accompanied by gestures.

When David entered Ives, he was small for his age. His smile, shy yet expressing the desire to make contact, lit up his face and eyes. He held his body rigidly, approaching both people and activities with caution. The teachers saw him as "handsome, neat, clean, extremely quiet, unsure of himself, and lacking spontaneity."

In the beginning, David was fearful of all activities, but by June, after turning 5, he had made real progress. He was jumping on the trampoline, riding in the wagon, and riding the tricycle. In the physical education program, he participated willingly in swimming. His end-of-the-year report from Ives said, "David has changed a great deal. He is trying to speak louder (he whispered in September). He is in a reading program and recognizes and understands 12 words, picking out the correct word to go with the right picture. He teases and even has some silly moods. All in all, he seems more relaxed and sure of himself."

David started speech therapy in his second year at Ives to help him overcome his lack of spontaneous speech. The therapist used a dollhouse, small dolls, and play furniture, and soon David could name all of them. The therapist said that his interest lay in things rather than in people. She said his visual memory seemed much better than his auditory memory but that he soon learned to complete nursery rhymes by supplying the missing words. He responded to his name by echoing it. He wanted desperately to learn how to write it and worked on that daily with the therapist.

He was told to look her in the eyes when he talked and to say his words clearly. This took much patient, firm repetition.

By the time he was 6 years old, David was talking so he could be understood. He no longer whispered or covered his eyes. He played with other children, although it was still more of a side-by-side play than a true give-and-take. He could even, on occasion, become gently aggressive.

After 2 years at the Ives preschool David was ready to go on to the newly established public school program for children and adolescents with developmental disabilities. There, he went into the state-funded communication disorders program, where he learned sign language. He blossomed and began to make fantastic strides. He quickly progressed from signing to talking, at first hesitantly and then quite fluently. He soon read, spelled, and wrote, although his teacher reported that he had some difficulty mastering verb tenses. The teacher also said he loved to read aloud, especially history books.

The director of the program was enthusiastic as she talked about David. She emphasized the role his parents had played. They had been responsible, cooperative in every way, and caring of David.

Socially, however, David still had severe problems. He could not adapt to change easily, and he was still "remote" in his contact with others. As with so many of these young people, he had trouble understanding feelings or making contact emotionally. He had some peculiar behavior traits as well, such as talking to himself, and he teased and taunted his peers, often without apparent reason. David also had temper tantrums, and it often was difficult to know what triggered them.

When an Ives school teacher observed him in his "higher ability" vocational-training class, David spoke with dignity and clarity, although he was repetitive. When he said "hello," he was friendly, although he had a "touch-me-not" quality. In his work, he was careful and precise. He made sense as he talked and was clearly in touch with reality—very aware of people and his surroundings. Nevertheless, there was a lack of give-and-take in conversation, a lack of spontaneity in his social and emotional reactions, and a lack of depth in relationships with the people around him.

In the communication disorders program, David continued to improve in his ability to handle social situations. He participated in nonclass activities such as lunch, trips, athletics, and recess. David was considered the star achiever of his group. Academically, however, it was believed he had reached a plateau.

After graduation from the special education high school, David joined a supervised workshop at a local *community house*, where he stuffed envelopes, labeled packages, and performed mail-sorting and collating jobs. He worked in several community businesses for a couple of years, such as a dry cleaner, a printing company, and a buckle company. But at that point, the state of Connecticut had no money for job coaches, so David was limited to his workshop and couldn't find subsidized employment elsewhere. He seemed a little less in touch—more withdrawn than at the time of his graduation from high school.

The following are selected quotes from the staff of the workshop that convey a picture of David as an adult:

> David socializes often with peers and staff, although he prefers staff interaction to peers. He is for the most part cooperative and will participate in program activities. . . .

> He is currently on a behavior program to increase his peer interaction. He handles conflicts by talking out loud to himself and handles his problems by asking staff for assistance. David can be bothered over the smallest thing, which can make him very upset, but he has no major disruptive behavior or problems at the present time. He has excellent hygiene and dressing skills. He has shaving skills and is aware of matching his clothes. He is aware of neighborhood surroundings, and he walks to the store and other places in his neighborhood independently. . . .

> David currently uses the community house van to travel to work. He has good table manners and is aware of cleaning up after he finishes eating. In the area of functional education, he has basic reading, writing, and math skills. He has basic knowledge of safety rules and survival skills.

David's leisure time remained a problem. He continued to live at home while attending the supervised workshop and had little exposure to the recreation he should enjoy as a young adult. His protective family rejected all suggestions that he live in a group home.

Growing up, David was most fortunate to have such dedicated parents. They were devoted to him and did everything they could for his well-being and development. Mr. Ellis held a good job as a machinist in a factory and was a man of determination and character.

Mrs. Ellis wanted to stay home while David and his three younger brothers needed her, though later she worked for many years in a public school cafeteria. Both parents were youthful, attractive, and very dignified, yet warm and friendly. David was constantly encouraged by the loving support of his parents, and later by his brothers as they matured.

When David was at home, he kept to himself, often to such an extent that it seemed like he was "not there." He appeared to be unaware of the presence of other people or of their conversations. Mr. Ellis tended to be firm, even stern, with David and conveyed a sense of distress that his oldest son would never be independent, able to hold a job, and able to support a wife and children. When David was a senior in high school, Mr. Ellis thought he might teach David to drive. He dropped this plan after the school social worker pointed out that his son did not notice physical landmarks and that, because David was socially "at sea," he was easy prey for strangers.

In the early years, the Ellises were bewildered by the challenges David faced. They recognized that he was getting excellent care at the Yale Child Study Center and trusted the people at the Ives pre-school, but they still had difficulty understanding and accepting that their child was different. The social worker at Ives explained that it was natural for any caring parent to feel angry, confused, and worried. When the Ellises joined a parents' group at Ives they were able to share their feelings about David and respond to guidance about managing his behavior. They also received help, especially educational guidance, from the physician at the Yale Child Study Center. At one point, David's mother repeated several times to his teacher at Ives, "Without all of you, David and us—we would have been lost."

Compared with the child who entered Ives rigid, withdrawn, and speaking only five words in a whisper, the adult David is a trib-ute to his intelligent, unflaggingly supportive parents; to the sensi-tive teachers and speech therapists who taught him from preschool through high school; and finally to the social workers, supervisors, and work coaches in his work program. Nevertheless, his maladap-tive behaviors remain as noted in his testing at Yale: poor eye contact, overdependence, little social contact, and trouble with concentration. His conversation sometimes seems "out of context." Improved though David is, the basic characteristics of autism spectrum disor-der remain.

Now in his mid-thirties, David has always lived at home at the insistence of his parents. Over the past 15 years, he has worked at a dry cleaner's and at various discount stores, such as Caldor's, where he worked as a packager and loader. Recently, when business was slow, he became unemployed and returned to the sheltered workshop. Then, when business improved, he went to a McDonald's restaurant. From there, he moved to another restaurant in his small town. For David as well as for other adults with autism and their families the ability to work at a paying job in the community is, of course, very important and a matter of immense pride.

At the age of 22, as is shown by his scores, David was on the borderline between mild mental retardation and typical development. This is borne out by his achievement in several areas: his speech, which became quite fluent and socially oriented; his academic performance, which was good; and his leadership role in the Communication Disorders Program at the Area Cooperative Educational Services (ACES), a state-supported regional organization that provides special education.

Dr. Fred Volkmar once said that David's highly protective family had limited their son when they discouraged him from living in a group home, where his socialization skills would have been given a chance to develop. His VABS scores did, in fact, show how his speech and general adjustment had blossomed during his high school years at ACES. However, his native intelligence and ability, as shown in his IQ scores, definitely played a part in his early strides both at Ives School and at ACES and his later ability to work at paying jobs successfully.

In the spring of 1999, after a talk I gave to a group of parents and professionals, one of the young parents stood up and announced,

> I am the mother of a 6-year-old, diagnosed with autism, who is doing very well in kindergarten with a special aide. But I am *so careful* of him! I watch him all the time. There is a summer camp for children with special needs in my town. I have been told he should go. I was *not* going to let him go. But after hearing what Dr. Volkmar said about how David might have benefited from less protection by his family, I have decided to turn my son loose. I *will* send him to camp this summer.

In December of 1999, I went to David's home for a visit and to take a picture of him as he is today. David's mother greeted us warmly, and David also came to the front door saying, "Hello, Mrs. Sperry."

On a visit I made to their home 2 years previously, David had seemed less mature. Now, he seemed fully "grown up." He stands about 5 feet, 6 inches tall, still a stocky figure, and was neatly dressed in navy blue pants and a white shirt. He now appears as a handsome, self-confident, and very dignified young man. Yet as I observed him, he still had that impervious quality. His shining eyes and broad smile lacked spontaneity, as his teachers had described him years ago.

His mother, a woman with a sparkling personality, urged us to sit at the dining room table so we could talk. She told me, "David still works 1 day a week at a local restaurant where he pours water and cleans off the tables." On other days, he goes to his community house workshop.

Once a month, on weekends, David goes with friends to a camp where they hike, dance, and keep busy with many other activities. David smiled as he talked about the camp. I sensed that he really had a good time on these outings. On other weekends, a counselor from the state DMR takes David and other friends bowling. His sister, an attractive young woman who works at a large university, chimed in that, of course, she and other family members take David out to eat or to the movies. All in all, I felt that David's life had fallen into a satisfactory pattern.

When asked if he remembered a former schoolmate, he replied, "Yes." Then he added, "And what about Eric? How's he doing?" He was pleased to learn that Eric was doing so well. It was at least 14 years earlier that David had last seen Eric, and his memory amazed me.

After taking pictures outside the house, it was time for the good-byes, and David's mother added warmly, "Have a Merry Christmas." Without prompting, David shook hands, smiled, and said, "Have a good holiday!"

*   *   *

In October 1987, at age 22, David was reevaluated at the Yale Child
Study Center. The testing session included both the WAIS–R and
the VABS. David's father was the informant for the VABS. David's
speech was stilted and halting, and he was reluctant to talk. He
refused to say that he was finished with a task and persisted in giving nonverbal cues (sitting back in his chair) instead. He had appropriate eye contact during testing but unusual motor movements:
pointing to his chest and stroking his legs. He muttered to himself
as he worked on nonverbal items. When he used this verbal medi-
ation, his test performance improved.

David achieved the following scores.

TEST SCORES

WAIS–R
Verbal IQ score: 70
Performance IQ score: 69
Full-Scale IQ score: 69

VABS

Domain	Standard score	Adaptive level	Age equivalent
Communication	45	Low	9 years 2 months
Daily Living	57	Low	8 years 11 months
Socialization	49	Low	7 years 4 months
Motor Skills (estimated)	73	Moderately low	4 years 3 months
Adaptive Behavior Composite	47	Low	8 years 6 months

ABC
78: Probably autistic

On the WAIS–R, David achieved a Full-Scale IQ score of 69 in the
mild range of mental retardation. There was no significant difference between his Verbal IQ score (70) and his Performance IQ score
(69). In view of David's enjoyment of reading history, it was interesting that he showed a relative strength (in the typical range) on a
task requiring the placing of pictures in a logical sequence. This test
evaluates the ability to comprehend and evaluate a situation

utilizing nonverbal reasoning. Anticipation, visual organization, and temporal sequencing are involved.

On the VABS, David obtained an adaptive behavior composite score of 47. This test examines communication, daily living skills, and socialization. David's score on this test placed him in the low range of typically developing adults in his age group. He was not stronger in one area than in any other. These formal test results are congenial with other evaluations of David, which showed him as having made great improvements over the years, while continuing to be impaired in aspects of intellectual and social functioning.

9

Karen Stanley

Desiring to Relate to Others

born May 14, 1962

When Karen Stanley was 3½, her family pediatrician referred her to the Yale Child Study Center for developmental and psychological diagnosis. He suspected she might have autism. Karen did not talk and seemed slow in other phases of development, such as toilet training, understanding simple instructions, and engaging in play with her age-group peers. Her physical development had been somewhat slow, and she was sensitive to sounds. The Stanleys said that Karen said only three words: "mine," "mama," and "ghetti." They felt that Karen at times put a wall between herself and others. Often they were not sure whether she understood them or not, but they were beginning to suspect that she understood more than she acknowledged. The Stanleys added that Karen did not seek out other children and had no idea of cooperative play. The interview concluded with a description of the Stanleys as "a warm family."

Serial observations by the developmental pediatricians and other members of the Yale Child Study Center staff were performed to measure Karen's level of skill on developmental tests, her social relationships, and her emotional development.

In the clinic's intake report, her mother described Karen as "vivacious, happy, strong-willed, persistent, likes to rock on a rocking horse, to empty drawers, spin pan lids, play in the sand pile. She seemed to enjoy members of the family and loves her kitty." She was also "sweet, charming, vigorous, active, and quick," but minimally interested in toys, often quite content to be alone, not seeking affection and not speaking. Her mother found it difficult to say why Karen had seemed "fragile" and "somehow different" from birth, in spite of being physically healthy and growing normally.

In addition to her generally delayed development in motor skills, problem solving, and speech, Karen exhibited a lack of interest in social interaction and social communication, absence of communicative speech, restricted patterns of behavior, pervasive anxiety, unusual preoccupation with objects and sensations, and deficits in the ability to play. Her deviant unresponsiveness and her precarious attachment to and lack of social communication with other people were especially conspicuous. No physical or neurological abnormalities were found. After the evaluation, the specialist at Yale told Mrs. Stanley that they had diagnosed Karen as having "atypical development with autistic behavior." She then described infantile autism to Mrs. Stanley, who, at first, was shaken and bewildered.

The doctors who examined Karen believed her developmental disorder was most likely inborn, and that she would require specialized education and other services in order to achieve her potential. While the long-term outlook was admittedly bleak, the doctors created an appropriate plan for handling Karen's behavior: to begin "putting her in touch with her emotions," and to find the best school for her. Karen's parents soon began to set the plan in motion.

Once the diagnosis had been made, Karen's parents were very eager to have answers to their questions and to have help with her. Professor Stanley, Karen's father, was described as "soft-spoken, deliberate, dispassionate," as if he were presenting the doctors with an academic problem. His concern for Karen, nevertheless, was evident in the many questions that he asked. Mrs. Stanley, a warm, direct, and intensely vocal woman, was to prove indefatigable in her pursuit of what was best for Karen. Mrs. Stanley asked in the intake interview, "Is her development pattern serious . . . or will she catch up at her own speed?" Many parents will empathize with the ambivalence and confusion this question reflects.

Mrs. Stanley, explaining Karen's condition to the rest of her family, wrote this: "Karen has no brain damage or physical impairment of any kind. Her difficulty lies in her personality structure, and it is a constitutional one. Her personality is described as atypical. Lacking the usual resources of a child, her growth and learning have been slowed. Her problems fall within the limits of what is now described as the autistic child." She concluded her letter by saying that not knowing what was wrong with Karen was far worse than knowing. She also added that whether Karen would achieve "normal" maturity was a great question still.

In the spring of 1966, when Karen was 4, she entered the Elizabeth Ives School for Special Children. She was apprehensive about everything and clung, frightened, to her teachers for safety and reassurance. Characteristic of her behavior at the time was her compulsion to flush the toilet. She would stand by the toilet, jumping up and down, flapping her hands, hypnotized by the whirling water. Her teacher was kept busy running to the bathroom, where she would inevitably find Karen. One of Karen's strengths, however, was her apparent desire to relate to people. In this respect she differed from most of the other children with autism at Ives, and indeed, other children with autism spectrum disorder in general.

After several months at Ives, Karen had made some academic progress, though this was quite limited. She knew the numbers from 1 to 3 but could not really use them for practical applications; and she could follow simple, one-step spoken directions. She was able to recite the alphabet, although she was unable to associate the sounds of the letters with their written form. She was beginning to read and learn the basic vocabulary of a preprimer, but she had difficulty following sentences from left to right because she did not see words as a whole, and therefore could not follow a word-to-word progression. (Later, at Karen's boarding school, her teachers used cardboard frames to teach her to read.)

Karen had some severe visual-perception and visual-motor problems. She could not, for instance, cut with scissors (she was 20 before she could cut out a valentine), zip a zipper, or snap a snap. When she came to Ives, she could not hold a stencil with one hand and at the same time control a pencil with the other to make an outline. She could not coordinate this until the end of her second year at the preschool.

During her second year at Ives School, Karen's teacher took her home for the afternoons. This teacher worked with Karen on self-identity and body image. She would show Karen the body parts of a doll and compare them with Karen's own body parts until Karen acquired some awareness of her own physical makeup. The teacher also had Karen do perceptual exercises, such as crawling under a broomstick held a foot or so above the ground, to show her how her body related in size and form to other objects. Through such patient instruction, Karen developed some sense of her own size and body.

When Karen was 6 years old, she went to a private summer school for typically developing children, accompanied by her Ives teacher. There she was helped with her anxiety around other children and slowly became used to being in a group. Her general level of anxiety and apprehension also lessened, and this helped her with some of her academic tasks: She began to be able to say four- and five-word sentences and to put several sentences together. At Ives, she began to stay with the children of her group consistently, although she tended to relate to other children most often through teasing them.

The next year it became clear that Karen was ready for a more advanced program than Ives could offer, and after discussions among the people at Ives, the Stanleys, the local public school system's social worker, and the doctor at the Yale Child Study Center, the decision was made to send Karen to a private elementary school for children with developmental disabilities, many of whom had emotional problems also. This proved to be inappropriate for Karen. She was overwhelmed in a class of six and unable to relate to the other children or participate in group activities. The following year she was sent to another local private school for children and adolescents with more severe learning disabilities. She stayed in this school from the time she was 9 until she was 12. As Karen got older, this turned out to be a pattern: progressively she had to be placed in groups of younger and/or children who were less able because of her impairments.

Between ages 7 and 13, Karen was treated by a child psychiatrist who helped her to develop and begin to use her innate capacities.

This psychiatrist was able to enter Karen's world—her obsessions, her interest in birds and plants—and bring out her ability to relate to people. He began, with Karen's help, by dismantling a toilet, explaining each step as he went. Karen was enthralled. His technique was to involve Karen as much as possible in the learning process. With her participation, he went on to introducing her to bird books and recordings of bird songs, and from there to plants and insects. Karen began to acquire more self-confidence through this therapy. Soon she knew many birds' and insects' names and types of habitats, and could recognize particular birds' songs. She also learned how to look up their names in the index of her bird book, following three-digit numbers. As Karen improved, it became apparent to the therapist and her teachers that she had a remarkable memory.

As Karen approached adolescence, she was ready for a more structured life among her age-group peers, and so, at 13, she was sent to an out-of-state residential school for teenagers with developmental disabilities. There, she had peer companionship on a 24-hour basis and was subject to peer models and pressure, which, it was hoped, could be helpful. The danger of a residential school was that Karen and the other teenagers would become isolated—increasingly unable to interact with typical children their age. Nevertheless, apart from its limitations, the school offered a good total program of special education, peer-group living with supervision, psychotherapy, medical care, and prevocational training.

At first Karen responded well to the new school, but, after a time, she became anxious and unhappy and developed "negative behavior." Karen had been placed in a house with several teenage girls with psychotic tendencies. This was the closest the school could come to an appropriate place for her. Because Karen was, and still is, very sensitive to loud noises, the screaming and violent behavior of her housemates was unbearable for her, and she reacted with emotional explosions and out-of-control behavior. The school's response was to put her on medication—Loxitane [loxapine]—for the first time in her life. Instead of helping, however, the medication produced in her emotional withdrawal, sadness, and a subdued manner. Karen's previously happy sparkle flickered and threatened to go out. The medication was continued for 1 year, then stopped. In time, Karen bounced back, and although she remained subdued, she began to enjoy herself and make progress.

Karen responded particularly well to the prevocational program at the school, which taught self-care basics: what to wear if it was cold or hot, and what clothes generally were appropriate. These were things that typically developing children learn readily but that children with emotional and developmental disabilities have difficulty understanding. Karen had to be taught to wear a slip underneath a sheer summer dress, to wash her hair and her face, to use a deodorant, to understand menstruation, and to care for herself in matters of cleanliness. She learned good personal hygiene and became quite interested in clothes and proud of keeping herself looking well. Karen's favorite courses were sewing and cooking.

Karen's basic anxiety had not been eliminated, however. She was still tense and avoided eye contact. On a psychological reevaluation performed when she was 17, she tested, on average, at a second-grade, 6-month level. As evidence of her perceptual and visual-motor deficits, she showed distortions and an inability to copy a whole geometric design or to complete one she had started. Her view of the world was global: She had no ability to discriminate among the different facets of her environment. As a result, generally she saw her environment as threatening. She dealt with everything in structured, constricted, concrete, nonabstract terms. The evaluation summary concluded that Karen suffered from moderate mental retardation, a high anxiety level, withdrawal from personal relations, depression, low self-esteem, poor reality testing (i.e., her anxiety prevented her from seeing reality clearly), and severe visual dysfunction.

Karen's parents, teachers, and doctors concluded from these results that she would probably always need to live under supervision. But they also believed that she needed a new residential environment to help her develop some independence. A boarding school for teenagers and young adults with autism, run by a group called Pioneer, Inc., had just opened in a town near Karen's home. Karen transferred there when she was 17 years old.

At the new boarding school, Karen roomed with two girls who became like sisters to her. The staff at the school worked to "reach" Karen and help her use her own capacities. Although she was afraid and timid at first, Karen slowly began to open up. Her self-confidence was encouraged by some small but significant cosmetic changes. She had her hair cut and styled in a bob she could care for on her own. She went to an orthodontist for braces, which not only straightened her teeth but also improved her appearance and, consequently, her self-esteem. She took renewed interest in dressing attractively, matching her hair ribbons to her dress. The increased pride she had in herself improved her ability to relate to people. At times she was even playful. Once, when her teacher spilled some coffee, Karen exclaimed laughingly, "You slob!" (a peer contribution to her vocabulary). She had a boyfriend among the residents of her house, and she often said to him, "You hate me, Joe," while her eyes sparkled. She had learned increasingly to understand feelings and to express her own feelings directly. She learned how to get her boyfriend to say he loved her. To another boy who was leaving school she said, "We'll miss you, Dan." Another time she remarked, "I'm really sad. I miss my folks."

The Pioneer school ran a number of vocational training programs, among them bottle sorting (for recycling), furniture refinishing, silk-screening, and bakery work. Karen took part in bottle sorting and silk-screening T-shirts. She also worked in the bakery and as a clerk in the school's gift shop.

Karen was at ease with her family. At a lunch that a teacher of hers attended, Karen helped to get the meal ready, chattering all the while to her mother. She passed the wine and crackers, and members of the family affectionately joked with her. When lunch was delayed, Karen chastised her father for holding things up by shouting, "Dad, lunch—come on! I'm starving!"

When Karen turned 21, her living situation changed again, this time out of bureaucratic necessity. At that time, funding for special education and other programs—provided by the local public school system from a combination of state, federal, and local sources—stopped when a child reached 21. As far as the Stanleys were concerned, in light of Karen's abilitiy to function well and improved flexibility in personal relationships, she could live at home. But at home she would have no meaningful job, no peers, no community involvement, and no tightly structured life designed to handle her deficiencies.

In Karen's residential program, there had been 17 other young adults who were older than 20 years of age. Because all of their parents faced the same funding problem, with the cooperation of the Pioneer school, they organized a group under the guidance of the state DMR to find an answer. In Connecticut, the DMR takes responsibility for placing such adults older than 21 years in living and job situations in communities. The parents felt that a supervised living situation was still clearly needed for most of their children. None of these young adults with disabilities would be able to continue to progress without a carefully designed and executed program—which, of course, involved peers and skilled teachers. The parents also felt that the large, impersonal institutions, with their inadequate staffing and large number of "patients," would rob these young people of their chance for continued independence and development. Moreover, these young adults were not patients. They were not sick; they had disabilities that partially could be overcome.

The parent group was determined to provide for their children a residence designed for training in independent living. After a year of strenuous activity, meetings, and fundraising (in which the young adults also took part), and after some of the parents had contributed personal funds, they had sufficient money for a down payment on a small apartment building and the beginnings of the new program: Maple Avenue House. In conjunction, Pioneer, Inc., rented a store nearby to house a silk-screen shop and a gift shop. The school also had overall responsibility for the apartment building and the vocational training.

Maple Avenue House was ready when Karen was 21. She lived there for 4 years with five other young adults and two staff supervisors. The residents organized their own lives and did their own shopping, cooking, and housekeeping with the help of the staff. Each one had a job in the community.

Karen at first worked at silk-screening T-shirts and helping with secondhand items to be sold. Because of her appealing way with people, she was to be trained as a clerk. But waiting on customers confused her, so when the bakery opened the following year, she was placed there.

At Maple Avenue House, Karen had her own studio apartment. She took her lunch to work and had dinner in the communal dining room. She took a bus to the bakery where she helped with baking bread, doughnuts, cookies, and pies. She was paid $35 a week. She used her salary for buying jewelry and tapes of bird songs and for going out for pizza, movies, and similar group activities.

Karen still retained her pervasive anxiety, vividly illustrated by an incident that occurred during a visit I made to her room. Mrs. Stanley was there, but had to leave the room briefly. She was careful to tell Karen that she was going to the bathroom across the hall. Although Karen knew me, she was immediately uneasy, as if what kept her organized and safe had gone. She knew that her mother was nearby, yet she started pacing the floor, muttering. When I told her her mother would be back immediately, Karen said, "I'll go find her." She ran out of the room and down the stairs to the main floor, but had acquired enough self-control not to run out of the building.

When Karen was 26, the director of Maple Avenue House met with Karen, the Stanleys, and the supervisor of the regional program to assess Karen's progress. The feeling was that Karen was ready to move to a facility where she could live a bit more independently. She had improved quite a bit in general and was more outgoing: She had even taken long bus and airplane trips by herself (with the help of Traveler's Aid) to visit family members. The participants tried to create a "road map" to help others make better plans for Karen's future.

Karen showed enjoyment and intense interest in the meeting. At one point, the director asked, "Who is important in your life, Karen?" She then showed Karen a drawing of a large circle containing concentric circles with Karen's name in the middle. Karen named her roommates, her cat, and her boss at the bakery readily, but she thought of naming her parents only after some prodding.

They then went on to Karen's likes and dislikes. For her "likes" she quickly mentioned shopping and jewelry, as well as her cat, fishing, cleaning fish but not eating them, and audiotapes—especially of bird songs. Karen seemed confused when asked to describe her "dislikes," so her mother mentioned that Karen had always hated loud noise and confusion. She was afraid of parades, for instance. Karen spoke up at once to say, "Hate carnival rides." Her impaired depth perception was probably responsible for her fear of amusement park activities, and she still panicked at the prospect of going down a steep incline of any kind.

Throughout her life, what was successful in treating Karen was "repetition and immersion." Karen had accomplished the most through constant repetition and by being with someone who demonstrated and coached as she performed a task. Mrs. Stanley added that whenever Karen wanted very much to do something, eventually, through her own perseverance, she was able to do it. From early on she had sought contact and relationships with other people despite her problems in doing so. As an adult, she has been motivated by pride in her achievements and by praise from someone she likes.

It was also noted that Karen's consistent weakness in living skills was the shallowness of her social contacts. She had also been unable to defend herself against taunting, teasing, or the aggressiveness of others, but in that she had improved. Her poor visual-motor skills, poor verbal intake, and limited verbal expression all continued to play a part in her difficulties.

Karen was rated by her vocational counselor as about 50% independent and responsible in general. She initiated and carried out getting a haircut, which involved using the telephone, although dialing was difficult for her. She took good care of her cat, using a chart of chores to be performed. Her grooming and personal care were good, and she took her vitamin C without having to be reminded. At the bakery, however, her poor concentration and visual-motor ineptness, and her inability to take sequential instructions, made it hard for her to learn new skills. In spite of some improvement, it was clear that the bakery was the wrong placement. Karen would always need a job coach, but her advisors agreed that she might be able to share an apartment with another young adult with a disability, because she had conquered each preceding step of development.

As a result of this meeting, Karen transferred to Algonquin House, a supervised three-bedroom house also administered by Pioneer, Inc., where she lived with two other women with developmental disabilities. A crisis occurred several months after Karen moved there. Because of funding problems, Algonquin House was threatened with closing. The crisis was averted, but the bakery where Karen worked had to be sold. She and her work mates began working in the regional vocational center, where they cooked and served lunch.

Karen participated in trips to places such as national parks, sponsored by Pioneer. She was able, with a supervisor, to go to a supermarket and shop from a grocery list successfully. She still couldn't make change, however, so the clerk had to take the money and count it out for her.

Karen has made almost miraculous progress from the delicate, vulnerable 4-year-old who arrived at the Ives School. Her perceptual impairments have been modified through patient training, although they continue to limit her behavior and personality. It took her many months, at the age of 22, to learn how to flute a pie crust, for example. She managed to ride an escalator independently for the first time when she was 25. And, although she is more in touch now with the people around her than at any time before, there are still times when she seems lost, remote, and tense, gripped by an anxiety she cannot control.

As an adult in her twenties and early thirties, Karen still did not talk spontaneously most of the time, and she avoided eye contact. Her speech, though often clear, was nevertheless staccato and limited in vocabulary and phraseology. When she was tired of a conversation, she would turn away as if the other person were not there. Karen still had compulsive gestures, and occasionally, when she was talking, she covered her face with her hands in a sudden convulsive movement of her body. Yet, in general, her relationships with others had improved. She would even, if asked, offer her cheek for a kiss, which was quite unusual, as people with autism are generally uncomfortable with such intimate contact.

At age 37, Karen moved into an apartment by herself, which was close to the seashore. She had spent summers with her family on an island, and there she developed an intense love of the seashore. She insisted that her first independent apartment be near water.

After working for a time at the cafeteria of the local rehabilitation center, she then took a job at the cafeteria of a nearby college. She later worked in a large warehouse discount store similar to the Price Club. She was thrilled to be making more than $7 an hour. Her boss said that Karen was worth every cent because she was so dependable and pleasant.

Similar to Tom, Karen was in an autism clinic research group, sponsored by the Connecticut Mental Health Center, which studied obsessive-compulsive behavior in autism and the effect of medication on behavior. She, too, was put on Luvox, which much improved her social awareness and ability to focus.

Karen's main interest from childhood has been flowers and birds. With her incredible memory she is able to paint flowers and birds in exact detail, to describe types of nests, and to recognize the songs of birds. Now very verbal and spontaneous in her speech, she is a different person today from the shy, frightened, delicate child who came to Ives School.

She still acts like she can't have enough jewelry, gets a manicure every 2 weeks, and always has at least two pets, a fish and a bird.

She is surrounded in her apartment by paper of every kind: note-books, catalogs of clothes, and field guides to birds and amphibians; as well as pens, pencils, and markers.

Karen's original diagnosis was "atypical development with autistic behavior." As a child she was barely able to speak and seemed surrounded by an invisible, impenetrable wall. Yet, through this wall, one felt that she wanted to relate and, despite overwhelming anxiety and shyness, she responded to patient one-to-one teaching. Her remarkable memory certainly played a part in her acquisition of speech. Her speech at this point has become comparatively fluent, though the listener must be willing to make a leap of imagination to bridge between her actual speech and its meaning.

Two incidents from a follow-up visit in 1998 illustrate the complexity of her thinking. When I asked her if she knew the restaurant where she and her family often went for lunch, she responded that she could show the way. But after two false tries, it was clear that she could neither give the directions, nor, when asked, could she recall the name of the restaurant. However, despite her remarkable memory, it seemed more likely that her intense anxiety blocked her ability to put directions into words.

We found the restaurant through trial and error. As soon as the car was on the right street, Karen delightedly recognized the area and pointed out the right place.

In contrast, a short ride down to the shore after lunch showed Karen's abilities in another light. Standing and looking out across the bay, Karen's demeanor changed as she stood and watched the bird life on the water. A gull flew up and Karen said, "That's a herring gull. There goes a white heron," as she pointed to a white flash with extended legs settling on the water. She was entranced by the proximity of the birds. She lost her anxiety—no more spasmodic covering of her face with her hands. She was totally involved, glued to watching the birds. Her intense interest in them gave her focus, wiping out her confusions and all-consuming anxiety. I was struck by her manner: At the harbor, observing the water and the shore birds, she was so absorbed and self-confident. What a contrast to how she looked when I left her that day: a stocky figure with football-player shoulders and hands clasped behind her back, walking disconsolately toward her apartment. My heart ached for her. This picture was indelibly printed in my memory.

In the summer of 1999, I made a date with Karen through her caseworker. As I searched for her new place of residence I thought about that last image of Karen trudging away. So when the search for her new apartment proved frustrating—the building was only two stories high and the number on the door miniscule—it was with relief and joy that I recognized Karen's familiar silhouette as she stood on the street corner, quite clearly watching for her visitors.

To shouts of "Karen, Karen!" she turned and ran toward the car, smiling.

Her new apartment was smaller, but complete with alcove kitchen, bedroom, living room, and bath. It was very neat and comfortable. Her case manager had laughingly described the increase in Karen's pet collection. There were now two fish tanks, with fish, crabs, and frogs. She also had two parakeets. Karen introduced each pet to her visitors by name. Occasionally she would croon to one creature or another, as a mother might to a small child. This reminded me of a previous visit, when Karen had called out to two gulls, "Come on, eat your lunch, eat your lunch." She described which of her pets she had to feed, and which were able to nourish themselves from the environment of the tank.

Karen was enthusiastic about posing for pictures, both with her pets and alone. I was happy to see that there had been a great improvement in her appearance. Her stocky figure had trimmed down, although her wide shoulders remained. She wore a white blouse, hand appliqúed with pink, blue, and green flowers. Her short matching skirt showed off slim, very feminine legs. These counterbalanced the impression of the masculine shoulders.

The biggest change was Karen's face. Rosy cheeks, very faint eyeshadow and penciled eyebrows, and a stylishly shaped boyish haircut completed the picture. With this new attention to grooming, and the addition of accessories such as pretty gold and pearl earrings, Karen was stunningly pretty. She gave the impression that she was quite aware of this, and had gained a subtle self-confidence from it. She had, even as a child, been clothes conscious, but it was as if all her artistic sense, as seen in her drawings, jewelry and choice of clothes, had come to fruition.

At a very late breakfast at a nearby diner (which we again had difficulty finding because her anxiety prevented her from giving me correct directions), she confirmed that she still works several days a week at a discount store where she puts away stock. On other days she works at a country club in the kitchen, "cleaning up." Both of these are paying jobs. One day a week she volunteers at a park run by the Audubon Society, "picking up trash." I gathered this information by asking her questions to which she gave brief answers, but always with a smile and a subtle air of self-confidence.

Karen goes frequently to the library where, according to her case manager, she invariably chooses books about nature, flowers, birds, snakes, and forest animals. Karen showed us these books at her apartment, and clearly she had read some of the text. This was amazing to me, as I recalled the little girl who spoke only four words when I first taught her. Her visits to the library to pick out books, pursuing her interest in nature, is another sign of her improved self-image. Her skilled makeup and very becoming outfit testify to this growing maturity. As she walked past an acquaintance, the friend said, "Oh hello, Karen. So pretty, as usual!"

Many things have improved for Karen, not the least of which is her speech. It now flows smoothly and easily. Usually, she answers questions in three or four words; however, her enunciation is clear and less stressed. When I mentioned having a bad knee, Karen asked, "Will your knee get better? My mother had knee surgery!"

She seemed settled and self-confident in a way that would have been impossible to imagine a year before. Her job was going well; Karen is now working full-time in the kitchen at an assisted living retirement center. Although she still covers her face with her hands, and occasionally is shaken by an almost imperceptible tremor, her intense anxiety has lessened greatly.

Karen's continuing development is a tribute to intense one-to-one teaching; the unceasing, intelligent care of her parents, particularly her mother; and of course the highly professional supervision of doctors, social workers, job coaches, and case managers.

As to the relevance of the test scores when she was 24, they clearly reflect her intense anxiety. When comparing her test scores with what she has accomplished, Karen has achieved more success than the scores might indicate. However, as the communication scores showed, she needed help in interpreting the social world, and this still remains true. She's very happy, and her parents are very proud of her.

Postscript

Interviewed in December, 1999, Karen's mother disclosed that Karen had been invited to be part of a research study at the Yale Child Study Center where, as a 4-year-old, her disability had been diagnosed. The research project is looking into the function of the brain as it affects the development of autism.

Participation in the study meant that Karen would have to undergo a magnetic resonance imaging (MRI) scan, a procedure many patients find frightening. But Karen's mother was impressed by the care the investigators took to ensure Karen's understanding of the test. She was brought into the laboratory several times prior to the day of the actual test to look at a model of the MRI machine, and the sounds that the machine makes were played for her. By the day of the test itself, Karen fully understood what would happen, and she seemed confident.

When Karen first went into the tunnel, her mother reported, she was delighted to look into the mirrors and see her mother's eyes reflected there. During the procedure, her mother stood at the end of the tunnel and gently squeezed one of Karen's toes or her foot, sending a silent message, "I'm here, Karen. Don't be afraid." She herself found the machine's clacking noise startling, but was astonished that Karen could lie so absolutely still. There was only one moment when her mother sensed that Karen was beginning to get upset. She then stroked Karen's leg, and felt her daughter relax.

Thanks to the researchers' skillful and thoughtful handling of the examination, Karen was able to complete it successfully. When it was over, she viewed images projected on a large television monitor. Her mother laughed when she heard Karen call out excitedly, "Mom, come in here and see my brain!"

*   *   *

Karen was tested in October 1987, when she was 25, at the Yale Child Study Center, where she achieved the following scores:

TEST SCORES

WAIS–R
Verbal IQ score: 62
Performance IQ score: 52
Full-Scale IQ score: 55

VABS

Domain	Standard score	Adaptive level	Age equivalent
Communication	20	Low	4 years 3 months
Daily Living	49	Low	7 years 9 months
Socialization	44	Low	5 years 9 months
Adaptive Behavior Composite	27	Low	5 years 11 months

ABC
126: Autistic

As measured by the WAIS–R, Karen placed in the moderately retarded range of intellectual functioning. Her Verbal, Performance, and Full-Scale IQ scores were all consistent with one another. It was striking to note, however, that Karen earned one of her highest scores on Similarities, a test of verbal abstract reasoning. Such relative skill in an individual with limited overall cognitive capability is rather uncommon. It suggests that she may have the capacity for some degree of conceptual, reflective reasoning.

On the basis of an interview with Karen's mother using the VABS survey form, Karen obtained an adaptive behavior composite score of 27, which places her in the low range when compared to all adults in her peer group.

The psychologist described Karen as a slightly overweight young woman with dark hair, heavy eyebrows, and a fair complexion. She was dressed casually in bright, stylish clothing. She was friendly and cooperative throughout the assessment. She volunteered that she was soon going to have her ears pierced and that her brother was going to be married, and she seemed quite happy about both events. Karen tried hard on all assessment tasks. However, when unsure of an answer, she would not attempt to guess.

"I had to identify her emotions for her . . ."

by Elizabeth Stanley

1994

In early 1966, after several months of careful examination and study, the Yale Child Study Center told me that my 3-year-old child was different—"atypical" was the word they used. They went on to say that her atypicalness fell within the broad syndrome known as "autism." I had never heard the term. They told me that she was born with built-in deficits, with no cause yet known. It was simply the way she was constitutionally constructed. This basic personality, along with its limitations, would be hers always. We had to accept and live with that.

I was terrified—at first by the cloud of mystery, and then by my gradual awakening to what it really meant, which was worse. Karen, this lovely baby we had so wanted, who was adored by all of us, including our other four children and relatives, would never be normal. Since then there has been no significant disagreement among the different specialists we have consulted on Karen's diagnosis and prognosis. All observed that Karen was not capable of imaginative play; she was withdrawn and unable to relate normally to other children. She was obsessive and perseverative. She was autistic.

By the time Karen was diagnosed, I had already known for some time that there was something wrong with her. When she was 2, our family lived for a year in a large city in the Orient. Before we left the United States, when getting the necessary immunizations at the pediatrician's office, I hesitantly raised my hidden fears about Karen. Although none of her development was out of step with what I knew to be normal, she seemed slow: She wasn't speaking; she felt limp; she lacked ordinary aggression (my other children at her age would have been all over the doctor's office, climbing on chairs, or pulling papers from his desk). I said she seemed docile, too quiet. Was something wrong? The pediatrician mulled that over a bit, gazed thoughtfully at Karen, then reassured me: All children develop at different rates and over different spans of time; she was within normal bounds.

Our voyage abroad by freighter was a lively experience: 2 months at sea, visiting many ports in the Mediterranean, the Red Sea, the Middle East, and India. But I grew more troubled about Karen. Although I took two trunks full of toys, games, and books for the children, she touched none of them. She would not play with any of us, although she enjoyed it when we tossed her about and tickled her. The only amusement she found was splashing in the sink or bathtub in our room, and being carried about by the crewmen, who adored children.

After our arrival in the East, following the custom there, I employed an aide to take care of Karen. I also enrolled her in a small nursery group. But while all the others joined in play or listened to stories or sang songs, Karen sat on the fringe poking at the sand at her feet. She stood all alone, isolated.

After a while, we started to refer to Karen as "the quiet one." We began to feel increasingly cut off, even rejected by her. At her age, after all, children look at you, hear you, laugh at and with you, and annoy you. Not Karen. I suspected that she needed medical help, and, so far from home, I became increasingly worried and at times nearly frantic.

When we returned in the fall of 1965 I immediately took Karen to the Yale Child Study Center to undergo professional scrutiny. While we awaited the outcome, friends and family tried to reassure us. But in those assurances I dimly sensed their need to protect me from some horrible truth they themselves had begun to fear. "After all," they reasoned, "what do you expect? All of you dote on her and baby her to death. She doesn't have to talk or do anything. Before long she'll get tired of that, and then you will see a big change. Einstein, you know, didn't talk until he was 3." We needed to believe them, so we did.

Meanwhile, we enrolled her in a nursery school, and our experience there prepared us for the reality the extensive testing would soon reveal. The teacher was completely baffled by Karen, so much so that she began to question her own competence. Finally, she insisted Karen must be deaf. Worse, she worried that Karen didn't like her and therefore would not respond to her as the others did. She felt hurt, a failure. I felt the same.

After 3 months of careful examination, observation, and con-
sultation by the staff of the Child Development Clinic at the Yale
Child Study Center, our doctor there told us the tragic truth. Karen
was not deaf; she could hear a pin drop. This developmental specialist, her eyes full of a dread her professionalism could not hide,
said Karen suffered from autism, an affliction for which there was
no known cure. Education was the only possible therapy.

The problem was that deficits in the formation of Karen's personality were interfering with its normal development. Karen had
no sense of her own identity, and she could not locate and use her
own emotions. "You must get through to her, press yourself upon
her, barrage her, make her hear you and respond. We are certain she
can. You must reach her." I could not miss the desperate insistence
in the doctor's voice.

The doctor went on. She said there was one other thing I had to
do: I had to identify Karen's emotions for her, and then interpret
them for her and teach her what they were and the appropriate
responses to them. I had no idea what this meant. For a long time
Karen had seemed incapable of feeling or expressing any emotion.
Now the doctor was telling me that she really had emotions but
could not understand what they were for or how to express them.
Likewise, the doctor said that Karen had intelligence but could not
use it. She could not relate normally to people or even to her physical surroundings.

As I listened, my mind whirled and my throat went dry. It all
seemed unreal. I realized Karen's responses and behavior were dis-
tressingly impersonal and sometimes bizarre. Now I was told I had
to develop some way to force her to do what she apparently could
not do on her own—hear me, respond to me, deal with me, act like
a human being. My God, what was she? Even dogs lick your hands,
jump on you, invite you to play. Was she a sub-being of some sort?
Could she even learn, respond naturally? What if she couldn't?
Would she become a "vegetable" and have to be "put away"? There
are no words to describe those moments, the pain and terror I felt
as I walked out of that office.

On arriving home, I opened the door. Full of apprehension, I
went to the kitchen and put my purse on the table. Karen stood in
the hallway. She acted as if I was not there. I looked at her. She did
not look at me; I wasn't "there." "Karen," I called softly, "come
here." She did not move, "Karen," I said louder. She looked at the

door. "Karen!" I shouted. She did not move. Tears of desperation filled my eyes. With both hands, I picked up a fat cookbook, lifted it over my head, and slammed it with all my might on the table, sending the salt and pepper shakers flying. "Karen!" I screamed. She turned and looked at me. She heard! I had reached her! She could respond! I was stunned. I knelt before her, gathered her in my arms, and sobbed. This was where I had to begin. What to do? Who would help? What would happen to her, to all of us, to me? Karen said, did nothing. So began the long trek to today.

Karen and Our Family

At the very time in the life of a child when one expects the beginning of social interaction, Karen withdrew from us. She was rigid in body, fragile in bearing, vulnerable, and very frightened. All stimuli confused her unbearably and caused her either to recede or to engage in what we thought of as bizarre behavior. She seemed to be deaf. She found refuge in the bathroom, where she flushed the toilet endlessly; or she sat on the floor and rubbed the feet of a bronze statue we had brought with us from the East.

She immersed herself in things, in objects, in meaningless behavior. She was withdrawn, out of touch. Her gaze fixated at times on certain objects, such as the reflector pan of the stove or a crack in the table top. She screamed in terror when we blew up a balloon. She poked things repeatedly that caught her glance: a piece of jewelry on another person's dress or a mole on the neck of a friend.

And the greatest problem of all for her future was her very poor reasoning ability and severe thought disorder. She had little to no ability for abstract thinking: She learned by rote, retaining what she held in her unusual memory. Pain, sorrow, anger—all these were beyond her. Such concepts as *under*, *over*, *near*, and *far* were like a foreign language to her, to be learned and routinely applied.

Her speaking as it emerged was often unrelated to anything and made little sense to others. She repeated a word or phrase over and over. As she learned speech, it was echolalic—automatically repeating what another person had just said.

She had no idea of spatial relationships, or similarities, differences, or opposites. She had little sense of her own body or of her body's relationship to the space around it. She seemed not to know that she had arms and legs, ears and eyes, or what they were for.

She insisted on objectifying anything (including living things) so she could touch it, handle it, mouth the words for it endlessly. She treated animate things as inanimate and inanimate things as animate. She turned people into things to be poked. She would pat and stroke a desk, or put a barn door hook-and-eye latch in the baby buggy and push it about. Records were for spinning, not for listening. Dolls were for pulling apart. She even tried repeatedly to pull off her own head or stick it in the toilet.

She was tense and fearful. When frustrated, she would hit herself, pull up her skirt, or recede into a corner, thumb in her mouth. She dug at her fingers until they bled.

In all, this one fact stood out: She could not relate to people as people. Locked inside this vacant isolation, Karen virtually was unreachable by anyone, beginning with her family, and of course I feared she could eventually back out of human contact entirely and into a world none of us would be able to enter. The prospects were horrifying.

Worst of all, she did not know us, who we were, or that she was our baby girl and our other children's sister. She had no idea who she was, that she was a girl, a daughter, a sister, a playmate, a person. She did not play with her siblings or delight them as babies always do. This was, I felt, a loss for my other children beyond speaking. Likewise, she did not know me as her mother: I had no special meaning for her. She could easily walk off with the next stranger on the street, and sometimes did. She didn't know the difference. It was years before she knew who her parents and siblings were, and where and what home and family were. All of us felt rejected.

I was nearly crushed. If you can penetrate the heart of a mother and perceive what really feeds her inner being and makes her enjoy being a mother, it surely includes the wonder and excitement and ineffable satisfaction of the response of her child to her. But this could not be; it was impossible to mother Karen. I was screened out. I had no cue from her to go on; I was at a dead end. I could only do things for her or to her and see that she was fed and clothed. The distance between such care and mothering is vast.

In those early days I could only think that I, in some way unknown to me, had caused her problem. I am sure every mother of an autistic person suffers this torture. But in time I came to understand that the cause stemmed from Karen's own constitutional

makeup and her consequent development. Slowly, I began to realize that these symptoms of autism were not rejection of me or of us
but rather her escape from impossible-to-endure confusion and
inner turmoil over which she had no other control. The symptoms
were, in fact, her very means of survival. We would have to find out
how to get around or through them to help her take control and
release the real person within.

Parents and Family At Risk

The difficulties an autistic person brings to a family are enormous,
especially for the mother. You go on being a wife, a mother to the
others, a neighbor, a friend, a relative—taking up those relationships while you try not to allow the autistic person to absorb you to
the detriment of your life. You try to avoid feeling guilty, for if the
mother feels guilty the problem is only compounded. And no matter how much you give, the autistic person still needs more.

Siblings often feel abandoned by a mother given over to the care
of an autistic child. They feel neglected, or worse, they feel guilty
that their demands might increase their mother's already too-great
burden. It is easy for them to fear that adding to their mother's worries might push her over the brink. They do not feel free to express
what might be ordinary discontent about their situation.

In such circumstances, how can a normal adolescent work
through the ambivalence and the complexities of growing up? This
was especially true in the 1960s and 1970s when Karen was young,
which was a time of great social upheaval and disenchantment of
the young with the establishment of which we, the parents, were of
course a part. So, Karen's siblings became mute and tended to go
their own ways, missing sorely what they needed from their parents.

Their apparent alienation made things difficult for me, too.
Because they were normal, I expected them to do a lot for themselves and to help with Karen. It was very easy for me to feel everyone left me with the burden, isolated and alone. Such feelings on
my part only increased their worries and drove them further away.
And the problem worsened.

My husband was usually not directly involved in the day-to-
day care of Karen. Some men, my husband included, find the pain
of having and caring for an autistic child simply too great to live
with intimately and still carry on their work. I now see that it might
have destroyed him, as he feared it would me. He had to protect

himself, and this meant distancing himself as he could from the everpresent trouble.

My husband did help where he could—with the transportation of the children to their social and school obligations and of Karen to her numerous appointments and programs. He did keep steadily at his job and its demands and supported the family. He sometimes made it possible for us to get away alone where we could restore ourselves and be refreshed. He involved himself in every decision. Although relating to Karen baffled him, he cared about her and in one way or another built a strong relationship with her that today serves her well. Now, he delights in her accomplishments, growth, and presence and participates in the new challenges we face with her. He often picks her up at her residence to take her shopping and to dinner at a restaurant, a treat she always accepts with much pleasure.

Once, speaking to a parent group, my husband said he often felt as though we were in a lifeboat. Karen had fallen overboard and I was about to jump in after her, even though I didn't know how to swim. His job, he said, was to steady the boat and keep me from jumping. (It is the mother, after all, who jumps. How could I possibly sit there and watch my child drown?) He once told me flatly, "If it is a choice between you and Karen, I choose you." Well, in a way I was reassured and in a way threatened. What did choosing me mean? Giving up Karen? I had to keep Karen and myself stable so that such a choice would not be necessary. So I kept quiet.

And in that is the essence of the deepest isolation of all the mother of an autistic child feels. I couldn't imagine giving up on Karen, yet I couldn't express to my husband or children what I was feeling, for I knew it hurt them and drove them away from me. So, I increasingly felt alone, trapped. I have since learned that most mothers of autistic children do.

Karen's Education

At the time Karen was diagnosed, there was only one small school in our area that was trying to deal with autistic children: the Elizabeth Ives School for Special Children. The doctors at the Yale Child Study Center suggested we enroll her there, which we did.

In all, Karen has gone to five schools, some of them new and experimental. From her earliest years, schooling for Karen followed a consistent pattern. She had a succession of wonderful teachers who were committed deeply to her, and who believed she could be made to hear them and to learn. Many of them believed firmly that she had a concealed intelligence and emotional sensitivity, which they sought desperately to reach and to activate. These forceful and persistent people provided Karen with the necessary structure and support for her to begin to participate in life, to respond, to speak, to know herself and to let herself be known.

Fundamental to the method used was the drive to get a reaction from her. They, the teachers, and we, the parents, *demanded* a relationship with Karen, and in demanding it from her, we began to get it. She *had* to look into our eyes, hear us and respond to us. We *insisted*. It was a gut job, not a paper exercise. It made us sweat. Teaching her reading, writing, and arithmetic at that stage seemed less relevant than nurturing a relationship in which we helped her to identify pain, anger, affection, humor, hurt, and grief and express them appropriately.

Karen's education and training went on at school and at home. Her disabilities forced us to teach her survival skills—what she had to know and do to adapt to a world she could not understand. We demanded, so far as we could, acceptable behavior. She gradually learned to look after her personal care, to take her own shower, to tidy her room, to understand and manage menstruation, to dress nicely, to greet people. Each acquired skill prepared her to learn the next and to grow in the art of being human.

There was an additional, extremely potent, force at work for Karen. It lay within her. She *wanted* to relate to us. She *wanted* to learn and be independent. All the while she was growing up, she had not been really so out of touch as her withdrawal had made it seem. As time and schooling went on, the layers of resistance and withdrawal peeled away, and we learned that she wanted to laugh, to sing, to dance, to be with us, to draw, to pile up blocks and knock them down, to swim, to walk, to listen to records, to watch the birds, to learn the names of flowers and trees, to go places and do things.

Speech came awkwardly. At first it was hollow and regimented, then slowly her own speech emerged, clear and crisp. She learned to assert herself and defend her possessions and her privacy. She wanted friends. As she learned to express her pleasure in people she began to elicit the affection of those with whom she came in contact. Her smile took over and the pleasant person she is emerged. For all her stilted speech, she won interest and affection, and more and more people made their adjustments to her difficulties and peculiarities and related to her. They not only made her happy, they helped her to learn to live. It all came with glacial slowness. It was only after long spans of time had passed between what she had been and what she was becoming that we knew progress was being made.

As Karen learned to relate to people, her ability to learn the fundamentals of the simplest survival skills and elementary academics improved, and her inner disturbance began to give way bit by bit to inner calm. She began to take control of herself and emerge as a person. She learned more and more of the social skills that are essential to normal living. In time, we found she could not progress very much academically. We had to learn when to stop our pressure.

Over the years, Karen has been examined, evaluated, and treated by competent psychologists, psychiatrists, social workers, and educators. We have employed helpers and teachers privately. Connecticut during these years was in the forefront in taking governmental responsibility for the education of all children, even those with impairments as serious as Karen's. So, happily for us, the state bore part of the horrendous cost of educating and treating her.

Adulthood and Supported Independence

After many years living at home and in group homes, Karen now lives with two other women with developmental disabilities in a semi-supervised apartment in a nearby city. The state DMR provides 20 hours a week of staff supervision for this semi-independent living program. In Karen's case, the staff person is a capable adult who helps Karen and her apartment mates organize their home, provide food and necessary supplies, schedule medical visits, and plan and take part in social and recreational activities. A vocational counselor helps locate jobs in the community. Thus, Karen is more and more thrown on her own resources, and often she is able to develop her own skills to meet her emerging needs. However, she still needs much help—the most difficult sort to provide—in taking responsibility for herself, and in planning and executing the means of satisfying her needs.

Given her basic impairments and the long-term care by staff members, her progress toward increasing independence is slow. She still has no concept of numbers or money, and quite confidently empties her wallet in front of store clerks, who are then expected to take only what is needed. So far, her trust has not been betrayed. But this illustrates how much we who parent such autistic people, must trust the fragile and often dangerous society into which we launch our children, hoping not only that they can manage, but that others will give them a hand and not harm them. With Karen, our trust has been rewarded, but I can never give up fearing for her. Even crossing the street is a major hazard because, with cars coming, she will start across the street, all the while assuring me she has "looked" and, having looked, is free to go. Looking, assessing what she sees, and transferring that into appropriate action is still a very complicated process. For Karen learns not so much by instruction as by immersion. I was never one to throw a child into a swimming pool and say "swim," but now I do it all the time with Karen. There is no alternative if she is to be able to live in the world as it is. For that goal I am willing to risk her life, to take the chance that she will make it. This is not a testimony to rashness but to my desperation and her need.

Any program in semi-independent living for an autistic person is full of risk and uncertainty. Karen is frequently on her own, busying herself at her home, traveling over the one bus route she knows to a mall which, I have learned, is like a village green, opening to her the world of shops and the possibility of meeting a friend. She takes up formerly impossible tasks such as getting herself bathed, dressed, and outside ready to meet a van that takes her to work each morning. Even managing not to lose her house key and actually being able to put it in the lock, turn it, and open the door without a helper in sight is a major step ahead, and a building block upon which she develops more confidence and other skills. The two people who share her apartment are good friends, and they all help each other in many ways. Their apartment has become a kind of informal gathering place for others in nearby semi-independent programs. They celebrate birthdays, go out together to special events, send out for pizza, and watch TV and videos. They hang out.

Efforts are made to help Karen and her friends explore and use resources in the community, such as churches, YMCAs, health centers, libraries, movies, concerts, and eating places. Like most adults, they move about in a circle they come to know and can handle on their own. Up until 2 years ago, Karen lived in group homes under 24-hour supervision and had never been left alone 1 day in her life, even at home. Until she was 30, her entire life was programmed, supervised, and carried out under close staff supervision. She could not use a telephone or take a bus or taxi. She could not prepare her own meals, organize her daily life, plan and carry out what she wanted to do, or pay her own bills.

Now she can use the telephone and, most of the time, dial it correctly. She helps clean the house and does her own laundry. She can open canned food and microwave TV dinners. She is often alone in her apartment, even for an entire weekend, sometimes preferring that to coming home to her parents. She can take the bus on a limited basis; she can call a taxi when needed. She can walk alone down her street a couple of blocks to a variety store to buy milk and bread. On Sunday she takes a taxi to church (having telephoned the previous day to arrange to be picked up). She goes to work each morning, still in a semi-supervised job, but increasingly on her own.

Karen still has major deficiencies that would confound any normal person. She cannot handle the telephone reliably: She will frequently pick up the receiver and not say anything, expecting it to talk to her. She does not get messages straight. She cannot read or write beyond primitive levels. She gets lost if a well-defined route is interrupted. She still does not approach others to ask for help or directions. Her recreational outlets are few, her friends limited to those at least as limited and impaired as she is. When frustrated, she may "act out" by screaming and breaking things, not yet knowing how to express her feelings appropriately and work out her frustrations in a more useful way.

As inadequate as it sometimes seems, I know Karen's life depends on the resources the state can give her in living independently and learning to manage her own life. Although I cannot see very far down the road, I am sure she can grow more and more into a life she can manage on her own. Increasingly, she will become independent, a goal once so far beyond the realm of possibility. Never in my wildest dreams did I imagine it could happen. Well, it hasn't yet, and every week is fraught with problems. But, we muddle through, and in the end, I am sure Karen will survive as her own person in her own life.

10

John Stark

Unpredictable and Turbulent

born June 20, 1961

When John was first at Ives, visitors, misled by his typical appearance, would often ask, "Why is that child here?" Now, as an adult, he retains a quick, flashing smile and a responsive sparkle in his eyes and has an outgoing manner and appearance. He is overweight and has lost the perfect complexion and boyish features of early childhood, but people are still mystified when told of his disability. They ask, "Isn't this young man perfectly normal?" But he isn't.

John was a very difficult baby—fussy, high-strung, and crying almost continuously. He was hard to comfort, although at times he quieted down when he was held and rocked. As he grew older he developed sleep problems. He was late in sitting and did not walk until he was 16 months old. Between 1 and 3 years of age, he often reacted with extreme fear to a variety of noises and changes in his usual environment. At other times, and more often after the age of $2\frac{1}{2}$, he appeared jovial and very likable, but had spells that a physician at the Yale Child Study Center described as "ornery."

John was undiscriminating about people. Anyone could care for him as long as they gave him undivided attention. He attended a general nursery school when he was 3 but got into difficulty because of his hyperactivity and impulsiveness. He was very demanding when his mother was present and insisted that she be involved in all of his activities.

His mother had become increasingly upset with John's behavior and said that most of the time she was screaming at him and in tears. She often reached the saturation point. Both sets of grandparents were critical of him and of her handling of him.

John was evaluated at the Yale Child Study Center twice, the first time when he was almost 3 years old and again about a year later. The developmental evaluations at age 4 described him as generally awkward in motor development, with difficulties in hand skills and eye–hand coordination. His performance scores on nonverbal problem-solving tasks placed him in a developmental range of between 30 and 42 months old, substantially below his age level. He became easily disoriented and overexcited or distracted, and his attention span was short. His social relationships were superficial, and his affect was bland, as though there were an emptiness within.

John used toys appropriately, but his play was fragmented, and he flitted from one activity to another. His speech production and comprehension were within normal limits. He enjoyed stories and knew many nursery rhymes. He seemed to want to be with other children but became overexcited and disoriented when he was with more than two others. He reacted intensely and with panic to certain noises and situations.

John was diagnosed as being a "neurologically impaired, emotionally disturbed" child. Yale recommended psychiatric treatment for him after his second evaluation, but his parents were not ready for that. (Later he would have a period of psychotherapy.)

John entered Ives School at the age of 4 years and 3 months. He was a short, well-built child with a pink-cheeked, round face; large blue eyes; and a beguiling smile. During his first week, he was agreeable and anxiously conforming. That disintegrated rapidly into hyperactive, angry, often hysterical behavior.

John required the total attention of his teachers. His favorite place to play was the doll corner, and with constant teacher attention and praise he could play with a toy for 1 or 2 minutes. He could not tolerate a lapse in teacher presence, and he reacted hysterically to efforts to introduce another activity or include another child in his play.

During John's first year he improved, despite absences caused by a broken leg and eye surgery to correct strabismus (a disorder in which the eyes cannot both be focused at the same time). He came to realize that, largely because of his verbal skills, he could do easy academic tasks better than his classmates, and this gave him some self-confidence. Gradually, though still distractible and anxious, he learned to stick to an activity for a short while, and he pushed and shoved far less. He was obsessed by domestic play, such as pushing the vacuum cleaner and pretending to cook, and he spent a lot of time in water play. He also began to play, albeit superficially, with other children. Even with his progress, however, teaching John remained a daring enterprise. Despite his verbal ability, there seemed to be an intangible wall between him and everyone around him.

After 3 years at Ives School, John was transferred to a private day school for children and adolescents with disabilities, where he remained for 8 years, to age 15. While there, he made painfully slow progress in academic areas such as math, written English, and the sciences; performed moderately well in reading; and improved his motor skills through athletics. He did well in music and at school assemblies, where he distinguished himself as a master of ceremonies, ad-libbing humorously. He seemed happiest when entertaining a group and blossomed with this success. Oral reading, singing, and acting were his strengths. He remained emotionally explosive.

During most summers between the ages of 7 and 15, John went to a residential camp. His ability to relate to his peers improved but nevertheless remained "insubstantial," according to camp reports.

John's family tended to have unrealistic expectations of him. Mr. and Mrs. Stark were both achievers: She was an accountant, and he was a teacher in a public school. The atmosphere at home was often chaotic. John was unpredictable emotionally and could dissolve without warning into hysterical crying or shouting. Life at home was a "constant screaming match." Because John was so verbal and had such a "normal" appearance, his parents had difficulty accepting the fact that he had a genuine and permanent functional disability.

At age 15, John went to a residential school for emotionally disturbed adolescents. This relieved the stress in the Stark's home somewhat, and John's parents thought it would help his socialization. Again, however, his improvement was minimal.

When John was 17, he returned home to enter a new special education program set up by the state, offering small academic classes and vocational training. He did fairly well during his 4 years in this setting. He was the star speller of his class, did well in reading and in English, and learned how to use a typewriter and a calculator. He remained unpredictable emotionally, however, and at the end of his first year he started group therapy. Significantly, in this group he could interpret his classmates' feelings but not his own. He could tell the members of the group how they were feeling, but he could never describe how he felt.

John started prevocational training his third year, working as kitchen help in a fast-food restaurant, and he did well. His employer was interested in adults with developmental disabilities, and gave John support and direction. In his second placement, in another fast-food restaurant, John did not fare as well; here his employer had little understanding of his disabilities.

During his high school summers, John went to a camp where he worked as an aide, and through this camp he participated in track and the long jump at the Special Olympics.

In his final years at school he worked 4 days per week doing more food preparation and less cleanup. He was paid hourly for the first time.

After graduation, John worked in a downtown cafeteria (he had long since learned to ride the bus) and then as a volunteer custodian in the public schools. He was discouraged not to be earning money, but his biggest heartache was his social isolation. Because for many years his family had regarded him as fairly capable, they believed that he did not belong in the social programs sponsored by the Association for Retarded Citizens (now the Arc of the United States). John had had only casual friends at school, and none in his neighborhood. Fortunately, he was in a special catechism class at his local church and in a special Boy Scout troop. Still, John had little else to do.

Finally, however, John's outward charm began to draw people to him. Four friends from high school began to call him; this happened so often that John's father gave John his own telephone. He began spending the night at friends' houses and, in turn, had a friend stay with him. He also developed enough self-reliance to spend long weekends alone at home when his parents went on vacation. John's self-confidence grew as a result of this increased independence.

At this time, a test given to John by a vocational psychologist showed him to have impaired sensory function. He was able to discriminate items by shape with only 50% accuracy. Discrimination of objects by size, texture, and configuration was quite difficult for him. This limitation narrowed the range and kind of work he could perform. For the first time, his family accepted the fact that he had mental retardation. His parents had him evaluated by the DMR's local regional center, which suggested that John apply to a special needs school for young adults.

Thus, at the age of 23, John was in a school that featured dormitory-type living, where he shared quarters with three other young men with developmental disabilities. They were all expected to have jobs, keep the apartment clean, buy food and cook meals, and participate in recreational activities. Although he did comparatively well in daily living skills and in his job as an aide in a nursing home, John frequently refused to join in group activities because of his emotional passivity, although he would go out for pizza or to a movie with others. He was more interested in activities within the apartment and in solo activities, such as listening to music. At times he had difficulty adhering to the structure of the program, and he had not done well in vocational tests administered by the state DVR.

There was a turn for the better, according to John's father, when, after repeated parental requests, the DVR agreed to retest John. The results showed great improvement, and he was permitted to enter training in the DVR fast-foods program. So, in his late twenties, John increased his participation in group activities and subsequently graduated from the school.

Since 1987, John has held different jobs, all in restaurants or involved with food. His last paying job was as a dishwasher in a large cafeteria. He broke down in tears, however, under the pressure caused by the cafeteria's need for speed and efficiency and was again asked to leave. After that, John worked as a volunteer, first in the small restaurant at a community center, then later in the dietetics department of a hospital. But in this capacity he faced logistical and emotional problems: He was asked to work on Sundays but no buses ran to the center that day, which meant he had to take a taxi. Though the center promised to reimburse John for his taxi fare, it frequently failed to repay him. When the restaurant managers gave him the opportunity to work on the cash register, this, too, proved difficult as the pressure, though subtle, became too much for him. When that happened, he would shout at a customer. As he said recently, "I quit, just as the center was about to let me go."

When he was 30 years old, John moved into a condominium with another graduate of the special needs school for young adults, whom he has now lived with for more than a decade. Together they take care of all their own needs: They shop, cook, clean, and generally maintain their own apartment. The condominium is located in a convenient area of the city, where John is able to keep in contact with his friends, who to this day include many of the graduates of the school. His case manager comes in several times a month to help John reconcile his finances and help with any personal problems he is having. He rarely needs more assistance, however. This living arrangement has worked out well, although John wishes his roommate were not so obsessively efficient.

"When I'm baking cookies, he puts up my utensils sometimes before I've used them. I have told him to *please* stay out of the kitchen when I'm cooking!"

John's charm and good nature have always made him well-liked. But his emotional instability became such a clear hazard that he himself recently took matters in hand. He has taken courses in stress management, ceramics (for fun!), and computers. He has been adamant that he would *not* see a psychologist. He has, through visits to the gym, use of an exercise bicycle, and walking, controlled his weight. At the same time, he pursued a job with the guidance of his case manager. On his own initiative, he got an application for a volunteer job in the dietetics department at a local hospital, filled it out, sent it in, had several interviews and, within the year, started working there and has been there since.

In describing this, he repeated proudly, "Yep. I did that all on my own. No, siree—nobody helped me!"

John still requires some guidance from the case manager and supervision at work: With someone in control, he feels safe. He can still disintegrate emotionally when he is too excited or when he is under certain unpredictable pressures, such as when he needs to make quick decisions or be flexible about a change in routine. But now he is far less likely to break down than in earlier years.

For someone who was unable to describe his feelings, John now seems to have a good perspective about himself. He describes himself as "not so moody as I used to be. I've noticed that in myself. I've just been figuring that out in my head. I *hate* going to pieces. When it happens, I say to myself: Where did I ever go wrong? Why was it always me? But now I can begin to sort out my feelings. I can open out more after one of these storms, and I do apologize to everyone." John is aware of how far he has come. "I am proud of myself," he says.

In the spring of 1997, over coffee at his condo, John talked to me about his life in general. I was touched by his description of his attacks of hysteria, which still cause him to break down in tears. When he feels an explosion coming on, he said, he tries to isolate himself.

"When I do that, when I start to cry, I say to myself, 'Why?' But I'm better now. I try to get by myself until I'm quiet again."

When asked what plans he had for the weekend, he replied that he was having a group of friends over for dinner. I exclaimed "John, are you cooking for that many people?"

"Oh, no," he replied. "I'll go out to Stop and Shop, and bring it back on the bus." This is another example of John's unusual independence and initiative.

John agreed to one last interview in the summer of 1999. He was waiting for me out in front of his condominium, leaning against a lamp post in a casual "man-of-the-world" stance. This obviously exaggerated pose was amusing to see.

Seated in the dining room of his apartment, John described his work at the hospital, which consists primarily of helping with the dishwasher and setting up trays for patients.

"The steam is taken out by a fan," he explained, shaking his head "but the heat is brutal man, it's brutal!"

He leaves home at 7:00 A.M., is through by noon, and gets home an hour later, via a commute that requires transferring from one bus to another.

When I reminded him of his teenage talent as a master of ceremonies at his school's shows, John smiled with satisfaction at the recollection and said, "I'm never shy!"

John sang solos as a child, but noted that he doesn't sing now. However, he is "into crafts." He proudly showed off a foot-high red rocket that he had made. Enthusiastically, he described launching the rocket in a field near his condominium.

He is also taking a computer course, and still enjoys ceramics class. In the latter, he made two life-size statues of cats, which he proudly showed me. They were very life like, with alert expressions. He was pleased when I told him that he had real talent in art.

"I know," he replied, adding that his teacher had also complimented him. John said he had been surprised when his art teacher exclaimed in school one day, "Boy, John, you are great."

On the computer, he uses e-mail and surfs the Internet. (Individuals with autism are often notably good with computers.)

John feels he has "enough hobbies" at the moment. Currently he is doing latch-hook work to create a wall hanging featuring Tweetie Bird. After that, he added, he will work on making a stained-glass window. Then he will be "through with art!"

When reminded how well he had done at his special education high school, receiving recognition as the top reader and speller, John recalled how surprised he was to be asked to graduate with his general high school class.

"I was nervous in the inside. But I did all right!" He was obviously very proud of this accomplishment.

John's parents have never been entirely convinced that he has autism characteristics. But, once again, his case is an illustration of the vast differences that exist within the spectrum of autism. John looks one directly in the eye; he has a surface ease in social situations. But, in fact, even going back to early childhood schooling, his contacts and understandings have been described as lacking depth.

One other instance of the conundrum of this disorder was revealed as John described his father's heart attack several years ago. John winced, shutting his eyes as he talked about this.

"Don't even talk about it! My mother called me and told me. Oh, it was awful! Things were going through my mind that you wouldn't believe."

His father is fine now. In recalling this painful time, John expressed such true depth of emotion, of shock and horror—and so verbally. *Most* uncharacteristic of people with autism.

In considering John's current situation, his family, like Tom's family, declare themselves "content." John is independent, with some minimal supervision. His father checks on him regularly. His caseworker comes in once a week to make sure his checkbook is balanced and that all is well. John, incidentally, is quite proud of never being overdrawn. "My checkbook is *always* balanced!" he added.

He has grown in both his self-knowledge and self-discipline. So, as of now, John is one more example of someone who has achieved "fragile success" despite the odds.

*   *   *

In October of 1987, when tested at the Yale Child Study Center at age 26, John had an overall IQ score of 68, with a verbal score of 73. This placed him at the borderline of average intelligence. In the VABS his low score in Communication is illuminating. John *communicates*, but with no depth of understanding. Most indicative of his "fragile success" today are his scores in Daily Living, Socialization and Adaptive Behavior Composite, which are surprisingly high, but again illustrative of the contradictions in John's personality.

Dr. Fred Volkmar labeled John's ABC score of 52 as "possibly autistic."

TEST SCORES

WAIS–R
Verbal IQ score: 73
Performance IQ score: 65
Full-Scale IQ score: 68

VABS

Domain	Standard score	Adaptive level	Age equivalent
Communication	65	Low	11 years 3 months
Daily Living	119	Moderately high	18 years 11 months
Socialization	111	Adequate	18 years 11 months
Adaptive Behavior Composite	92	Adequate	18 years 11 months

ABC
52: Possibly autistic

The supervising psychologist's report reads as follows:

Behavioral Observations

John Stark . . . cooperated fully with all aspects of this evaluation and appeared to give his best effort. He appeared extremely proud and smiled a great deal following responses he perceived to be successes. Throughout the testing session, he made appropriate eye contact, and he initiated several conversations. For example, he spontaneously described his job at a pizza restaurant. On the way to the testing room and returning, John appeared very unsure of himself in terms of his orientation in physical space. He appeared unsteady in a hall that has a slight incline followed by a slight decline and he raised his foot very high to move over a colored area rug.

Summary of WAIS–R and VABS Interview Data

John's level of cognitive functioning was assessed with the Wechsler Adult Intelligence Scale–Revised (WAIS–R). On the WAIS-R, John achieved a Full-Scale IQ score of 68, which places his performance in the mild deficit range of mental retardation. . . .

On the basis of an interview with John's father using the Vineland survey form, John obtained an Adaptive Behavior Composite score of 92 . . . plac[ing] his adaptive functioning in the average range and corresponding to the 42nd percentile when compared with all adults in his peer group. John had significant strengths in daily living skills and socialization.

"Never take 'no' for an answer ..."

by Carole and John Stark

1994

We have always had a lot of confidence in John and have always wanted the best for him. Maybe it was that we saw through the surface; we felt that he had potential and could succeed despite his autism. We hoped to work through his limitations and help him succeed. We were dedicated to the idea that John would continue with his education and take advantage of all of the opportunities available, pursuing whatever he could to find out just what it was he could and couldn't do. As a result we have often had to fight state agencies that felt that, according to their test results, he wasn't up to "par" for the competitive world.

It is John himself who has given us the confidence we have in him. He has always conveyed his ability to maintain a semblance of normality and to live in the community. While John was growing up, however, it seemed that every school he went to was only giving him about half the kind of education he needed, and he did not progress as we felt he could. Finally, when he was 21, we found the right school for him, one where they had the living skills program— job skills and so on—to give him the necessary background to be in the competitive world and able to live on his own with a roommate. He has handled everything very well.

We have always had difficulty with the administrative agencies and their attitude toward John and his capabilities. It seemed they were always saying he couldn't do something, while we thought he could. At the last school John attended, one of the requirements for graduation was that the student work at paid employment for a period of 6 months. The school worked in conjunction with the DMR, which dealt with handicapped individuals. The DMR did vocational skills testing to find where each student's job skills were strongest. After John was tested, they felt he would be best suited for general maintenance work (e.g., mowing, raking, general cleaning). He was sent to several jobsites, and his performance was evaluated.

The evaluation proved to be poor. John was found to be lethargic and lacking interest in his work and the physical stamina for that type of job. The DMR decided that John was not suitable for competitive employment in the community. We were outraged. They had ignored John's experience, acquired before he entered this school, of working for a cleaning service for several months and, for many years before that, working for a local restaurant as a dishwasher and food preparation person. The DMR recommended that John wait for placement at a sheltered workshop, and advised a thorough physical examination, although their own physical examination had not revealed any health problems.

While he waited for placement, John worked at a variety of volunteer jobs. One was at a home for older adults, where he worked as a transporter, taking patients to physical therapy and returning them to their rooms when their therapy was over. He did this well, but every now and again he became a bit bossy and had to be reprimanded gently. He would also enter uninvited into conversations, and although patients enjoyed his friendly nature, the staff was sometimes a bit put out. The staff would correct John when his behavior was out of line, and he stayed on that job for several months.

By then it was time for another planning and placement team meeting at his school. The PPT was a group of professionals, comprising of a school psychologist, teacher, vocational teacher, the program director, and parents, who met to help plan the balance of John's academic and social skills program and, most important, to decide in what area he could earn a living. After much discussion, we decided to ask the DMR to retest John's vocational skills, this time in the area of food services. The reason was that John had shown many changes in attitude and ability since his previous tests.

We heard from the DMR very soon after the PPT meeting. They informed us that John's name had come to the top of their list for placement in a sheltered workshop. We told the DMR about the recent PPT decision and emphasized that his improvement over the past year was the basis for our desire to have him tested again. The DMR insisted that it was highly unlikely that anyone, in such a short period, could have made an improvement significant enough to warrant a retest. They said that they had discussed it with the school and that they all—DMR *and* PPT staff—felt that John should take this slot at the sheltered workshop or he might not get another chance. The DMR also strongly implied that if John did not, his file might be closed. This would mean that John might not be able to use any DMR services in the future. We felt a good deal of pressure, even threat, in what the DMR said to us.

As parents, we were surprised and extremely upset with the professionals, especially those at the high school who had done such an about-face. It was the height of hypocrisy, this change of mind without even meeting with us, but this was more or less what we had experienced through the many years of John's earlier education. In previous cases, we had gone along with the professionals. We felt that, after all, they should know what was right. This was different. As John's mother, I decided we would not accept a unilateral decision.

Taking time from my work, I locked myself in a private office and prepared to do battle with both the school and the DMR. After several hours of making telephone calls, I finally convinced the DMR that John should be retested. The testing would take place at one of their worksites and would be for 5 days, not the 1 day originally allotted for it. We did not feel that John, or any child really, could be evaluated properly on the basis of 1 day's experience. The DMR also agreed to hold open the sheltered workshop until all of the results of John's tests were evaluated. This was much more than I had ever expected to get out of the DMR.

Both of us then sat down with John and tried to get the message across to him that his entire future depended on this evaluation. We were convinced that since he had already held a job or two in the community, he could do it again. We had to ignore the pressure we might be putting on John. This was a rare second chance, and our message to him was, essentially, "Don't blow it, kid!"

When the test results were ready, the three of us met with DMR staff and counselors from the school. The evaluation was reviewed, and the DMR counselors were amazed at the complete turnaround in John's performance. Where in the previous testing he had been considered "noncompetitive" in nearly every area, he now tested out "competitive" (i.e., motivated to work and able to stick to a task through its completion) in just about every aspect of the food-services test. The DMR now felt he could and should be considered a candidate for a regular job in the food service area, such as in a restaurant. John was assigned to a pizza restaurant with a job coach to help him adjust. He subsequently was able to graduate from the school. He got an apartment of his own, which he still shares with another young man.

John's job ended when the restaurant went out of business. His father, his vocational coach at the time, was able to find him another job at a diner, and he worked there for several months. It was only a part-time job, at minimum wage and with no benefits, like most of the jobs for young people like John.

We then heard of a dishwashing job at an executive cafeteria. This job was at least 30 hours a week, with a starting wage of $7 an hour and benefits. It was a great opportunity, and we felt that John had a shot. My husband took John for an interview with the manager, a very pleasant man who, despite little experience working with people with disabilities, was willing to give John a chance. The cafeteria was very busy, and they did not have time or the ability to train or work with someone who could not keep up. John worked a week on a trial basis and then, with the manager's approval, started full time.

After John had been on the job about 4 weeks, however, the manager called us and said that John was having difficulty. He was becoming unstrung emotionally and was not able to keep up with the work load. They apparently served a large number of lunches. The dirty dishes came in fast and furious during the 2-hour lunch period and everyone had to keep up the pace or the whole system fell apart. My husband went in and worked with John for several days to see just what was happening. It seemed that there were several things working against John. First of all, the kitchen was extremely hot, dishwashers had to stand in water, and the dishes coming out of the dryer were so hot that your fingers would tingle for days afterward if you handled them without gloves. In addition, other people on the line were not holding up their own ends, and this made the pressure on John even greater.

My husband spoke to the manager about all of this. He asked whether, if we could procure a trained job coach from the local DMR, the manager would be willing to work with John a little longer. The manager was agreeable, so we called the DMR.

We remembered the difficulty we had had with them before, but this time they were delighted to help and gave us a job coach within 24 hours. (It turned out that they had been trying to get an "in" at this company to place clients and had not been successful. So they took this as an opportunity to do a little PR and get their foot in the door.) The job coach was unable to solve John's problems, however. He did not know John and had never worked in a kitchen before. In any case, he did not know how to deal with John's emotional problems and only, I felt, aggravated the situation. The DMR, of course, had a different point of view. They felt that John was overwhelmed with the job; that he was placed in a job beyond his capabilities; and that he should not have been there to begin with.

Again we had a difference of opinion with the DMR, but this time it worked to our advantage. Because the job market for people in John's category was bad, the DMR felt that John would have a hard time competing and suggested that we apply for disability income for him. We had not done this in the past because we always felt that he would be able to support himself. Now we were beginning to have our own doubts. We were approaching the age of retirement and were concerned about how we were going to provide for John if he could not keep a full- or even a part-time job. If he could work at minimum wage for only 12 hours a week, he would never be able to support himself, nor would he ever be eligible for medication or other benefits. So we followed the DMR's recommendation. They wrote the report that got John approved for disability. And because it was made retroactive for the previous year, John immediately received a sizable check.

John has now been receiving disability payments from Social Security and state welfare payments for almost 2 years. He is also covered by Medicare. We feel that we have provided for his future, and that's all we can do. We still would like John to work out there in a paying job. He needs that for his own morale. He could still handle a job at a supermarket, bagging, or a job at a fast-food restaurant in their food-prep department. But those jobs are either not currently available or very difficult to find, and employers are going to take the applicant with the better qualifications.

For the time being, John volunteers at the home for the aged where he started out 7 years ago. He is well-liked there. They feel that he is doing a good job, that he gives his all. Once, in the past year, we received a telephone call from the DMR saying that John was becoming emotional on the job—teary-eyed—and he couldn't express his feelings enough to say what his problem was or what might be causing his upset. We were able to work out what was bothering him, but the people at the home were very concerned. They like John and want him to continue to be a volunteer, but they don't have the time to deal with his emotions. So we have to keep an eye out so that John can continue to work there.

That's where we stand now. We have felt right from the beginning that John belonged on the outside. We still feel that he does not belong in a sheltered workshop. He is now out in the world with people, helping, smiling, making someone's day, and this is where he belongs—this is something he's capable of doing. He's in the community. He has friends. He entertains and is invited out by many people. Although he still needs counseling, and he still needs support from his family, he handles most of his affairs himself. He's succeeding, and in his own way he's happy.

Sometimes we wonder whether the DMR or we were right. The way things have turned out, maybe we weren't right. We have our doubts. But we know we can only try to do the best we can. We've worked on this together for nearly 34 years, and we hope that we'll be around for a while longer to give John the advice and reassurance he still needs.

The lesson we learned as parents was that one should never take "no" for the final answer until all avenues have been explored. Mental health professionals are very busy people, and sometimes rules and procedures and even costs get in the way of their judgment. It takes love and understanding of a young person's problems and desires to know just how far he can go. And when the chips are down, it takes extreme tenacity. Stick to your guns; it is not impossible to fight city hall. It just means that you have to fight harder for what you believe in. In the end, it is well worth it.

At this time, John is working part time at a fast-food restaurant. He has adjusted very well to the new job, with the support of a coach. He has expanded his social activities to include going to small dinner parties (he loves to cook), attending some classes offered by the school, and taking part in occasional dance parties. He walks for exercise and recreation and attends some sporting events. He is involved with many family functions and is still interested in what his former classmates, relatives, and family friends are doing. He uses the telephone like a lifeline to others. He is happy.

11

Larry Perelli
Emotionally Blocked

born May 8, 1964

Larry Perelli, who came to Ives at age 5, died in his sleep in February of his 23rd year. After many years of what had appeared to be negative achievement and feelings of failure, he had been on the verge of a happier life. He was gaining some control of himself. He was receiving praise at work from his workshop supervisor and at home from his mother and stepfather. For the first time he was feeling some solid success. He had been accepted in a group home and was joyfully preparing to move into comparatively independent living. The autopsy revealed no identifiable cause for his death.

When Larry was 4½, his pediatricians referred him to the Yale Child Study Center for diagnosis because of his delay in motor and speech development and his problems in emotional behavior.

Larry's mother, in a series of interviews, displayed perplexity at her son's difficult behavior. She said that he had changed from a well-behaved child to one often out of control. Complicating whatever innate problems Larry had was his chaotic and emotionally charged home life. His infancy and toddlerhood had been rendered confusing, distressing, and probably frightening by the conflict between his divorced parents, and by the strained relationship between his mother and maternal grandmother, with whom Mrs. Perelli and Larry then lived. The evaluations at Yale noted that Larry was an emotionally disturbed boy of basically average intelligence whose cognitive functioning was impaired by his personality disorder. He was extremely anxious and fearful and was beset with preoccupations and confusion of thinking that manifested themselves in odd, idiosyncratic associations to objects, pictures, and phrases. It was not clear whether some degree of inborn predisposition to deviational development had existed in Larry from early on, but it was clear that the adults responsible for him were unable to create a favorable child-rearing environment and that he had experienced emotional deprivation and trauma in an inconsistent, turbulent environment. Autistic and psychotic features in his behavior made the outlook for the future uncertain.

The autistic component in Larry's personality lay in his "unreachableness," his imperviousness to social contact. He related minimally to people, with no awareness of the impact of his behavior on others. Although he talked incessantly, it was rarely *to* anyone, with little conversational give-and-take. He was a dramatic example of the heterogeneity of autism—a mixture of typicality and apparent intelligence, yet totally removed, as if by a wall, from social relationships.

In spite of his disturbances, Larry showed an ability to relate to the psychologist and so was referred to a child psychiatrist for treatment. His mother accepted this referral and seemed eager for the assistance. Larry, at 5 years old, began treatment that continued for 3 years, with some interruptions because of changes in therapists. (He had three therapists in that 3-year period.) At the same time, his doctor at the Yale Child Study Center referred him to the Ives School for his educational needs.

Larry had a puzzling mixture of qualities; he was intelligent and able to relate to people and the environment; nonetheless he had sudden violent, out-of-control outbursts of screaming, racing around the room destroying everything in his path, grabbing his teachers, mouthing or biting shoulders or breasts, repetitive swearing, and running out of the classroom. When these episodes occurred, Larry's teacher would hold him firmly but gently. Sometimes she might need the help of another teacher for a few minutes to help him calm down. She would take him to the "isolation" room, where she would help him to regain control of himself. There never seemed to be a specific cause for these outbursts.

Because of his behavior, Larry spent his first year at Ives largely apart from other children, in a classroom with one teacher. He joined his class only for snack time, and even this often ended in chaos—spilled juice; much mopping up; and negative, critical comments from the other children. He would often bolt out of the classroom, and his teacher would have to pursue him and return him to the isolation of his individualized program. It is indicative of his responsiveness that when so removed, he would become frightened and then winningly obedient, saying: "Are you angry with me? Don't be angry with me! I'll be good!"

By his second year at Ives, Larry had developed enough self-confidence and inner control to remain in the classroom with other children. In certain ways he had a quick intelligence, and on his good days he could outperform his classmates. By the end of his second year, he had mastered simple addition and subtraction and could read in a beginning first-grade reader. He initially refused to write, and when he finally attempted to form letters, he reversed many of them. He did very well with puzzles and loved to build with blocks or play with trucks. He also was able to use the outdoor play equipment appropriately.

At Ives (and throughout his life) Larry was, in a way, his own worst enemy. He was a bright little boy, and when he was in good shape, he mastered beginning academics—reading, math, and spelling—more easily than others in his class. But he was at the mercy of his uncontrollable emotions and could learn nothing when he was in an uproar.

Larry remained at the Ives preschool for 5 years, until he was 10, at which time he entered a residential treatment center. At age 13, he entered the local special education high school, where he was placed in the communications disorder section. He was soon transferred to the higher functioning group there.

Larry was tested for that program. The results described him at age 13½ as having a mental age of 8 years, 6 months. The psychological summary concluded that in all academic skills he showed an immature and concrete approach, meaning that he was weak in abstract reasoning. He had special difficulty in visual-motor integration; he was weak in sound–symbol integration, and he relied on structure and form to decode words in reading. He was reading on a third-grade, 8-month level, and his math ability was on a second-grade level.

There were nine children in the higher functioning group of the program, and Larry's performance was among the highest. Each child sat at a desk somewhat removed from the other eight, creating a feeling of privacy for each child, combined with a warmth of togetherness. There was one teacher and an aide. The classroom routine was highly structured, yet each child was working on his own program at his own speed.

When Larry was 16, his biological father insisted on seeing him. He had remarried, had two sons close to Larry's age, and was living in the same town. Mrs. Perelli agreed to this and set up a schedule of weekend visits. For the first visit, Larry's father took him out to dinner with his two other sons. Larry, wild with excitement, raced around the restaurant, and the two half-brothers followed his lead. The father managed to quiet Larry down, and afterward Larry began spending whole weekends with his father and stepmother.

By age 17, Larry had made great progress at school. Academically, he was high-functioning compared to the rest of his group. He used a calculator and read on a third-grade level. But although he had improved a great deal in his ability to control his behavior, he was still unpredictable, and at times he exhibited inappropriate behavior and excessively repetitious conversation. Throughout high school, Larry lived at home. Although things were better there, and his mother was pleased with Larry's teachers and the school, she found keeping Larry at home was still a trial.

At age 18, Larry was retested by his public school system's psychologist as part of the normal procedure for assessing "special problem" cases. The results confirmed his placement in the communication disorders program. At that time, Larry's teacher had detected that his eyesight was terrible and recommended that he see an ophthalmologist and obtain better glasses. At this same time, Larry's mother had given birth to another child, and the plans to see an ophthalmologist were scrapped in the face of Larry's bad reaction to the new baby. The arrival of the baby apparently had made him even more susceptible to losing control, and his mother felt that neither she nor the ophthalmologist could have managed him successfully during an eye exam.

On the advice of Larry's teachers, he might have returned to a residential treatment center, but he remained in the communication disorders program after the planning and placement team advised that he stay in one consistent, low-key program. Thinking of the future, his teachers felt that because Larry was high functioning, he would eventually do well in a structured group home.

In his high school vocational class, Larry was unable to concentrate on the job. He talked erratically and nonstop and often seemed to be totally absorbed in his own world. His eyes—slightly cock-eyed—were always moving, yet he never looked at anyone directly. His hands were never still, and he stopped work every few minutes to change the radio station. The vocational teacher could not let Larry work independently and checked on him every few minutes. Larry's tension and hyperexcitement often seemed on the border of becoming uncontrollable, yet he responded to correction and would calm down if a teacher told him to.

During his last year in high school, Larry was in group therapy at school. He also began therapy with an out-of-town psychiatrist whom he liked. As a result, he improved in the consistency and control of his behavior. That summer he worked as an aide at a special education camp and got good reports from his supervisor.

Larry graduated from his special education high school at age 22, and after an evaluation at the local rehabilitation center, he was placed in its workshop. At first, erratic and constantly asking questions or screaming, Larry was often impossible to control. He once disappeared from the workroom and was discovered by his frantic supervisor lying in the street, head on the curb, long legs out in the street, inviting destruction by the next car.

Larry's caseworkers set up a highly structured program for him, consisting of behavioral contracts that established limits, rewards, and daily objectives. Through these contracts, Larry's inappropriate and erratic behavior lessened. His improvement was such that he was accepted in a group home, much to the pride and delight of Larry and his family. Then, for no apparent reason, he died one night, quietly, in his sleep.

The tragedy of Larry's story lies not only in his early death but also in his day-to-day struggle to control himself and permit his intelligent functioning to show while he was alive. It is sad that death came to rob him of the fruition of his desire just as it seemed attainable.

12

Eric Thomas

Mute and Angry

born May 23, 1965

Eric came to the Ives School in the late spring, when he was 4 years old. He was referred to Ives by the Yale Child Study Center, to which he had been sent by the Yale–New Haven Hospital Pediatric Outpatient Clinic because of his lack of speech. Aside from this delay, his development was considered typical. He sat at 6 months, and stood and walked at 12 months. He had made baby sounds at age 1, but only between the ages of 3 and 4 had he begun to say a few words: "mama," "eat," "baby," "tata," and "no." Otherwise, he made little effort to communicate, either with or without words.

Eric tended to play alone and be in his own world a great deal of the time. Although he loved music and danced to television at home, when children his own age came to play, he shut himself in his room and rocked on his bed. He was able to play normally with

175

trucks but just looked at most other toys. He was fascinated by noises, particularly of cars starting.

Eric appeared jealous of his siblings and had severe tantrums. His mother had a history of mental illness, for which she had been hospitalized several times. Eric's brothers and sisters helped to take care of him 5 days a week, yet undoubtedly Mrs. Thomas's uncertain mental health had made adjustment harder for him.

The physician at the Yale Child Study Center described Eric as a well-developed, handsome boy whom she found very difficult to test. He clung to the materials he liked and wailed when they were taken away. Although he vocalized in an expressive, animated jargon in which some sounds and phrases could be distinguished—"whee" and "there it is"—he totally ignored questions and commands. His self-absorption and detachment from the environment made him almost impossible to reach. The frequent changes in his behavior without any obvious outside reason, as if he were responding to an inner stimulus, made him even more of a challenge.

Through the testing, Eric was found to have well-developed fine motor skills. He liked and clung to pegs, blocks, and crayons. He could build a tower of five blocks and find a hidden toy. He also scribbled.

Eric's test results were affected by his imperviousness. He was successful at a 21- to 24-month level on some test items, and this seemed to indicate that he possessed at least a minimum of ability. The physician who tested Eric summarized her assessment by stating that Eric had an impairment of personality development, probably inborn, known (at that time) as congenital autism.

When Eric came to the Ives School, he was a little boy with a snub nose and a cherubically round face. He had a beguiling smile, which, however, was not aimed at anybody or anything. He was endearing, but for the most part he represented a defeat for the teachers at Ives. His smile and unfocused affability were at first mistaken for responsiveness to others, but he was soon found to be surrounded emotionally by an "invisible wall" that made communication difficult. He shared this personality trait of imperviousness with several other children at Ives. Eric's characteristic behavior was to walk, compulsively yet apparently aimlessly, around the play yard, with his head cocked to one side, smiling. He never played with any of the other children or with outdoor equipment unless supervised and, usually, assisted by a teacher.

Midway through his second year, Eric began to show marked regression. He had spells of trance-like abstraction alternating with hyperactive aggression and fits of temper. He became aggressive toward his classmates and started having tantrums. Twice he ran unnoticed out of the classroom. Each time a frightened teacher found him wandering around the building.

When Eric was put on medication to treat this behavior he became less aggressive and less prone to tantrums. He was still unmanageable at home, however, and ran away several times. One time he was found by the railroad tracks and another time, down by the harbor. Because his behavior began to exceed that which Ives was capable of handling, he was referred to the autism unit of a state hospital in a neighboring town. There were no openings at the state hospital, however, so pending a more appropriate placement, Eric remained at Ives.

Though his behavior was erratic, academically Eric did continue to make strides. By this time, Eric could sort by color, shape, and size. He could string beads, place pegs in a pegboard, and color—left-handed—in scribbles. His school reports nevertheless still described him as out of touch with reality.

When Eric was 6 years old, he transferred from Ives to the communication disorders section of the public school special education program. He remained in that program until he graduated at age 21.

Eric was tested several times over the course of his schooling. One test administrator described him as a healthy and cute 12-year-old boy who was functioning far below age level in all respects. He was described as inattentive, impulsive, hyperactive, and very unsure of his perceptions of the environment. He required support and encouragement in order to respond to the test items and was so confused that when he did answer, he often gave several responses to each question.

The examiner concluded that he was "functionally retarded" in all areas measured by the test. He had a maturational age of 3 years, 6 months, with an IQ score of 36. The tests also found that his comprehension was particularly impaired in auditory sequencing, meaning that other people's speech came to him as a jumbled series of noises from which he could not extract meaning. This neurological impairment affected his thought processes and emotional control, which perhaps explained his rages, inability to adjust to change, and frustration.

His greatest strength lay in his ability to follow visual cues, which helped him make sense of his environment. But the inability to understand speech or to express himself even minimally caused great frustration for Eric and exaggerated his high anxiety level. He required supervision and remedial help, concerns being addressed by his special education program.

Eric continued to have problems as an adolescent. By age 15, he had a history of violence against women and had beaten up several teachers, including his own female teacher. He had to be watched carefully by the staff, and a male teacher's aide accompanied him at all times and stood behind his desk in class.

Eric still frequently exploded into wild tantrums, and when he did, he had to be removed to a small, padded isolation room, where he was locked in until his violent anger subsided. During these spells, he kicked and hammered the door and occasionally loosened the padlock. He brought his rage under control only after being told repeatedly that he would not be let back into his classroom until he calmed down.

According to his school file, Eric was working on basic tools of learning. He had mastered some sign language and could understand simple oral directions and questions if they were given with gestures from the teacher. He could sign the action words "walk," "stand," "hop," "eat," "drink," "blow," "break," and "pull," but not spontaneously. He responded to "open," "close," "pick up," "turn off," "turn on," "color," "draw" (a circle but not a triangle or square), "fold," "pour," "sand," "sweep," and "mop." He could use a pencil, sponge, scissors, and crayons correctly. He could color and print with teacher participation. In gross-motor training, he could roll, crawl, hop, and skip, and with help, he did exercises in imitating physical postures (e.g., copying the teacher's gestures or movements).

Eric's social skills were minimal. On a good day, he could be part of a group and listen and obey with teacher supervision. His visual-motor skills consisted of the ability, again with prompting, to match pictures, reproduce a pegboard pattern, string beads according to a pattern, put two halves together, and trace. In early pre-vocational classes, he had learned to water houseplants.

Later, Eric entered vocational classes structured for the lowest functioning group, with two teachers and eight students. The classes began each day with one of the teachers saying and signing "hello." Eric could sometimes repeat this in a hoarse voice, but primarily he signed. All eight young adults were asked to follow the basic directions: "wash hands," "dry hair," "brush teeth," and "wait." After each of the eight students performed one of these actions, the teacher rewarded him by saying: "You earned a raisin for good waiting," or "for brushing your teeth." Later in the day, the students performed manual tasks, such as painting blocks of wood. Eric was consistently able to stick to his job and do it well.

The director of Eric's vocational program said that Eric had definite skill in carpentry and woodworking. This seemed to bear out his early evaluation of good fine motor skills. The possibility that Eric might be able to pursue a vocation, however, was limited by his history of emotional instability and violent behavior, which, even though it had improved, made placement in a sheltered workshop very doubtful.

During these years, Eric's family was very supportive. Eric's mother was serious and concerned. She kept all of Eric's medical appointments for shots, checkups, and dental work, and she spent her Aid to Families with Dependent Children allotment on sensible food for a well-balanced diet for all of her family. Her niece-in-law, girlfriend, and brother-in-law helped with Eric but stopped as he grew older and more aggressive. Mrs. Thomas's father, sister, son, and grandson took turns giving her a few hours or a weekend off from caring for Eric. There were times when Eric's bouts of violence and running away drove her to think about putting him in an institution, but neither she nor the family ever contemplated this seriously.

After Eric graduated from his special education high school, at age 22 he was placed in a sheltered workshop program in which he continued to receive job training and to try to improve his social and verbal communication and control of his behavior. Although Eric often complied with instructions quietly and willingly, at the same time he communicated a sense of tautly controlled violence that might erupt at any moment. He would stand and raise his arms, gesturing with his hands, up and down, simultaneously looking at the sky and seeming to address an unseen presence with incomprehensible gibberish. He would frequently try to parrot the last word or phrase of other people's sentences. His enunciation was slurred and indecipherable.

At the workshop, Eric's control of his violent behavior started to improve in some ways. He saw a psychiatrist at a state mental health clinic and was taking medication, which was monitored at the workshop. When he was in control of himself he did well in jobs that involved fine motor skills, but the instability of his behavior interfered with his productivity. Close supervision was required to keep him on task. He became confused and disoriented easily. He had one particular chair in one special place at his workbench. If this familiar routine was changed, he had a temper tantrum. Usually in the first hour after his arrival, he was visibly upset, sullen, perspiring, and in a physiological state that his supervisor felt was due to a general frustration. His supervisor came up with a strategy: The first hour at work Eric often was allowed to sit quietly listening to the radio. After this, he was able to settle down to his job.

For a time, Eric's future appeared uncertain. To send him to an institution (as had been expected when he was in high school) would be disastrous for him and an admission of defeat for his family and all who were involved with him, including his case manager, his social worker from his school system, his teachers and supervisor from the sheltered workshop program. His family remained concerned about his aggression and wanted to see him in a group home where his behavior could be managed and contained appropriately. They felt encouraged that this might be possible after his name moved high on the list for such a placement. Certainly the fact that he was able to live at home and was being considered for a group home was solid progress and success compared with institutionalization, which had seemed inevitable when Eric was younger.

By the time Eric had reached his early thirties, happily his situation had much improved. When I visited Eric in 1997 at his mother's apartment I was pleased to see how he had turned out: a well-dressed, nice looking, 32-year-old man. He shook hands with me and smiled, giving me a gibberish greeting. ("Hello," perhaps?) Then he went into the kitchen, picked up a laundry basket, and went downstairs to do the laundry. This indicates a socialized, purposeful behavior that he would have found impossible 10 years ago.

How satisfying it is to report that everyone's dream for Eric—a group home—came true shortly after this visit, and he has been living there successfully for several years. Eric stays there during the week and comes home every other weekend. For a time he came home every weekend, but his mother found his behavior at night too difficult to handle. He now spends his weekend days with his mother, but returns to the group home at night.

Like some of the other former Ives pupils, Eric, too, was part of an autism research group at a local mental health center, in which he was put on a drug called Risperdal (risperidone). At first his mother and his social worker reported a dramatic change for the better. He was far less aggressive and, for most of the time, seemed amiable and even cooperative! However, the benefits of Risperdal turned out not to outweigh the drawbacks. His mother reported that when Eric would come home on the weekends he would tear up the beds and pillows in his room, and he "made such a mess" that she requested that he return to the group home for closer supervision at night. In a way, this behavior suggested the "old Eric," before he was put on Risperdal. He was taken off this drug because of side effects and put on another medication.

For my last visit to Eric's home, he was dressed in his usual athletic outfit: blue shorts that came below his knees and a crew neck, short-sleeved jersey with "Michigan" on the back.

Similar to Tom and Karen, Eric has become more focused. The sense of violence simmering beneath the surface was there no longer. He smiled brilliantly and shook hands, saying, "Hi," again followed by something that came out in gibberish. His whole attitude, in his stance and his directness of gaze, is now much more in contact with reality. I felt that he really *saw* me addressing him, and that he had a greater understanding than he did when I visited him the year previously. For example, he is able to say words, mostly repeating others after they speak to him. But it is clear that he understands the meaning behind the words. For example, when we told him that we were planning to take pictures of him and held the camera up for inspection, Eric smiled and clearly said, "Pictures." Then he put his hands up, spread them about 4 inches apart, and imitated taking a picture. This was a dramatic change from the previous year's visit, when he still, as in years past, did not seem "with it" or in any way "in touch."

As Eric posed for pictures against the wall of his living room I said, "One, two, three, smile . . . !" Eric immediately added, "Four, five, six!" Again, this was almost a miracle, considering his testing at age 12, which showed that he did not hear words as words, but only as sounds.

Eric's mother quietly observed the photo session. She remains a pretty woman with eyes that sparkle when she talks. She conveys a surprising sense of composure, despite, as has been noted, her history of mental illness. She commented that Eric was "fine," and that she likes and trusts all the staff at his group home.

By watching Eric form the beginning sounds of words I could tell that he had had some speech therapy. For example, Eric was echoing a word beginning with *b*. He clearly formed the phonetic |b| ("buh") and then said the word articulately—an unimaginable achievement, even a year before. (Eric's speech certainly seems to have improved in general over the years: During a recent talk to a group of professionals and parents of children with autism, I was interrupted by a member of the audience who announced, "I am a social worker, and Eric is one of my clients. He is now saying whole words clearly!")

His mother updated me on the status of her two daughters: One has received a degree in registered nursing, and the other is a technician in a cardiac laboratory. When I asked Mrs. Thomas if she had wanted to go to college, she smiled and said that, despite knowing that she was a good student, she had wanted only to be a mother!

Eric's mother goes biweekly to a psychiatrist at a local mental health center, as does her son, and she believes that these visits have helped her to cope.

At the time this edition of the book was written Eric was working in one of the workshops run by the Shoreline Association for the Retarded and Handicapped (SARAH). His mother noted that one of his responsibilities for this job is to ride in the delivery van, in which he helps deliver products made in the workshops. We agreed that this interaction with other people is an extraordinary outcome for Eric.

At the suggestion of Eric's mother, I arranged to visit his group home. All the staff involved with Eric's care, including the director, the assistant director, and the counselor who is specifically assigned to Eric, were present to greet me. Eric himself, dressed in neat blue jeans and a short-sleeved plaid shirt, shook my hand, flashed his brilliant smile, and said, "Hi! Hi!"

Sitting at the dining room table, the staff listened intently, shaking their heads and murmuring with surprise and concern as they heard about Eric's early years. They were clearly astonished to learn of his severe impairment at that time; the professionals' conclusion that he heard words only as sounds, without understanding; the gloomy prognosis; and the violence. Then, with smiles of pride and pleasure, they spoke of Eric's astounding improvement.

With prompting from the director, Eric filled me in on his current schedule. For Monday through Friday, Eric said, "Work"; but when it came to Sunday, prompted by the director again, Eric said, "See my Mamma."

"And then what?" the director asked.

"Eat lunch. Barbecued chicken . . . [hesitation], string beans . . . , *apple pie*!" I was appropriately enthusiastic.

When discussing his schedule, the staff revealed that the group home residents go for walks in the afternoons, and on Thursday evenings they go to a music class. When he heard this, Eric beamed and began to sing, "Old McDonald had a farm. . . ." To the refrain, "Ee-I-Ee-I-O. . . . And on that farm there was a duck . . . ," Eric happily made "Quack, quack here" sounds (albeit unclear), to general applause.

Eric does not have regular speech therapy at the group home, although staff said he had received this at his former special school, which confirmed my earlier impression when I had heard him pronouncing words. When the director had a speech therapist come in to evaluate all the clients, the speech therapist said that Eric, without help, could identify 100 pictures of objects and people.

When it was time for me to leave, the director commented, "Eric, remember that we see our guests to the door." Eric immediately stood up and came over with his hand extended. To proud smiles and gentle applause, he took my hand and escorted me to the door.

* * *

In October 1987, in his early twenties, Eric was tested at the Yale Child Study Center. His mother could not attend, so the VABS was omitted, and he was only tested on WAIS–R and the ABC.

TEST SCORES

WAIS–R
Verbal IQ score: 51
Performance IQ score: 51
Full-Scale IQ score: 46

VABS
(Mrs. Thomas was unavailable to answer the questions for this test.)

ABC
101: Probably autistic

The psychologist conducting the tests observed

> During the administration of the WAIS–R Eric asked for water several times, drank it and made a squealing sound. He evidenced repetitive and stereotypic behaviors, lip smacking and raising his arms when he was excited. He repeated the last words in an echolalic fashion, and, in doing motor tasks, his coordination seemed quite awkward. His Full-Scale IQ score was 46, classified as in the severe deficit range of mental retardation with no difference in verbal and performance. Eric . . . showed relative strength in placing a series of pictures in logical sequence, which shows ability to comprehend a situation using nonverbal reasoning in which anticipation, visual organization, and temporal sequencing are involved.

It is interesting to note that although as a child he was diagnosed as congenitally autistic, Eric's score on the ABC was rated by Dr. Fred Volkmar as "probably autistic." At the same time, Dr. Volkmar also made the comment that, of the former students profiled in this book, Eric, with an IQ score of 46, was the most typically autistic.

13

Jane Thompson

A Study in Contrasts

born June 15, 1978

The story of Jane, added to expand readers' perceptions of the variety that exists within a set of related syndromes, differs greatly from the other case studies in this book. In the preceding case studies, the individuals, by 1999, were in their thirties, their adult outcomes clearly marked. As children, they were characterized by traits that distinguished them as different: for example, lack of speech or delayed speech, with a remote, impervious (a word used by their specialists) appearance.

In contrast, at the time this edition was published Jane was just entering her twenties. Until she reached the age of 4 or 5, her development seemed typical to those around her. Diagnosed as having pervasive developmental disorder-not otherwise specified (PDD-NOS) at age 10, Jane's experience is a vivid illustration of the contradictions contained within this paradoxical diagnosis, as described by Kenneth E. Towbin in 1997:

> Although PDD-NOS is a single diagnosis in DSM-IV (American Psychiatric Association, 1994), it is not a uniform clinical entity. The conditions encompassed by PDD-NOS do not share a specific etiology. In describing PDD-NOS one attempts to specify the common

characteristics of a group of disorders that are "not otherwise specified" . . . a diagnostic term derived from a conceptual model of pervasive developmental disorders. This model regards all [of] the
conditions under PDD, including autism, as a set of related maladies
that exist along a hypothetical spectrum bounded by severe autism
at one end and by a condition of being nearly normal, save for a dis-
tinctive life-long social or empathetic "blindness" at the other. (pp.
123–125)

Jane's difficulties—hyperactivity and an inability to pay attention
or to obey directions—became apparent at around age 4, when she
started nursery school. Her family was at that time living in the
midwest. It was in kindergarten, however, at age 5, that Jane's continued difficulties began to cause her parents and teachers to feel
deep concern.

The kindergarten had 60 children; even with an aide helping
the teacher, this was too large a class for any child, much less for a
child with Jane's problems. Jane's mother was active in the school,
volunteering and helping to train other mothers as volunteers. But
for a child with Jane's difficulties, it became an increasingly impossible situation.

Jane's parents were having marital problems, but these did not
become critical for another year or so. The fall after kindergarten
Jane was placed in a "transitional class" rather than first grade, but
again her hyperactivity, short attention span, and high level of anxiety were clear to observers. At her mother's request, Jane was
tested at age 6 with these resulting scores:

WISC–R (Wechsler, 1974)
Verbal IQ score: 88
Performance IQ score: 65
Full-Scale IQ Score: 75

The year from 1986 to 1987, Jane's seventh year, was not a happy
one for the family. Jane's mother decided to move east and stay
with her mother and father to allow her personal situation to cool
down. Jane had a younger brother, age 3 at that time. Jane's mother
and grandmother drove east with the two children and this, in contrast with the previous months, Jane remembers as fun.

It was early summer when they settled in with Jane's grandparents. One can only imagine the bewilderment and anxiety of a
young girl undergoing these multiple moves exacerbated by the

stress of the breakup of her parents' marriage. According to Jane's mother, the child suffered separation anxiety, which exaggerated her other, already serious, problems.

Jane entered a general first grade the following September. She was referred for testing by her classroom teacher because of her inability to organize her thoughts and to pay attention. The evaluation found that she had serious visual-perceptual problems, which led to poor visual memory. Her auditory memory was excellent, but her impairment in logical thinking worked against this strength. She was so eager to please and, at the same time, so aware of her deficiencies that she became belligerent and "bossy," attitudes which she probably adopted subconsciously as defense mechanisms. In short, she began to exhibit behavioral problems in the classroom.

In January of that year, she was moved to a self-contained special education class for children with a variety of disabilities. Her family and school staff thought that both her learning and social adjustment problems could be better addressed in this classroom environment.

The following June and July, at the request of her mother, her therapist, and the school system, Jane was referred to the Yale Child Study Center for evaluation. This was not only so that an effective program could be planned for her but also to give her mother and grandparents a clearer understanding of her strengths and weaknesses. The results of the evaluation was as follows:

> Jane is an 8-year-old girl who is currently functioning in the low–average range of intelligence with significantly impaired performance on tasks subject to interference from anxiety and difficulties with sustained attention. . . . She is currently having difficulty in organizing the world in conventionally meaningful ways, feels isolated in interpersonal relationships, and is experiencing a significant amount of internal distress.

She performed adequately in reading and below average in math.

About this time Jane began to see several psychotherapists who, over the years, provided valuable input to the family on the best course of action for Jane. It was recommended that Jane continue in a small structured class setting, and also that there be clear, consistent, consequences for her behavior, such as time-outs and verbal rewards. She needed guidance, the report continued, to improve her skills in social relationships with peers. In reading she needed assistance in the phonetic decoding of words, because she learned words as "whole" words. The use of an appropriate medication to help Jane focus and center on a task was also suggested.

In September 1988, Jane began classes in a self-contained special education second-grade classroom. At the end of that year, her teacher reported that she was an expressive reader, who had some ability in creative writing and good "expressive skills." As will be seen, Jane exhibited these strengths throughout her school career.

In terms of social skills, it was noted that Jane had improved her ability to accept criticism, yet still had scattered attention and had developed a "giggling" problem.

Math on the second-grade level was very difficult for her; including addition and subtraction, telling time, making change, and simple measurements. This bears out the finding that individuals falling within the autism spectrum usually have trouble with conceptual processes, such as math, punctuation, and language that involves feelings or ideas.

In the third grade, when she was 10 years old, expressive skills continued to be Jane's main strength. But one report from that time stressed her good fine motor skills in arts and crafts. Math and social relationships remained the areas of concern. It was noted that Jane had a habit of giving unwelcome "constructive criticism" to classmates, perhaps another defense mechanism against what she believed to be her own inadequacy.

The end-of-the-year report recommended that Jane enter the special education fourth grade but that she be mainstreamed for fourth-grade physical education. So, at age 11, Jane was placed in a social skills counseling group. She was commended for being a neat and a hard worker. She wanted desperately to learn. She was faithful about her homework and again her language skills were her predominant strength. However, the teacher reported that expectations of Jane must be modified to suit her need for structure and slower-paced teaching. She needed guidance to help her improve her interaction with peers.

Math was becoming even more complicated and frustrating for her. Jane lost focus, and also had difficulty processing language-based concepts. Her reading and work in language arts (writing, stories, grammar, spelling), for example, were on the third-grade level (1 year below grade level.)

Jane then went into a mainstream fifth-grade class in which she could progress at her own level. She was sent to the resource room for math and reading. She also saw the school social worker once a week.

At the end of her fifth-grade year, Jane was transferred to middle school and to the general sixth grade. There she was classified as "learning disabled." Academic expectations were modified. Content, materials, and pace of teaching were adjusted to suit her through cooperation between the special education teachers and her general education teachers. Each day, Jane met with her special education teacher, who helped to reinforce the mainstream academics and Jane's organizational skills. She was still reading a grade below her grade placement. Her individualized education program noted that directions must be clear and specific and that she could not do an assignment that used a separate answer sheet. Her math skills continued to lag behind, much below grade level. She had counseling once a week. Her peer relationships continued to be poor, and her family relationships were difficult.

There were some positive signs, however. At the middle school, Jane adjusted to switching classes and working with different teachers. In the middle of her sixth-grade year as Jane celebrated her thirteenth birthday, she was making several strides: her grades were improving, there was less complaining and, in counseling, she could admit to "having problems." She still had difficulty in spelling, grammar, and specific writing skills.

The end-of-year report noted that Jane no longer required special transportation, and could now go on the regular school bus. This was progress, because prior to that she had experienced anxiety over riding in a crowded school bus and had taken the van for special education students instead.

Encouragingly, in the fall of that year as she entered the seventh grade, her mother reported that Jane was "up about school." A special education teacher met with her daily to check assignments, and she continued to do well in English.

Early in the ninth grade, however, Jane's behavior took a turn for the worse. She refused to go to school and hid in the basement, and she even mentioned suicide. This led her desperate family to seek additional help.

There were two private schools for children and adolescents with special concerns in Jane's town. Her mother and grandmother visited both, choosing the one that addressed a broader range of special concerns. Jane was interviewed and accepted. Certainly, at this difficult time, the input provided by her longtime psychother-apists and other service providers helped both Jane and her family.

Jane entered this local private special education school at the ninth-grade level 2 months after the school year had started. The late start might have been a major drawback for Jane, but reports at the end of the quarter all indicate that she was trying hard to do her best. Considering the discomfort she must have felt, this determi-nation was to her credit.

Comments from the end of the second quarter revealed the contradictory nature of her disorder. In math, an evaluator noted, "Jane's recalling of facts and the process of solving basic operations is not automatic. She requires continual reinforcement. She was encouraged to use the calculator and manipulatives." In English class, she actively participated, reading *Uncle Tom's Cabin*, and "shared many interesting insights." In her writing assignments, however, Jane needed constant help from her teacher. At first she was intimidated in her biology class but, with encouragement, "took risks" and joined in class discussions. In history class she answered only when called on, was "quiet," but was successful on all of her tests.

Comments from the school's director showed the understand-ing, compassion, and infinite patience that went into helping Jane adjust to her new school. The director compared her first 2 years at the school to a roller-coaster ride, with all its ups and downs. Dur-ing her first year Jane was constantly in hysterics, frequently stomp-ing out of the classroom. In the beginning months, she would often refuse to go into the class. The director would stand with her, talk-ing softly and slowly, and gently try to ease her into class. The social worker was upset with this procedure, calling it "coddling." The director replied, however, that Jane needed this reassurance in order to develop trust. The director also went into Jane's counseling group, hoping to help her develop a sense of security.

Jane adapted to the structure of the school and began to use self-enforced time-outs, which helped her exercise more self-control. She struggled to "maintain appropriate boundaries regarding her behavior." She became active in the school's community service program, which was compulsory. For her activity Jane chose to work with animals in a nature center. She enjoyed the work and being outdoors. In her art class, she particularly enjoyed working with watercolors, but lacked confidence in starting new projects. She was considered a "pleasant" student. In physical education she was "timid" but, with encouragement, began to improve.

The most telling comment was her teacher's time-out summary. Jane was told, "When you stay calm and discuss only what led to the time-out, you do well. When you complain about hating this school, or your life, or certain people, time-out is not helpful. Time-out is a place to SOLVE PROBLEMS, not a place to get attention." She was told she should "avoid problems by not taking everything personally in class."

The end-of-year report in May of 1996 noted that Jane had refused to come to school 1 day of each week. These absences were not excused, and she was given detentions. Her absences were caused by her fear of riding in the van, fear of the field trip bus or the bus to the theater, "and/or problems with interpersonal relationships within the classroom."

Her behavior toward her peers continued to be inconsistent. If anxious, Jane would be cuttingly sarcastic and cynical. She was a stubborn opponent, always having to have the last word. She found it next to impossible to recover and apologize to classmates. Rather she would refuse to go to school for a day after a confrontation in order to recover what school staff regarded as "her generally sweet and animated disposition."

Throughout the year, though trying hard, Jane continued to struggle against the same difficulties. As has been written in her report, she needed constant and clear directions, with teacher support. In English class, after reading a story, she could rarely give a good example from the story to illustrate her ideas. She lacked the insight of a good reader, and "did not reflect the fully developed ideas."

The physical education report from that year named all the sports in which Jane was expected to participate, but it noted that she gave up easily and became frustrated with her peers, frequently walking out of class. Yet the report said she exhibited "good sportsmanship."

Again, this contradictory element in Jane was evident. She could be "cynical, sarcastic"—wanting the last word in an argument—yet in general she had a "sweet and animated disposition." She walked out of gym class, presumably because of performance failures or arguments with her peers, yet the report commended her for "good sportsmanship."

By the spring of her ninth-grade year, Jane's school test scores on nonverbal ability were too low to interpret, and her verbal ability was low as well; she performed better than only 3% of ninth graders nationally.

To summarize, in Jane's first year at her new school, the impairments she had exhibited as an 8-year-old were still impeding her struggle to do well, although she was clearly making progress.

About this time Jane was tested again, using the Wechsler Intelligence Scale for Children, Third Edition (WISC–III; Wechsler, 1991), and the VABS. Her evaluation ended with a list of suggested interventions, including the need for teachers and counselors to focus explicitly on Jane's adaptive living skills, and also to begin immediately to approach the issue of vocational placement with Jane's active involvement. Jane's final tenth-grade report stated that in none of her subjects had she achieved the academic goals but that these were "in progress." Also by this second year at the private school, Jane had progressed; she had fewer problems with her peers and her bouts of hysteria were less frequent. In the second year, limits were put on Jane's behavior. She was often told, "Jane—stop it. That's it!"

Again, mathematics was her weakest subject. She could add and subtract whole numbers, but could not calculate in her head. She needed to use paper and her fingers or a calculator. She could not multiply or divide consistently, and still she was unable to tolerate the frustration of failure. She could only measure "a foot" or "an inch." In English, her strength with vocabulary came to the fore. "When vocabulary is introduced with a new concept," the report stated, "Jane will often retain this information and be able to define the word at another time." In art, Jane made straight As.

She showed greater effort in her academic work, but at the slightest difficulty, would give up unless supported by constant, consistent teacher attention. Socially and emotionally, however, she had grown to the point of being able to stay in group counseling, even when it became uncomfortable for her.

The usual spring achievement tests showed progress in verbal ability. She now scored higher than 13% of the national group of tenth graders. However, her test results still fell well below the national norm.

By the eleventh grade, Jane had been put on the antidepressant Zoloft (sertraline) by her psychiatrist with very good results. She herself said she felt "better." She could focus, and therefore achieve in school through this newly gained self-confidence. Academically she continued to perform below average, well below average in math. She still had little tolerance for frustration and change, and exhibited difficulty managing her moods. But she was said to be cooperative, hard working, sociable, polite, helpful, outgoing and personable, taking great pride in her appearance. Her eleventh-grade year ended with a clear triumph: On her report card she received As and Bs, with a B– in math.

As she entered her senior high school year, Jane was looking forward to the prospect of "What next?" She had started to explore job possibilities, working with the Bureau of Rehabilitation Services. Also, according to the school's director, Jane's volatile, sometimes histrionic behavior had disappeared. The director's exact words were, "Her senior year was an incredibly smooth, positive year!"

In the late spring of her senior year, Jane began her job training, first in the kitchen of a nursing home and next as a clerical aide at a hospice. During her training, she was asked to use the copying machine, but her math weakness made such a task a real struggle. Asked to make 30 copies in sets of 5, she found it impossible without the use of paper and pencil, or a calculator.

Jane's job preferences had been, in order of importance: 1) to work with older adults, 2) to do clerical work, and 3) to work with children. She had found the first two choices unsatisfactory, so she went next to a child care center for 1- to 3-year-olds. She worked as an aide with the youngest children. Her job coach acted as a liaison between the head of the day care center, Jane and Jane's mother, and the Bureau of Rehabilitation Services.

Jane's transition from school to the workplace had been undertaken by several organizations working together: The state Bureau of Rehabilitation and the Easter Seals Society had provided the job coach under the authority of the State Department of Mental Retardation. Jane had begun to participate in this process (again, typical of many young adults with special concerns) a year and a half before her high school graduation. It should be pointed out that perhaps none of this would have happened so efficiently without Jane's mother. In her words, she "gently urged" the public school system to begin the transitional plan for Jane in her junior year in high school.

Jane had two high school graduations. She was proudest of her graduation from her town's public high school. She would show her high school graduation diploma to older friends, saying matter-of-factly, "It took a lot of courage for me to do that."

When Jane was asked how she liked the private school she had attended, she said that she disliked much of it because it made her feel "different" from her friends in her general class. But, she added, she loved her teachers, and said she had been happy getting one-to-one attention and so much help academically and in many other ways—meaning with peer and adult social relationships.

In talking with Jane, her mother's friends were often confused by her apparent brightness and verbal ability. They often would ask themselves, "This is a girl who needed to be in a special school? Why?"

In essence, professionals might recognize Jane's hard-to-define, but still present, challenges. Her social or empathetic "blindness" which, combined with borderline typical intelligence, placed Jane truly "in a gray area" or, Towbin described it, she was "nearly normal." This had made it puzzling and sometimes difficult for those—whether bosses, friends, teachers, or job coaches—who were dealing with her.

On a visit with Jane I took her out to lunch and later said to her mother that Jane was such a fascinating, confusing, challenging combination of qualities: very young naïveté, sophisticated vocabulary, and surface maturity. Here is one instance of this paradox: When I asked if I might take a photograph of her she tossed her head, swept her brown page boy behind one ear, flashed a teasing smile at her mother and exclaimed, "Oh, good, Mom. Now all that money you paid for my braces will be worthwhile!" Everyone chuckled and smiled. Jane's charm was almost palpable.

Jane's mother pointed out that she was constantly advising the job coach *not* to take Jane at surface value. She told him to assume always that Jane needed clear, structured explanations and guidance, particularly in job situations. He thanked her and said that later, at the child care center, he found that advice indispensable.

The summer following graduation, Jane was two thirds of the way through her probationary placement with the child care center. She loved it and hoped that she would be hired, rather than being on trial. She worked with both 1- and 2-year-olds. She had had some "run-ins" with the head of the child care center. However, through the job coach, these situations had been straightened out.

Meanwhile Jane passed her courses in both first aid and in CPR and was glowing with pride as she reported this. She had started taking a course in early childhood development at a local community college, and reported that she was doing well in the class.

When the director of her private high school heard this, she was clearly astonished and delighted. She said, "Looking at her, as she came into freshman year, we *never* expected such an outcome. I *must* tell her teachers!"

For now, Jane lives at home, and her relationship with her family is stable. She dates, and occasionally sees some of her former and current classmates.

Jane's maturation is a work-in-progress, but for all the gains she has made already she may be considered another "fragile success."

*   *   *

In the spring of her ninth-grade year, Jane was referred to the Yale Child Study Center for a transdisciplinary evaluation, which included a speech-communication assessment, developmental and psychological testing, and psychiatric evaluation.

In discussing past evaluations, authors of the Yale report noted a significant discrepancy between her overall verbal skills and performance skills, favoring the former. Her notable weaknesses related to visual-perceptual and visual-motor skills, arithmetic skills, short-term auditory recall, and social judgment. Poor academic performance was associated with great frustration and refusal to attempt novel tasks.

TEST SCORES

WISC–III
Verbal IQ score: 82
Performance IQ score: 68
Full-Scale IQ score: 73

VABS

	Standard Score	Adaptive level
Communication	53	Low
Daily Living Skills	52	Low
Socialization	42	Low
Adaptive Behavior Composite	46	Low

In the assessment section of the report, the Yale team noted:

> [Jane] presents with an unusual history of developmental difficulties, marked problems in learning and social interaction, and persistent difficulties in dealing with anxiety and negative affects. . . . In the past, she has carried diagnoses of both learning disability and PDD-NOS. . . . The latter term has the advantage of indicating that she has problems in multiple areas including social interaction. It must be noted, however, that [Jane's] constellation of difficulties, like those of many other individuals, really do lie at the interface of learning and psychiatric difficulties and our current diagnostic systems probably do not characterize their problems. . . . The term PDD-NOS certainly

characterizes her major problems in social interaction associated with problems in the modulation of affect and behavior.

14

Where Does This Leave Us?
Summary Update

In the closing chapter of the first edition of *Fragile Success*, I described the lives of these individuals and their families living with autism spectrum disorders as being "bittersweet." Their situations appeared both encouraging, because of the strides they were able to make through intensive education and one-to-one care, and discouraging, because of the limitations they still faced in terms of independent living and their relationships with others. I noted, "But this book, fortunately, does not present the status quo." It is exciting to look back and to be able to say that at the time this new edition of the book was written, all of the eight former Ives pupils still living had made great—indeed in some cases, almost unbelievable—progress. This is also true of Jane, the subject of the added case study.

What emerges is a hopeful picture of inner growth and steps toward independence. Although they cannot all live independently or speak or relate to others with the ease of typical adults, these nine people have come a long way from the isolated, frightened children they were so many years ago.

In the year 2000, Tom is a self-confident adult, living independently, with some staff support, in his own condominium;

working successfully at the same job for 20 years; and commanding affection and respect.

Jimmy, one of the two individuals in these case studies considered nonverbal as a young child, has mastered elementary sign language to the point where he is teaching it to his mother! He is employed successfully as a gardener and as a delivery person for Meals on Wheels: a responsible job that, even 2 years ago, would have seemed impossible for him. Jimmy is now a dignified, confident man, whose pride derives not only from his weekday jobs, but also from being an "indispensable" assistant at his mother's church.

Polly lives independently in a condominium with a "condomate." She has regular paid employment, and gets to work by herself on the public bus. She seems sturdily sure of herself and her ability "to be responsible" in every way for herself; her determination to manage her own medication is just one example of her increasing self-confidence. She is proud of what she has achieved.

Bill, married and the proud father of two children, worked for many years in the *sales* department of Disney World and is now going to night school to get his master's degree in computer science. Also, through his work with Habitat for Humanity and his involvement in his church, he has developed into a leader, a description that never would have been ascribed to him several years ago.

David, who lives at home, works two jobs: at a restaurant and at his community house. With friends and supervisory staff, he goes camping overnight once a month and bowls every week. He speaks with relative fluency and seems to have a remarkable memory. I was astonished when he asked about former Ives classmate Eric, whom he hadn't seen since they were both 4 years old.

Karen's parents declare her a complete success. She works fulltime at a retirement community, where she is happy working in the kitchen and proud of her starched white uniform. Her parents feel that Karen's story is a lesson to all parents of children with disabilities; parents should not set their own goals for the child, but should help the child to do what he or she wants, and can do well. Both Karen's parents had faces lit with pride as they talked about her accomplishments.

John is one of the most independent of the former Ives pupils. As he proudly told me, he secured his own job at the hospital, where he is happy, and well liked. In view of John's problems with hysteria, this is surely a personal triumph.

And Eric—who at the age of 12 was described as hearing only sounds, not words; was totally nonverbal; and was often aggressive—has made quite a turnaround. Neither his family members nor his staff or teachers could have predicted the Eric of today. He now talks, with prompting, in short sentences, and makes it clear that he *understands* what is said to him. He lives in a group home, holding a job in a workshop where his carpentry skills can be put to good use. He also rides in a delivery van, helping deliver the workshop's products. His mother is delighted, and all the group home staff discuss his progress with pride.

Jane is attending a small college, where she plans to major in early child development. What an unlikely and happy outcome, considering her challenging childhood and adolescence!

Despite these encouraging strides, however, it is important to remember that such outcomes are, and will continue to be, dependent on many factors. When they hear of such high-functioning people as Bill and John, some parents tend to develop unreasonable expectations for their children with autism spectrum disorders. As Kenneth E. Towbin has noted,

> A very small number of autistic persons are able to attend college and live independently. Although many make obvious strides in achieving greater social awareness, they remain socially odd, and they require lifelong supervision and educational support. The largest portion, perhaps 60%, make modest gains or remain severely impaired. The outcome of autism has been directly correlated with overall IQ, language development, and appearance of seizures. (1997, p. 138)

Dr. Fred Volkmar of the Yale Child Study Center has often stated that intelligence is the defining factor in adult outcome. In the last few years, however, various medications have been developed that help calm individuals' anxieties and strengthen their ability to focus. Tom, Karen, Polly, Jane, and Eric take medication; Bill, John, David, and Jimmy do not.

Significant strides are being made in research into the brain function of individuals with autism spectrum and other developmental disorders, and the result will surely be more effective interventions, teaching, and treatment methods.

So, we may close on this hopeful note: Success, at least with reference to these nine adults, is not quite as fragile as it might have seemed even a few years ago.

Appendix A

Growing In and Out of an Autistic Mind

by Bill Kolinski

I've never heard, or at least understood, the word autistic until I saw the film *Rain Man*. And, although I never remember believing or acting the way Dustin Hoffman did in his award-winning role of Raymond, I have studied the subject some and have come to an understanding of why—in my early childhood—I would have to a lesser degree been labeled as autistic.

Because most kindergarten children are handicapped with language barriers, I thought you might like to know how I have battled my way out of autism to write stories and poetry, earn my bachelor's degree in journalism, and become successful out in the working and social world by claiming my faith.

As far back as I can remember clearly, I did live pretty much in my own idiosyncratic fantasy world. And as goes along with the definition of an autistic child, I remember not communicating much in the way of talking or facial expression.

It was in kindergarten where I remember first being blatantly eccentric and rejecting almost everything they were trying to teach me about dealing with the real world—including playing with my classmates. I prided myself on being independent-minded and using reverse psychology tactics on my teacher and others, except for my parents. Basically, I had no desire or motivation to deal with or adjust to most people and the world around me. I feared the unknown and as a result, change. Not caring what anyone thought of me, I had decided I would be happier making my own rules in the safe bubble of the dream world I had created (or that possessed me), and I wasn't going to let anyone come inside or threaten it.

Once, the school nurse told my parents I might be deaf because I didn't raise my hand when I heard the high pitch of her tuning fork during a hearing test. (I heard it very clearly.) I remember thinking it was fun to ignore and fool people like her. I constantly played mind games when people tried to reach me. Sometimes it felt like I was watching life around me on a large television screen, and I wasn't a part of it.

I was very good at analyzing and understanding people's behavior, including my own. But perhaps due to my excessive shyness and sensitivity, I was afraid of being hurt or rejected by my peers, so I felt like I didn't need any friends. I lacked the will to be accepted or to fight my way out of my trapped mind. So I turned almost fully to a nonreacting, nonjudgmental, intellectual/soulful friend that would please me unconditionally—music.

No one introduced me to any instruments or encouraged me to learn to play, so I've never found my full potential of any talent in music. But I could sit for hours on end listening to and memorizing almost every type of music I heard, down to the finite details of instrumentals and the structure of hundreds of songs and classical symphonies. I connected spiritually with music, but I didn't tell anyone.

I had already decided life in general was not as romantic as the stories and visions I interpreted from the music in my out-of-control imagination, so I began allowing my mind to blend the visions with reality to make existence more interesting—like may of the early Romantic European poets probably did. I suppose many people who smoke dope or take LSD to alter their senses try to capture the vivid surrealistic sensations with which I perceived the world in my self-absorbed fantasies. I knew what was going on around me and what people expected of me, but because I was unable to grasp the purpose of growing up from one stage to another, I chose not to snap out of my dream world.

I've read that most autistic children aren't able to really fantasize because of their limited comprehension. And although I remember having a short attention span (I felt hyperactive and would tune out reality because I didn't find concentrating on my responsibilities important or interesting), when I tuned out I daydreamed about things and ideas, including words. If something such as music, passages from books, or places fascinated me, I had a photographic memory.

One of my poet/rock singer idols—the late Jim Morrison—said of his own eccentric behavior that he was testing the bounds of reality because he was curious to see what would happen. That's how I felt.

Sometimes my fantasies would control my mind to the point of on-the-edge irrational fear. One morning I imagined that I would sink into the floor if I got out of bed, and it took me about an hour to muster up the courage to slowly step on it. When I had vivid dreams of someone—a teacher at Ives once—I literally expected them to remember being in the same dream and was stunned when they told me this is impossible. It was also at this time that I developed a great interest in art—especially drawing.

It was at Ives where they popped my fantasy bubble and forced me to become aware, even self-conscious, of my unpleasant eccentric behavior. All the bottled-up energy due to my withdrawal I would channel out by acting crazy—often deliberately—to get the kind of attention I sought. My cousin, who had just come from Poland, also stabilized me. I taught her to speak English, and she steered me into acting more like a normal American kid.

I did struggle with learning schoolwork, mostly because I couldn't get myself to concentrate. But one of the most important things I learned in the Ives program was to appreciate the purpose for being in school and growing through the various levels of life.

After Ives and through much of public school, I would still occasionally get a kick out of making a fool of myself to get laughs from peers—good or bad. My self-consciousness began to almost possess my mind and emotions like the early fantasies had, and severe shyness resulted. It became what I refer to as "emotional warfare" in high school, where I became crazy about girls and began to stutter. I wanted to make love to every girl in school but couldn't get myself to say hi to them.

In the tenth grade, I saw a psychiatrist for my stuttering, and though I loved talking to him, he couldn't give me any advice I did not already know. It was up to me to conquer my fears of failure (the cause of my stuttering), break through, and go for the gusto. How to exactly go about that, I hadn't yet gotten control of.

This coincided with me beginning to worship my older brother, Steve, who to me at the time seemed larger than life—like Jack Kennedy or a movie star. He did just about anything he set his mind to. What many, as myself, only dreamed, he went out and lived fully and with great style. Steve had a daring and charismatic way about him that made him a center for others, and I wanted to be that ideal center more than anything. I decided to fight and break through self-doubt and shyness and become as much like my brother as I had in me. Socially and academically I didn't get that far. But, I dressed more stylishly, became an outdoors fanatic, and even tried to grow my hair long, though my conservative dad always made me cut it.

Throughout my high school years I wanted to be a psychologist. From high school to college, I was greatly into theater and acting. Acting, like my eccentric mannerisms in the past and writing in later years, became a way to channel my dreams and desires in a productive way. I was in a few school plays, but I felt like an arrow trapped by its bow, unable to fly out to its full destiny.

By the end of my college freshman year, I knew I wanted to be a writer. I had kept a few journals throughout my teen years, but one night I had a great vision that I was destined to be a great writer like Charles Dickens or Mark Twain. I knew that was my purpose and talent in life: to translate my inner vivid impressions, my 100-frames-per-second runaway imagination, into romantic literature, poetry, or creative journalism. I was going to leave my mark in this world, to influence people's lives and make them think. I saw my life as a shooting star and believed there would never be another one like me. It was the summer of '82 and at age 19, with my new fire-filled dream, I felt like I owned the world. I began filling journals with my everyday ventures and thoughts, my own poetry and passages and ideas from novels. I filled pages with my own philosophical ideas about life and wrote a play based on who I wanted to be. I also became a voracious reader and began drinking alcohol—mostly beer—like it was going out of style.

I believed that as a writer I had to experience everything at least once and live every day with great style, like Napoleon, Hemingway, or my brother Steve. Drinking to me was a part of that free-spirit life, and I did it every chance I could, without reserve.

To stimulate my confidence even more, I began to believe I was a genius. To paraphrase another of my musical idols, John Lennon, I thought that If there was such a thing as a genius I was one, and if there wasn't I don't care. I could intuitively see spiritual forces that others didn't seem to see. Perhaps I had been learning disabled and was slow in ways, but if you set your heart and mind on a goal like I did, nothing can stop you from success in your own eyes, despite circumstances you have little or no control over. You aren't teachable and capable of maturing unless you believe yourself to be, and will it. Schools and teachers offer knowledge, skills, and guidance; it's up to you to take the initiative, open yourself up, and apply it to create who and what you believe you are best meant to be.

I became the arts and entertainment editor for my college newspaper and had a lot of authority, writing and assigning articles for the pages I designed. In my senior year, I also became president of the German club.

Many a day I would wander the ivy-covered Gothic area around Yale University, journal in hand, pretending to be Hemingway in Paris working on his novels. I would write about Connecticut and experiences based on my life and family, the way Hemingway did about Europe in the roaring twenties or Mark Twain did about life on the Mississippi. I fancied how high school and college students would read their assigned classics, which I had written, for their English classes. I pictured my name on the shelves between F. Scott Fitzgerald and John Steinbeck. Gifted students and professors would discuss and admire my life and works in the years ahead, over coffee.

Perhaps unconsciously I was trying to make up for my lost autistic years. Perhaps, you think, the dream bubble was reemerging. But I didn't feel conceited, and I was very practical. I still believe the road of experience leads to the palace of wisdom. As you can plainly see, I felt pretty much in my prime. Even close friends and girls were entering the picture.

Although I never became a professional reporter or freelance writer, as was my goal, I did have two articles published in two local Connecticut newspapers. I also had three of my poems published, one of them winning an award. I privately published my own volume of poetry and wrote a book on my family's history, in the literary biography style. I like to think of it as a basis of or internship for my first novel or perhaps a book of nonfiction.

During my 4 years at college, I went home to my parents most weekends, because it was a local school, and there weren't many weekend activities. So, even though I got a taste for liberal campus life and the real world, I never became fully independent for more than 2 weeks at a time.

When I went on a summer student-exchange program to Poland after graduation I was on my own for almost 2 months, except that everything was organized, and there were guides to fall back on if the going got tough. But, I was now learning quickly to adjust to sudden, unpredictable, illogical changes—something I remember not being able to deal with easily when I was autistic. Again, it really comes down to a choice of self-determination.

In the summer of '86, not having found a job, I decided to push myself to the limits and travel through Europe on my own for a full 2 months—no one to depend on but God and myself. This was my first real test to prove I could be successful in anything I set my mind to. In school you train yourself for your chosen career and acquire knowledge to enlighten the intellect or stimulate your social life. In travel you acquire knowledge and wisdom through intensified experience to enlighten the soul.

It was the first venture in my life that I had saved for, planned, and organized completely on my own. It was first a test of survival, part of the initiation from college boy to manhood (I was still following in my brother's footsteps); second, a self-imposed internship to train myself for a possible career in travel writing; third, a vacation. One dream at that time was to write a practical, insightful travel book, based on my experiences in Europe, with the intention of making mistakes that future travelers could learn from. Though I did not do this I did get to meet the Pope in Rome and paint my name on the former Berlin Wall.

If public schooling was my preparation for the world after Ives and autism, then college and Europe were the entrance exam. Moving to Orlando to become independent, successful in my career, and active in my church and in my personal life is then the intense education of life, while the future of marrying and raising a family in the image of the Lord is the final exam. Getting into heaven is graduation.

I am very much interested in girls—I've had crushes since I was 12. I did have a girlfriend in my senior year of high school, whom I dated through college when we were home on vacation. Annie was ambitious and highly intelligent and went to law school in Boston. I would take her out dancing; she encouraged me a lot as a writer. And there were others through college.

Much later in Europe I met an Iranian girl, Sima, on a train, and we spent the day in Amsterdam. We became pen pals (she lived in

Germany), and I visited her at her brother's place in Los Angeles the following year. I was more serious with her than I was with other girls and even asked her to marry me, but distance and different backgrounds hampered our relationship. Finally, after living in Florida a few years, I met Gloria at my church—the beautiful "angel eyes" of my dreams whom I was engaged to for a time. And of course I can't forget Margot, whom I met at culinary school. I was first in love with her, like I had been with hundreds of girls in my lifetime, but now we are just good friends.

While living at college with my roommates, and later on with one of my wild friends, there were many nights of spontaneous parties, bar-hopping, and of course lots of drinking. Ending up with a girl—any girl who was good-looking and willing, regardless of her personality—was usually the end of the means. And, it wasn't only fun, but a sort of initiation from boyhood to manhood. Also, I felt that sex gave me a greater air of confidence in relating to women, like the pride one might feel reaching the top of a high mountain, rather than just admiring it from below.

But lo and behold! I found out that this is really only psychological deception because of our passionate human nature. What I am about to conclude my testimony with tops off everything else in terms of life's worth. While at culinary school in Rhode Island, I joined the student Christian club and gave my life to Jesus Christ as my personal Lord and Savior, becoming what Jesus himself called a "born-again" Christian. My intention here is not to preach but to share the truth that set me free. I don't regret anything I've experienced (sex, drinking, living on the edge) because I've learned from it. I'm sure many people need to learn and experience lessons for themselves like I did, and that's fine. Sometimes you need to go through darkness to appreciate light. I have been successful in all my dreams, but then success is only giving everything with what we have, by what we feel in our heart. And, no one is excused, not even the once-autistic.

Appendix B

Autism as Portrayed in the Film *Rain Man*

In the 1988 film *Rain Man* a man explains to a nurse that his older brother is "autistic." The bewildered nurse replies, "Artistic?" That scene, though it might sound silly, in fact quite realistically portrays a rather common scenario in the lives of people who have or who care for someone who has autism. For a long time, and sometimes even now, to say someone has "autism" has been to invite a blank or quizzical stare in response.

The film tells the story of Charlie Babbitt (played by Tom Cruise) a fast-talking, opportunistic car dealer, and his 40-year-old brother, Raymond (played by Dustin Hoffman), who has autism and lives in a private institution called Wallbrook. The thematic core of the movie is the gradual transformation of Charlie into a caring, though still slightly frustrated, brother to Raymond, and the slight moderation of Raymond's symptoms brought on by his new relationship with Charlie.

By virtue of the considerable publicity surrounding the movie and Hoffman's receiving an Academy Award for his portrayal of Raymond, the public was shown for the first time what the experience of autism, or at least one type of autism, is like. There now seems to be more of a public awareness of the disability, if not always a true understanding of it. By publicizing autism, the film has allowed many people to face and accept people with autism in their own families and communities. One mother of a child with autism wrote to Hoffman that after seeing *Rain Man* her mother was able, for the first time, to discuss with her friends her grandson who had autism.

Scene by scene, the film skillfully outlines the nature of the disorder. Although Raymond exhibits fairly rare savant characteristics, he can be described as having the main traits of autism: an inability to deal with abstract ideas or reason logically; atypical speech patterns (articulate but odd, limited, echolalic); absence of eye contact; stiffness in posture and body movement; compulsive gestures; fascination with repetitive movement; overwhelming anxiety communicated through posture; hair-trigger tantrums; and the need for sameness and structure.

Throughout the first part of the film, Charlie and the audience, bit by bit, begin to see the dimensions of Raymond's condition. His imperviousness and rigidity come through in his monotonal recitation of a barrage of statistics on Charlie's Roadmaster convertible, his stubborn insistence that he drive the car "only on Mondays," and his inability to participate in conversational give-and-take. In one scene, Charlie encounters Raymond's extreme obsession with structure when Charlie takes down a book from Raymond's neat, book-laden shelves and Raymond erupts, screaming and hitting himself, then calling pleadingly to the attendant for help. Raymond's need for structure is typical of a person with autism and is also reflected in his absolute insistence, to the point of frenzy, on seeing the same television show at 4 o'clock every afternoon accompanied by his extreme anxiety when he thinks he will miss it.

The film also shows how the experience of having autism—the thought processes coupled with the inability to communicate one's feelings—can be so frightening to individuals with the disorder and to others who care for them. In a scene in the bathroom of a motel, Charlie innocently turns on the hot water for Raymond's bath. Seeing the steaming water, Raymond screams and again hits himself out of uncontrollable, overwhelming terror, crying, "*Burn* baby! *Burn* baby!" The cause turns out to be his horrifying memory of accidentally scalding Charlie when Charlie was a baby.

The frustration that relatives of people with autism experience is brought out well. As Charlie slowly develops from a selfish manipulator into an affectionate brother who wants to be emotionally closer to Raymond, he is blocked by Ray's imperviousness and emotional distance. In one scene, Charlie, exasperated, shakes Raymond, crying desperately, "You must be in there somewhere!"

The film never allows the audience to think of Raymond as an automaton. It goes to considerable effort to show his humanity. One of the most moving scenes occurs in the bathroom while Raymond is brushing his teeth. As he looks at himself in the mirror, he says, "Funny rain man." Charlie then realizes that his childhood imaginary companion, his "rain man," is in fact Raymond. Somewhere in the sequence of Charlie's questions followed by Raymond's abbreviated answers, Raymond leans over and pats Charlie on the head, experimentally and tentatively. The moment is significant: Raymond has broken through a part of his emotional isolation to some awareness of Charlie as his brother.

The optimism of the film is guarded, however. In one of the final scenes of *Rain Man*, the psychologist asks Raymond, "Do you want to stay with Charlie Babbitt or go back to Wallbrook?" Raymond at first answers, "Yeah, stay with Charlie Babbitt." To the repeated question he then answers, with the echolalic speech pattern characteristic of people with autism, "Yeah, stay with Charlie Babbitt, go back to Wallbrook."

Two years of research went into *Rain Man*. The most important concern of those involved, according to Gail Mutrux, the associate producer, was that the script depict this adult with autism accurately, as a person who is capable of only minor adjustments and who possesses characteristics of the disability that are primarily unchanging. Three directors quit *Rain Man* in the early stages of production largely out of frustration over the limitations placed on the character of Raymond. Each, in essence, found himself asking Hoffman, "You don't look at people? You don't talk? How can there be a story or a movie?"

The writers, producers, directors, and Hoffman himself all used a number of consultants for the film and visited a number of facilities for people with autism. The principal consultant was Dr. Bernard Rimland, director of the Institute for Child Behavior Research in San Diego, California. Another was Dr. Ruth Sullivan, director of the Autism Services Center. (Both Dr. Rimland and Dr. Sullivan have children with autism who served as models for the character of Raymond.) Other consultants were Dr. Bodel Silverstein, a behavioral therapist; Dr. Darold Treffert, a specialist on savant behavior; and Dr.

Peter Tanguay, a child psychiatrist on the staff of the University of California–Los Angeles Neuropsychiatric Institute.

The original screenplay modeled Raymond on a real person, Kim, a savant with mental retardation who had an unlimited ability to recall facts and figures. To help develop the character of Raymond, Hoffman met with Kim and adopted the way she moved and walked. In addition, Hoffman met with and used observations of three other people—all who had savant characteristics, including a man named Peter Guthrie. Guthrie was especially helpful because he had an active relationship with his brother, Kevin. Hoffman and Cruise spent time bowling with Peter and Kevin in order to observe the nuances in the interaction between the two brothers. From Peter, Hoffman acquired the nasal, monotone voice, the habit of spelling out names, and the obsession with statistics. The exposure to the actors playing a man with autism and his brother had an interesting reciprocal effect on Peter and Kevin. Two weeks after that first meeting, Kevin received a telephone call from Peter. When Kevin asked him what he wanted, Peter replied, "I just wanted to talk to you, K-E-V-I-N." Never in their 25 years together, said Kevin, had Peter ever said anything remotely like that.

Dustin Hoffman also prepared for his role by visiting several facilities, including a sheltered workshop, the Devereaux School in Santa Barbara, and L'Arc Ranch in Los Angeles County. Mutrux, who did a great deal of the research for Hoffman, visited other workshops and schools and taped interviews with a variety of authorities in different fields concerned with the lives of people with autism. Hoffman studied *A Portrait of an Autistic Young Man*, a film about Joseph Sullivan, Dr. Ruth Sullivan's son, and met with Temple Grandin, in her own words a "recovering autistic" and author of several books on autism, to discuss the complexities of the disability.

The last scene of *Rain Man* shows Raymond on the train sitting beside the director of Wallbrook. As the train slowly pulls away from the station, he stares impassively ahead, oblivious of Charlie, who is standing, waving, on the platform. Raymond is heading back to Wallbrook and life in an institution. Though dramatically effective, this ending is not entirely realistic in view of the opportunities available for people with autism. Because of the deinstitutionalization movement, now most people with developmental disabilities are in group homes or supervised apartments. Those who can work usually seek jobs in supervised workshops or in the community.

Improved educational opportunities exist for those with disabilities and a variety of private and public programs are available to help people such as Raymond acquire a degree of self-sufficiency.

The director's insistence that Raymond return to Wallbrook does serve one important purpose, however. Although it may not have been the most realistic ending, it does avoid false optimism about Raymond's ability to improve, and it almost certainly is the best ending for conveying to the audience a basic truth about autism: Despite the moderation of deficits and sometimes even dramatic improvements, most people diagnosed with an autism spectrum disorder never lose the inherent characteristics of autism, although with education and intervention some people can lead productive and satisfying lives.

Appendix C

Summary Chart:
Preschool Through High School

	Tom	Jimmy	Polly	Bill
Original diagnosis	Atypical personality disorder	Autistic symptoms, emotionally disturbed	Personality disturbance/autistic tendencies	Atypical personality with autistic features
Referred by	Clinic pediatrician	Clinic pediatrician	Clinic nursery school teacher	Public school kindergarten teacher and social worker
Reasons for referral	Clinging; bland; slow in all landmarks; limited, whispered speech	Aggressive behavior, no speech, hyperactive, has tantrums, is self-involved	Wild, violent behavior; is anxious; panics easily	Bizarre behavior; limited speech; babbles, shouts meaninglessly; is a loner
Strengths	Determined, cooperative, responds to teaching	Aware of people and surroundings, motivated and quick to learn; has "charm," sense of humor	Learns quickly, wants to relate, speaks normally, is determined	Responds to teaching, cooperative, interested in dramatics, has literary ability
Weaknesses	Remote, echolalic speech, very stubborn	Poor vision and motor development, physically violent (e.g., biting, pinching)	Unpredictable emotionally, can be unreachable	Distanced emotionally, rigid, panics easily
Education	Preschool, public school special education through high school, vocational and summer camp	Preschool, 2 years; residential school, 5 years; program for communication disorders until graduation	Nursery school, 1 year; clinic nursery school, 1 year; preschool public education program for emotionally disturbed (moved to program for individuals with mental retardation), 1 year; high school vocational program in special education high school; camp for individuals with mental retardation, 4 years	Preschool, 3 years; phased back to public school; college, 4 years; culinary institute, 2 years

Information on Jane is not included in this table due to incomparability of data.

David	Karen	John	Larry	Eric
Aphasia, mildly retarded	Atypical development with autistic behavior	Neurologically impaired, emotionally disturbed	Emotionally disturbed, autistic, more "psychotic" features	Congenital autism
Clinic pediatrician	Clinic pediatrician	Clinic pediatrician	Clinic psychiatrist	Clinic pediatrician
Delayed in speech and all developmental landmarks; placement to be diagnostic	Lacks speech—has only three words, remote, does not respond to people, exhibits high anxiety, is fearful	Hyperactive, impulsive, is "easily disoriented and hysterical"	Wild, uncontrolled behavior; exhibits "severe emotional problems," speech often unrelated and rapid (i.e., "shot-gun")	Lacks speech; is "out of touch," "unreachable"; has repetitive behaviors, tantrums
Determined, cooperative, wants to relate though hindered by disability	Wants to relate, some speech, available to teaching, remarkable memory	Very verbal; beguiling; relates well superficially; good singer, artist	Responds intelligently to one-to-one treatment, appealing and attractive appearance	Shows some fine motor skills, uses sign language, follows visual clues well, performs some tasks consistently
Distanced emotionally, talks in whispers, limited speech	Repetitive, echolalic, fearful, "often unreachable"	Distractable, explosive	Immature motor and verbal development, echolalic, swears	Inaccessible to teaching, rigid, anxious, demonstrates apparent friendliness that has no basis in reality—"like grabbing mist"
Preschool, public school special education communication disorders program, special education camp	Preschool, 1 year; private education school, 7 years; private special school; two residential schools (graduated from second)	General nursery school; preschool, 3 years; private special education school, 8 years; boarding school, $1\,^3/_4$ years; special education high school	Preschool, residential treatment center, communication disorders program, summer special education camp	Preschool, 2 years; public school special education communication disorders program through high school

Appendix D

Adult Outcomes: 2000

	Tom	Jimmy	Polly	Bill
Current living situation	Owns condominium, has several hours per day of staff and parental support	Lives at home with family	Lives in rental condominium with staff support, shares with another woman with a disability	Rents apartment; independent; is married with two children
Current occupation	Has worked as full-time dishwasher at restaurant for more than 20 years	Is a delivery person for Meals on Wheels, gardener: Jobs obtained through sheltered workshop	Works in biomedical factory part time because federal regulations prevent her from earning more and still qualifying for Medicare	Is in shipping department of an electronics company
Current income source	Social Security Disability Insurance (SSDI), state department of mental retardation pays for support team, paid employment	SSDI, Supplemental Security Income (SSI), provider organization, and a minimum state payment for staff assistance	SSDI, SSI, paid employment, also rent is partially subsidized	Paid employment only
Degree of mental retardation	Mild	Moderate	Moderate	None

Information on Jane is not included in this table because of incomparability of data. Information on Larry is not included because he is deceased.

David	Karen	John	Eric
Lives at home with family	Lives in rental apartment, receives several hours per day of staff support	Lives in condominium, which he rents from another person with a disability	Lives in group home
Does restaurant work 3 days per week, also works at a community house workshop	Does full-time kitchen work at a retirement center	Works as volunteer in a dietetics department of a large hospital	Works in a sheltered workshop and helps make deliveries from a delivery van
SSDI, paid employment	SSDI, paid employment, also state support	SSDI, SSI, state disability support, food stamps	SSDI, paid employment; also Title XIX, state agency supplement for personal needs
Mild	Moderate	Mild. People who know John do not think he has mental retardation	Severe. Eric's outcomes are very surprising in that he now understands speech and talks in brief sentences

Glossary

Affect   The external manifestation of how a person feels at a particular time. Anger, sadness, elation, and depression are all examples of moods that are expressed through affect. The type of affect, its appropriateness to the situation, and its persistence are important patterns that help determine a diagnosis. Affect can be a symptom of or a sign of a disorder.

Aphasia   Impairment or loss of the faculty of using or understanding spoken or written language.

Asperger's syndrome   A disorder at the mild end of the autism spectrum; children with Asperger's syndrome are poorly coordinated in movement, have average to above-average intelligence, and have circumscribed "intellectual interests."

Atypical personality disorder   *See* Pervasive developmental disorder.

Auditory integration training (AIT)   An emerging treatment for disorders of auditory processing. It was popularized through Annabel Stehli's book, *The Sound of a Miracle* (Georgianna Organization Inc., 1997), which described the improvement of her daughter's autism through this treatment.

Autism   A neurobiological syndrome beginning from birth or during the first 3 years of life, which is usually lifelong and which can be severely incapacitating. An inability to relate to others is its hallmark. It is characterized by slow development of physical, social, and learning skills. Three times more common in males than females, autism has been found throughout the world in families of all racial, ethnic, social, and economic backgrounds.

Community house   An organization within a town that offers a variety of services to the local community (e.g., day care and programs for senior citizens, workshop training for people with disabilities).

Concrete thinking   To take words literally, to attach limited meaning to words; an inability to think in abstractions.

Echolalia   Repeating words or phrases spoken by another. When it occurs in individuals older than 24 months, it is often viewed as a symptom or characteristic trait of mental retardation, a language disorder, or autism. In these individuals, the behavior can be especially pervasive and meaningless.

Facilitated communication   Developed in Australia, a system of teaching nonverbal children to answer questions using a typewriter or computer or pointing to letters on a letterboard with the help of an adult facilitator. The facilitator assists the child by placing a hand gently on the child's hand, back, or shoulders, but is not to guide the child's answers intentionally. This method has generated much controversy over the issue of authorship of the individuals' communication. Numerous studies have failed to determine whether facilitators (consciously or subconsciously) control the content of individuals' messages.

Fine motor skills   The ability to use the small muscles of the body, such as those in the hands, feet, fingers, and toes.

Fragile X syndrome   A genetic condition in which one part of the X chromosome has a defect. People with fragile X syndrome experience a range of cognitive involvement from learning disabilities to mild or moderate mental retardation. In childhood, individuals typically have long faces and large ears, and boys have large testicles. In later years physical features become less distinguishable from those of the general population.

Gross motor skills   The ability to use the large muscles of the body.

Inclusion (*or* Inclusive education)   An educational model in which students who have disabilities are educated in the general classroom environment, but with appropriate modifications and interventions as needed. These modifications and interventions are usually determined through collaboration between general education and special education teachers. See also *Mainstreaming*.

Kanner's syndrome   An atypical behavior pattern in young children observed in 1943 by psychiatrist Dr. Leo Kanner, which he described as early infantile autism. This behavior pattern, now known as autism, starts within the first 30 months of life and is distinguished by inability to form typical social relationships, atypical development of speech or lack of speech, and avoidance of eye contact.

Labile   Unstable, fluctuating emotionally.

Mainstreaming   The practice of putting a child with disabilities in general school classes for some—sometimes all—subjects. *See Inclusion*, which is preferred over mainstreaming as both a term and a practice.

Neuromotor   Physical movement controlled by the nervous system (e.g., cutting with scissors, walking, running).

Obsessive   Completely possessed by an idea.

Perseveration   Extremely repetitive movement or speech thought to be a result of a person's inner preoccupations; frequently seen in people with autism.

Pervasive developmental disorder-not otherwise specified (PDD-NOS)   Formerly known as atypical personality disorder, PDD-NOS is characterized by lack of responsiveness to others, resistance to change, oddities of movement, severe disturbance in social relations, abnormalities of language development, distortion in the development of affect, and vulnerability to unusually high levels of anxiety. This is a diagnostic classification used within the spectrum of autism disorders.

PET (positron emission tomography) scans   A technology that permits measurement of the metabolic areas of the brain.

Psychogenic   Having its origin in the mind or in a mental condition or process.

Psychosis   Any serious mental illness or abnormality existing at any one moment, characterized by a weakened ability or inability to distinguish between reality and fantasy.

Psychotic   Mentally ill, unstable, out-of-touch with reality. Characterized by amoral, antisocial behavior, and an inability to form meaningful relationships or to learn from experience.

Savant   A person with autism who exhibits one extraordinary ability in memory, music, art, or math (e.g., remembering the numbers of all the exits on the highways in a state, ability to do complicated mathematical problems).

Schizophrenia   A mental disorder associated with lack of motivation, social withdrawal, emotional flattening, hallucinations, and delusions. Not related to autism.

Sheltered workshop   Supervised employment for people with disabilities, usually run by a state agency.

Supported employment   Paid employment of people with developmental or other disabilities, usually supervised by a job coach.

Symbiotic personality type   A personality type that causes someone to cling to another (e.g., mother, teacher) almost to the point where the individual wants to become that other person.

Resources

Following are organizations that provide varied services and information to parents of children with autism and to individuals with autism themselves. For more information, call, visit their web sites, or write to request a copy of their newsletters or other publications. Organizations or branches of organizations also thrive at the state, county, or local level. Consult the yellow pages of your telephone directory or your library or local mental health association for these groups.

American Association of University Affiliated
Programs for Persons with Developmental Disabilities (AAUAP)
8630 Fenton Street, Suite 410
Silver Spring, MD 20910
301-588-8252
http://www.aauap.org

The Arc of the United States
1010 Wayne Avenue, Suite 650
Silver Spring, MD 20910
301-565-3842
http://www.thearc.org

Asperger Syndrome Coalition of the United States (ASC-U.S.), Inc.
formerly Asperger Syndrome Education Network of America
(ASPEN)
Post Office Box 49267
Jacksonville Beach, FL 32240-9267
http://www.asperger.org

Autism Research Institute
(formerly Institute for Child Behavior Research)
4182 Adams Avenue
San Diego, CA 92116
619-281-7165
http://www.autism.com/ari

Autism Services Center Hotline
Prichard Building
605 9th Street
Post Office Box 507
Huntington, WV 25710
304-525-8014

Autism Society of America
(National Office)
7910 Woodmont Avenue, Suite 650
Bethesda, MD 20814
301-657-0881
http://www.autism-society.org

Autism Training Center
Old Main 316
Marshall University
Huntington, WV 25755
304-696-2332

Federation for Children
(formerly Technical Assistance for Parent Program [TAPP])
1135 Tremont Street
Boston, MA 02116
617-482-2915

International Rett Syndrome Association
9121 Piscataway Road, Suite 2B
Clinton, MD 20735
301-856-3334
http://www.rettsyndrome.org

Joseph P. Kennedy, Jr., Foundation
1325 G Street, NW, Suite 50
Washington, DC 20005
202-393-1250
http://www.familyvillage.wisc.edu/jpkf/

Kids on the Block
9385 C Gerwig Lane
Columbia, MD 21406
410-290-9095
800-368-KIDS (5437)
http://www.kotb.com

Learning Disabilities Association of America
4156 Library Road
Pittsburgh, PA 15234-1349
412-341-1515
http://www.ldanatl.org

National Fragile X Foundation
1441 York Street, Suite 303
Denver, CO 80206
303-333-6155
http://nfxf.org

National Organization on Disability (NOD)
910 16th Street, NW, Suite 600
Washington, DC 20006
202-293-5960
http://www.nod.org

National Rehabilitation Information Center
4407 Eighth Street, NE
Washington, DC 20017
301-588-9284

Online Asperger Syndrome Information and Support (OASIS)
http://www.udel.edu/bkirby/asperger

Parent Educational Advocacy Training Center
228 Pitt Street, Suite 300
Alexandria, VA
703-691-7826
http://www.peatc.org

Paul H. Brookes Publishing Co.
Post Office Box 10624
Baltimore, MD 21285-0624
800-638-3775
http://www.brookespublishing.com

Rehabilitation Research and Training Center
Virginia Commonwealth University
1314 W. Main Street
Richmond, VA 23284-0001
804-828-1851

Sibling Information Network
University of Connecticut
A.J. Pappanikou Center
249 Glenbrook Road
Storrs, CT 06268
203-486-4031
http://www.parentsoup.com/library/organizations/bdfa009.html

Siblings for Significant Change
105 E. 22nd Street
New York, NY 10010
212-420-0430
http://www.specialcitizens.com

Special Olympics
1325 G Street, NW, Suite 500
Washington, DC 20005
202-628-3630
http://www.specialolympics.org

TASH (Formerly The Association for Persons with Severe Handicaps)
29 W. Susquehanna Avenue, Suite 210
Baltimore, MD 21204
410-828-8274
http://www.TASH.org

Treatment and Education of Autistic and related Communication Handicapped Children and Adults (TEACCH)
Division TEACCH, CB #7180
Medical School Wing E
Chapel Hill, NC 27599-7180
919-966-2174
http://www.unc.edu/dept/teacch/

Yale Child Study Center
230 South Frontage Road
Post Office Box 207900
New Haven, CT 06520-7900
http://info.med.yale.edu/chldstdy/autism

Bibliography

Ames, L.B. (1989). *Arnold Gesell: Themes of his work*. New York: Human Sciences Press.

Arnstein, H.S. (1965). An approach to the severely disturbed child. In P.T.B. Weston (Ed.), *Some approaches to teaching autistic children*. London: Pergamon Press.

Associated Press. (1989, February 19). Real rain man thrives with film. *New Haven (Conn.) Register*, p. A2.

Axline, V.M. (1947). *Play therapy: The inner dynamics of childhood*. Boston: Houghton Mifflin.

Barsch, R.H. (1967). *Achieving perceptual motor efficiency. A perceptual motor curriculum* (Vol. 1). Seattle: Special Child Publications.

Bender, L. (1942). *The Bender Visual Motor Gestalt Test for Children*. New York: American Orthopsychiatric Association.

—(1947). Childhood schizophrenia: A clinical study of 100 schizophrenic children. *American Journal of Orthopsychiatry, 17,* 40–56.

—(1956). Schizophrenia in childhood: Its recognition, description and treatment. *American Journal of Orthopsychiatry, 26*(3), 499–506.

Bettelheim, B. (1950). *Love is not enough*. New York: The Free Press.

Caparulo, B.K., & Cohen, D.J. (1983). Developmental language disorders in the neuropsychiatric disorders of childhood. In K.E. Nelson (Ed.), *Children's language*. New York: Gardner Press.

Cohen, D.J., Caparulo, B.K., Shaguritz, B.A., & Bowers, M.B.J. (1977). Dopamine and serotonin metabolism in neuropsychiatrically disturbed children: CSF homovanillic acid and 5-hydroxyindolacetic acid. *Archives of General Psychiatry, 34,* 545-550.

Cohen, D.J., & Donnellan, A.M. (Eds.). (1987). *Handbook of autism and pervasive developmental disorders.* New York: John Wiley & Sons.

Cruickshank, W.M., Bentzen, F.A., Ratzenburg, F.H., & Tannhauser, M.T. (1961). *A teaching method for brain-injured and hyperactive children: A demonstration pilot study.* Syracuse, NY: Syracuse University Press.

Cutler, B.C., & Kozloff, M.A. (1987). Living with autism: Effects on family needs. In D.J. Cohen & A.M. Donnellan (Eds.), *Handbook of autism and pervasive developmental disorders.* New York: John Wiley & Sons.

Dahl, E.K., Cohen, D.J., & Provence, S. (1986). Developmental disorders evaluated in early childhood: Clinical and multivariate approaches to nosology of PDD. *Journal of the American Academy of Child Psychiatry, 25,* 170–180.

Despert, L. (1951). Some considerations relating to the genesis of autistic behavior in children. *American Journal of Orthopsychiatry, 21,* 335–350.

Dunn, L.M., & Markwardt, F.C., Jr. (1970). *Peabody Individual Achievement Test.* Circle Pines, MN: American Guidance Service.

Elgar, S. (1966). Teaching autistic children. In J.K. Wing (Ed.), *Early childhood autism.* London: Pergamon Press.

Grandin, T., & Scariano, M. (1986). *Emergence: Labeled autistic.* Novato, CA: Arena Press.

Kanner, L. (1943). Autistic disturbances of affective contact. *Nervous Child, 2,* 217–250.

—. (1971). Follow-up of eleven autistic children originally reported in 1943. *Journal of Autism and Childhood Schizophrenia* 1(2), 119–145.

Kephart, N.C. (1960). *The slow learner in the classroom.* Columbus, OH: Charles E. Merrill.

Lieberman, D.A., & Malone, M.B. (n.d.). *Sexuality and social awareness.* Yalesville, CT: Benhaven Press.

Mahler, M. (1952). On childhood psychosis and schizophrenia: Autistic and symbiotic infantile psychoses. In *Psychoanalytic*

Study of the Child, 7. New York: International Universities Press.

—.(1968) *Our human symbioses and the vicissitudes of individuation.* New York: International Universities Press.

Marcus, L.M., & Schopler, E. (1987). Working with families: A developmental perspective. In D.J. Cohen & A.M. Donnellan (Eds.), *Handbook of autism and pervasive developmental disorders.* New York: John Wiley & Sons.

Matringa, S. (1990, February). Night of the rain men. *Cable TV Guide,* pp. 18–23.

Provence, S., & Dahl, E.K. (1987). Disorders of atypical development: Diagnostic issues raised by a spectrum disorder. In D.J. Cohen & A.M. Donnellan (Eds.), *Handbook of autism and pervasive developmental disorders.* New York: John Wiley & Sons.

Putnam, M.G., Rank, B., & Kaplan, S. (1951). Notes on John I.: A case of primal depression in an infant. In *Psychoanalytic study of the child* (Vol. 6). New York: International Universities Press.

Putnam, M.G., Rank, B., Pavenstedt, E., Anderson, E.N., & Rawson, I. (1948). Round table, 1947: Case study of an a-typical two-and-a-half-year-old. *American Journal of Orthopsychiatry, 18,* 1–30.

Rank, B. (1955). Intensive study and treatment of pre-school children who show marked personality deviations of 'a-typical development' and their parents. In *Emotional problems of early childhood.* New York: Basic Books.

Reilly, S. (1989, January 30). A welcome rain. *New Haven (Conn.) Register,* pp. 17–19.

Riddle, M. (1987). Individual and parental psychotherapy in autism. In D.J. Cohen & A.M. Donnellan (Eds.), *Handbook of autism and pervasive developmental disorders.* New York: John Wiley & Sons.

Ritvo, S., & Provence, S. (1953). Form perception and imitation in some autistic children: Diagnostic findings and their contextual interpretation. In *Psychoanalytic study of the child* (Vol. 8). New York: International Universities Press.

Sparrow, S., Rescorlo, L.A., Provence, S., Condon, S., Goudreau, D., & Cicchetti, D. (1986). Mild atypical children: Preschool and follow-up. *Journal of the American Academy of Child Psychiatry, 26,* 181–185.

Stehli, A. (1997). *The sound of a miracle.* Westport, CT: Georgianna Organization.

Terman, L.M., & Merrill, M.A. (1960). *Stanford–Binet Intelligence Scale.* Newton, MA: Houghton Mifflin.

Towbin, K.E. (1997). Pervasive development disorders–Not otherwise specified. In D.J. Cohen & F.P. Volkmar (Eds.), *Handbook for autism and pervasive developmental disorders,* (pp. 123–125). New York: John Wiley & Sons.

Volkmar, F.R., (1987). Social development. In D.J. Cohen & A.M. Donnellan (Eds.), *Handbook of autism and pervasive developmental disorders.* New York: John Wiley & Sons.

—. (1991). Autism and pervasive developmental disorders. In M. Lewis (Ed.), *Child and adolescent psychiatry: A comprehensive textbook.* Philadelphia: Lippincott, Williams & Wilkins.

Volkmar, F.R., Cicchetti, D., Dykens, E., Sparrow, S., Leckman, J.F., & Cohen, D.J. (1988). An evaluation of the autistic behavior checklist. *Journal of Autism and Developmental Disorders,* *18*(1), 83.

Volkmar, F.R., Stier, D.M., & Cohen, D.J. (1985). Age of onset of pervasive developmental disorders. *American Journal of Psychiatry, 142,* 1450-1452.

Wechsler, D. (1967). *Manual for the Wechsler Intelligence Scale for Children–Revised.* New York: The Psychological Corporation.

—. (1974) *Wechsler Intelligence Scale for Children–Revised.* New York: The Psychological Corporation.

—. (1991) *Wechsler Intelligence Scale for Children* (3rd ed.). New York: The Psychological Corporation.

Weston, T.B. (Ed.). (1965). *Some approaches to teaching autistic children.* London: Pergamon Press.

Wing, J.K. (Ed). (1966). *Early childhood autism: Clinical, educational, and social aspects.* London: Pergamon Press.

Wing, L., & Attwood, A. (1987). Syndromes of autism and atypical development. In D.J. Cohen & A.M. Donnellan (Eds.), *Handbook of autism and pervasive developmental disorders.* New York: John Wiley & Sons.

Index